Take Judaism, for Example

Chicago Studies in the History of Judaism

Jacob Neusner, Editor

Take Judaism, for Example

Studies toward the
Comparison of Religions

Edited by
Jacob Neusner

The University of Chicago Press
Chicago and London

For Hans Henry Penner

Jacob Neusner is University Professor and the
Ungerlieder Distinguished Scholar of Judaic
Studies at Brown University. Among his many
books are *Judaism: The Evidence of the Yeru-
shalmi, Stranger at Home,* and *Judaism: The
Evidence of the Mishnah,* all published by the
University of Chicago Press. He is the editor of
a thirty-nine-volume translation of *The Talmud
of the Land of Israel,* also published by the
University of Chicago Press.

The University of Chicago Press, Chicago 60637
The University of Chicago Press, Ltd., London

Library of Congress Cataloging in Publication Data
Main entry under title:

Take Judaism, for example.

   (Chicago studies in the history of Judaism)
   Includes bibliographical references and index.
   1. Judaism—History—Addresses, essays, lectures.
2. Judaism—Doctrines—Addresses, essays, lectures.
3. Judaism—Relations—Addresses, essays, lectures.
I. Neusner, Jacob, 1932–   II. Series.
BM40.T27   1983   296   82–16039
ISBN 0–226–57618–3

Contents

v

Preface

This is a book addressed to the comparison of religions, even though all of the chapters deal with problems of Judaism. The mode of address, however, lies in the shaping of questions appropriate to the analysis, description, and interpretation of religions. When we study any religion, we want to know how that religion relates to the society that believes and sustains it and shapes the culture that expresses and embodies it. We want to be able to define the religion under study. We seek a model for the interplay between religious ideas and the social group that holds them. We investigate the character of religious leadership within that social group. Common categories in religions are shaped by religious experience, worship, and mysticism; by religion in society, with special attention to the virtuoso and the community on the one side, and the interplay of religious belief and ethics on the other; and, finally, the place, within religion, of the religious intellectuals. When, at the end, we confront a religion within the contemporary world, that is, a religion that lives in our own day, we take up questions of interpretation on how that religion shapes its own past, how it imposes its vision upon the culture of living people, and, finally, how it sorts out the choices and challenges presented by modern times and circumstances. In laying out these general questions, I also have shown why this book follows the outline it does, from analysis (Part I), through description (Part II), to interpretation (Part III) of the history of Judaism in its ancient (I), medieval (II), and modern and contemporary stages of development and unfolding (III). But the history of Judaism is not the principal focus. Rather, at hand is an effort to exemplify a theory on how religions should be studied, and, it must follow, how also they should be compared.

The authors of this book are seeking both form and language for a fresh approach to the study of religion. We have in mind an experiment. The essays constitute laboratory exercises. What we seek is how to frame a problem that may be shared. We want to learn to express the results of inquiry in a way intelligible and useful to people investigating a congruent problem within another religious world than the one at hand. This effort is a beginning. If it succeeds, it soon will be made obsolete and seen to be primitive. Ours are voices in an, as-yet, one-sided conversation.

This book emerges not out of a world seeking understanding of religion but out of the studies and the classrooms of scholars who, to begin with, invented the subject of their labor. For in the world, in general, people who are religious study the religion they believe (if, as religious folk, they study anything at all). They do not learn about religion, but about religions, that is, about their particular religions. Such a result of theological study of religion is perfectly natural. It is only out of our own minds that an abstract category, religion, has come forth. In the world at large there is no such thing as religion; there are only religions, examples of something we-know-not-what, instances of something we are not experienced at defining. The labor of generalization so that, beyond religions, we learn something about religion as a phenomenon of humanity and society confronts scholars of humanities and social sciences. These are people who want to understand not only this particular person or that distinctive group but humanity and society, hence, too, not only diverse religions but religion.

For the work of generalization we must compare and contrast. Otherwise generalization is banal, too general to be interesting, too vast to be intelligible. Yet how to generalize about religion is not so clear. The way already explored by earlier scholars of the study of religion is generally called comparative religion. It consisted in what was essentially a large-scale labor of monothetic taxonomy. Questions of evolution, from simple to complex, exercises in unification of discrete and diverse experience, differentiation of rather general phenomena through similarity and contrast—these are the completed states. The goal, to be sure, has not been reached, whether it was to discover the origins of religion or to uncover what made a religion work. At best the answers appealed to ideal types, that is, to the form of a given religion described out of all relationship to historical context. The answers, moreover, required precisely that mode of thought, framed in terms of ideal types, because what was sought was encompassing taxonomy—not historical and contextual insight at all.

What was attained, by contrast, was ineffably dull generalization imposed from above, a set of statements so obvious and vast as to be of little use in making sense of religion as a force in history, culture, society, psychology, imagination—any of the ways in which religion is to be understood as a fundamental constituent of the world of humanity and of nations. "Judaism," for instance, was defined in terms so encompassing that anyone knowledgeable in some of its specific forms and diverse expressions over its long and complex history found the results puzzling. The "Judaism" of comparative religion was neither comprehensible nor relevant to the facts of Judaism. It was a caricature, ignorant and often bigoted. So it was with the other religions—"Islam," for instance—still more diverse and complex in their concrete, social exemplifications than Judaism.

A fresh approach has been aborning for some decades now. This book represents an experiment in talking about one religion within the framework of this other approach. For a new generation wants to know about religion in context. For that generation it is a commonplace that to make sense of something we must establish a context for meaning. We have to uncover a setting for sense and interpretation through comparison and analysis of choices affirmed and choices rejected. To study about religion is to define, analyze, describe, above all, interpret. Religions are not to be studied one by one, god by god, so to speak. There are too many of them. It also cannot be studied in general. Somewhere between the pure nominalism required by the study of only one specific religion (then only of one version of that religion, then only of one text of that version, and onward down to a single sentence, a single letter) and the encompassing realism required by the study of only religion in general, there must be a middle way. For the present we cannot say what that middle way is, except to lay down a simple fact. If we are to avoid the vapid and empty generalizations about religion left to us by our predecessors, we must know a great deal about specific religions in their historical circumstances and the writings that preserve their historical expressions in those settings.

If, on the other hand, we are to avoid the empty-headed claims to the self-evidence of the importance of a given corpus of data, an approach characteristic of experts in some one religion—the Classicist, Egyptologist, Semitist, Buddhologist, Iranist, Sinologist, insistent as they are upon philological monopoly over the facts of the matter—we must find some way of overcoming the narrow limits of ever more particular knowledge. We seek a mode of intelligibility for people who, to begin with, do not know the languages "we" experts know, the facts "we" deem essential. The way forward, it is clear, is to treat each fact as suggestive of something beyond itself, indicative of the traits of the whole of which it is a part. That whole, at one level, is the particular religion under study. The whole, at another, is religion in general, also under study at one and the same time. If we cannot speak an accessible language of generality, we end up talking to ourselves. But how to shape a suitable language, how to define questions the answers to which someone outside of a narrow circle of specialists will want and, yet, which a narrow circle of specialists will find accurate and representative—that is the challenge of our time.

I said we could not yet state that middle way. That is not entirely so. In fact, speaking for a diverse and broad spectrum of specialists in various religions who wish also to study religion, Jonathan Z. Smith has laid down a theory entirely suitable for the quest of our own day. This is what he says:

> For the self-conscious student of religion, no datum possesses intrinsic interest. It is of value only insofar as it can serve as *exempli gratia* of some fundamental issue in the imagination of religion. The student of religion must be able to articulate clearly why "this" rather than "that" was chosen as an exemplum. His primary skill is concentrated in this choice. This effort at articulate choice is all the more difficult, and hence all the more necessary, for the historian of religions who accepts neither the boundaries of canon nor of community in constituting his intellectual domain, in providing his range of exempla.
>
> Implicit in this effort at articulate choice are three conditions. First, that the exemplum has been well and fully understood. This requires a mastery of both the relevant primary material and the history and tradition of its interpretation. Second, that the exemplum be displayed in the service of some important theory, some paradigm, some fundamental question, some central element in the academic imagination of religion. Third, that there be some method for explicitly relating the exemplum to the theory, paradigm, or question and some method for evaluating each in terms of the other.

What Smith has said constitutes the contemporary program, the platform for the study of religions within the humanities and social sciences. If we propose to understand human imagination on the one side, and human society on the other, then religion must come under analysis as a principal human phenomenon. We take up the labor of explaining religions and how they work: the choices they make and reject. For that purpose we need to draw together a considerable range of examples, making the case that these examples truly do exemplify, do represent choices of importance. The exemplum has to be understood. It must be turned to the service of exemplification of theory, the testing of hypothesis. The question or theory has again to turn back upon and make some sense of the example. Interpretation is dialogue: a conversation in which people talk with one another, to a common point—and speak more than once.

The title of this book, then, is meant to lay down a challenge to the study of Judaism within the study of religions. *Take Judaism, for example*—but to exemplify what? If we move *toward the comparison of religions,* what is it about religions that, as scholars of the humanities, we choose to compare? Let me specify what I think we study when we study religion, and, even more specifically, what we study when we want to know about Judaism. I wish to know about Judaism. I wish further to explain why I regard the study of religion as urgent, not merely interesting—a necessity for society and a precondition for the future of humankind.

Humanistic study of a religion, or religion as a genus of human activity, asks what we learn about humanity from humanity's yearning for God, devotion to supernatural revelation, dedication of this life to the life to come, and vision of humanity as a sacred projection onto earth. The humanistic study of religion reverses matters. It is to see divinity as a secular projection onto heaven, religion as a principal datum for the study of humanity. Since the humanities encompass the study of history, literature, philosophy, art, music, and the other intangible treasures of human emotion, wisdom, and learning, the study of religion, to begin with, does the same. That is, we study the history, literature, philosophy, art, drama, music, and dance that people have made because they believed in a realm beyond this one, a God beyond themselves. But not these alone have people made. More than history, literature, philosophy, they have made temples on hilltops and cities in deserts, where they should not be, cathedrals of time in space they should not occupy. Society and systems of culture, ways of living out ways of seeing the world—these are what we study when we study religion, not a small or negligible thing, but rather the whole thing, seen whole. What is it, in particular, that as humanists we study in or about religion? It is not necessarily how people made things. It rather is why, or more really, how they told themselves the reason why, the insistence of cultures. To be concrete, we may study the ancient temples of Egypt without studying the religion of ancient Egypt—until we want to know why people built those temples. The study of religion in a humanistic setting is the study of what people have made, have felt, and have been, because they were religious.

This description of what we study does not suggest what we hope to find out. Nor do I propose that a study is worth our while without regard to what we learn. On the contrary, not all information, not every datum, is of value or interest or even relevance. It is more important (to state matters in our obvious way) to know how to cure cancer than how to string a tennis racket. So the critical issue is what we hope to learn by understanding what religion is and means in the context of human knowledge. Still more, what do we learn from studying religion that we do not learn from systematically studying any other expression of humanity?

The three most important results of humanistic study of religion deal with culture, history, and society. When we understand the religion of a group, we penetrate deep into its culture, its way of life. When we grasp the world view of a people, we understand how it makes sense of events: how a group transforms this event, that accident, into history and destiny. When we accurately describe the way of life and world view represented by culture and a sense for history, we grasp how a society hangs together, how religion serves to bond this one and that one into families, tribes, a coherent social group. So among the many things we learn about when we study a religion, the principal ones are, I believe, also critical to the interpretation of humanity at its irreducible and fundamental reality: culture, history, society.

The things people do every day because they are religious are not random. They are not mere customs and ceremonies. Rather, they fit together into a whole and harmonious unit, a way of conducting life. Religion is what expresses, as a whole, the ethos of a group. In its power to encapsulate in immediate and concrete words, symbols, or gestures, in laws and remissions from law, the deepest layers of culture and consciousness, religion reveals the whole as a whole. In an integrated and healthy system, there will be an interplay between (to use contemporary examples) the way we drive our cars and the way we fight our wars, the way we organize our economic life and the way we educate our children. That view of the interrelatedness of the constituents of culture presents no surprises. It is a commonplace, after all, to speak of consciousness and society, or of culture and conviction. Now, from the time of Marx, Durkheim, and Weber, it has been equally commonplace to recognize that the religious convictions of a community express the community's deepest values. Hence, they shape and form its economic activity. Accordingly, it is not to claim too much when I assert that when we study religion we enter into the deepest layers of the culture of a group.

How we live out our lives in a common culture requires not merely deed but deliberation. For, as we all know, we not only do things but explain to ourselves what we do and why. For that purpose every group tells itself a story of who it is. In the nature of things, the story accounts for how the group has come into being and what is important in the things which have happened to the group. History, as distinct from narrative, comes into being as the explanation and expression of what has happened to the group. That explanation, it hardly needs saying, makes sense in particular of the way of life of the group, what it remembers and what it chooses to forget. History defines the events it takes as paradigmatic and those it treats as inconsequential. The formative power of religion in accounting for history hardly needs specification. If you want to understand how events are transformed into an intelligible account of reality, how the everyday becomes noteworthy, and how what I do is dictated by what I think I have been and must become, you had best study religion. The reason is that, for much of humanity now and most in the past, religion has given shape and meaning to events. That is why religion as a mode of interpreting and acting out history constitutes the second of the three principal foci of humanistic study of religion.

These two—way of life, world view—demand yet a third focus. No system of living life and explaining it emerges from the pages of a book unless it enters into a social context, that is, unless it forms, and is embodied by, a society. To state matters simply: It is easy to explain how rites make sense of reason, and how ideas generate concrete action. For that purpose you write a book. No one need doubt that ethos and ethics are mutually explanatory. But to say of a system that it works and to explain how, we have to point to the society which gives flesh and blood to the ethos and the ethics. When we turn to examine a society and ask how it holds its members together, defines its family units and protects them, we turn to that third and critical component of the study of religion, namely, its power to bond society, to impart a shared vision and articulate a common cause. For it is religion which defines who is on the inside and who is on the outside: that is the beginning of the social group. The insider then is declared holy, the outsider unclean; the insider practices supernatural powers, the outsider magic; the insider speaks a language, the outsider says "bar bar bar." Where shall we find the source of these ubiquitous distinctions, the secret of what makes a group see itself but no one else as a group, if not in religions? That is so not only in the premodern West. It is so in all of the modern world, whether the Middle East or Europe or North America today.

This rapid account of some part of what we hope to learn in the humanistic study of religion—of human visions of the divine—brings us to its counterpoint in the humanistic study of Judaism. By Judaism, by analogy to what already has been said, I mean the history, literature, philosophy, art, music, and other things Jews have made because they believed they are Israel, a holy people on earth. I mean these, and also the towns and cities, the societies and systems of culture, all expressed and embodied in law, not a trivial matter. It is clear, I think, that nearly all of what the Jews have been and done throughout their history, they have been and done as Israel.

The questions to be addressed to the holy books of Judaism when they are read as documents of religion readily present themselves. What we want to know about is Judaism as a cultural system, Judaism as a mode of interpreting history, and Judaism as the means of bonding Jewish society. What I already have explained about what we principally study when we study religions and religion hardly demands extensive application to what we study when we engage in the humanistic study of Judaism. What we want to describe is how the various modes of human expression of Judaism fit together into a single and cogent culture. What we wish to analyze is how the things that happen to the Jews are transformed into history, made into a compelling statement of a unique destiny. That is, we want to know how Judaism constitutes a system for interpreting history and explaining why what happens is paradigmatic. When we have grasped the interplay between Judaism as a system of culture and Judaism as a mode of interpreting history, we have yet to complete the work. For at that point we turn to the critical issue of the interplay between Judaism and society, that is to say, Judaism as a means of bonding Jewish society, as the catalyst for the Jewish group. Once more we refer to the great exercise of Max Weber in asking about the interplay between economic behavior and religious belief. The larger question about how what I believe relates to my social situation is to be asked without in any way reducing belief to a function of sociology. These are three principal foci, then, for what we study when we study Judaism.

It remains to explain why I believe it is urgent to study religion, and, within religion, Judaism. When we consider the tensions among living religions, the power of faith to generate hatred of the outsider, we realize why it is necessary to study religions within an academic, humanistic framework. For any path to understanding opens roads to peace. The purpose of studying religion in the setting of the humanities is to understand why people do what they do in the name of God. Since, in Asia, the West, and the Middle East, so much that they do is for God's sake, so much is done by holy writ and at the word of holy men and women, it is time we asked a fresh set of questions. For up to now, within the reservations of the respective faiths, people see the outsider as not only the enemy, but the devil. That is to say, we do not understand, so we reject, condemn, avoid, declare crazy, unclean, unholy. We do not understand because we have no theory of the other, no way to make sense of the outsider, who lives by gibberish, so to speak.

Now there are two routes from one reservation to the next, one of good will, the other of learning. The former path serves few and leads nowhere beyond a wilderness of platitudes and clichés. As to the other—we do not know where it leads because it is the way not yet taken. And yet the way of learning is to be described. I mean a path paved not with facts—one group believes this, the other eats that, the third marks the moon's rise. It is a path not paved at all; it is marked out, rather, by guideposts. These are three: description, analysis, interpretation. Description puts facts together into meaningful structures, systems in which the facts make sense to someone, if not to all. Analysis makes sense of facts in yet another way. I mean not only as they fall together to the one inside but also how they make a different sort of sense to the observer. When we ask what sort of things people believe, and how what they do expresses what they believe, we describe in a coherent way. We turn facts into intelligible knowledge, exemplifications of generally accessible propositions. When, further, we take the system, now described, and ask analytical questions about how it functions within a larger social and political ecology, we find ourselves engaged in a labor of interpretation. To describe, to analyze—these prepare the way for the hardest work, interpretation, the exercise of taste and experienced judgment. We interpret religions when we see them whole and at work. That perspective—*to see the whole whole*—is made possible when we see the parts as segments of a larger context, when we ask questions of comparison. These are important, because they allow us to contrast one world with some other, to discover what is unlike because it stands upon a common continuum in humanity, to uncover what is common through scrutiny of what is not.

For in the end we shall understand the other best when we see the choices before us all and understand that we do make choices, because we have freedom to choose. By interpreting religions we mean to grasp the choices people make, to do some thing rather than some other, to eat this, not that, to live within some ethos rather than some other. To state matters simply, to describe religions we must become historians. To analyze religions we must become sociologists, for the social side of things, and philosophers, for the intellectual side. To interpret religions, we must turn ourselves into anthropologists of a certain sort, I mean merely into students of humanity, of ourselves. The work of interpretation, indeed, demands all of the gifts of the entire range of the humanities.

In all the world religions are studied. But it is mainly in America and Canada that religion, too, is studied. Everywhere, East and West, religions and their surrogates are cultivated—indeed, treated quite rightly as the binding of society, the core of culture, the mode of finding one's place in time and space and history, the condition of consciousness. But where societies are diverse, religions and their surrogates prove divisive. In America, from World War II onward, our common task has been to uncover the sources of unity among a people not only diverse but now at last disposed to honor difference. But how we are to live together in difference—this has been our national quest, our American dilemma. It is a country of differences, from the color of our people's skins to the shape of their noses. There are no commonalities but language and loyalty on

the one side, and a fear of commonality, of absorption into an un-
differentiated mass, on the other. That was the context in which the
humanistic study of religions was born. That is the frame within which we
who propose to describe, analyze, and interpret Judaism do our work.

Up to now I have treated as self-evident the importance of the
humanistic study of religions. Let me now spell out why I think this
approach to religion and to the study of Judaism is an urgent task. We
must make sense, to begin with, of why humanists turned to religion. Let
me therefore explain briefly, in just a few sentences, the history of the
humanistic study of religions, including Judaism, in America. Before
World War II, religions were studied only for theological purposes, that
is, as divine sciences, and religion was scarcely studied at all. Afterward
there was a sincere effort to study other religions than one's own. This
represented the beginning of the humanistic study of religion. There have
been three main stages. First, we organized departments of religious
studies in which Catholic priests taught mainly Catholics about Catholicism, rabbis taught Jews about Judaism, and Buddhist holy men taught
everybody else. Legitimate classroom discourse involved rabbis inter-
rogating Jewish students about why they were atheists. There was not a
department of religion; there were only diverse religions, each a specimen
of itself alone. We now look back on that period's departments and call
them zoos: each species in its cage. In the second stage, we tried to teach
several distinct religious traditions in a single context, so we organized
courses in Catholicism, Protestantism, and Judaism. There was, further, a
pretense of comparison, but mainly it consisted of much good will and
little shared comprehension. We had not left the zoo; we had merely
enlarged the cages.

Now, at the present stage, as is clear, our effort is to find a common
program of questions to address to diverse religions, that is, to ask the
questions of the humanities, to discover and define religion. Our work is
to treat the various religious traditions as exemplary of religion. Given
religions, at a given point in their history and society, may offer interesting data to exemplify a phenomenon of religion important beyond themselves. What is important only for itself teaches mere facts. What is
important beyond itself, what supplies an *e.g.*, so to speak, is what we
seek in the several religious traditions before us.

That is why I pointed to the power of Judaism to exemplify how a
religious tradition informs culture, interprets history, and shapes society.
At the same time, I repeat, when this work makes its contribution, the
result is to overcome polemic and to introduce a measure of understanding and mutual comprehension. For in the end, when we exemplify, we
address a world beyond ourselves. We reach out to the other and see
ourselves in the stranger, and the stranger in ourselves. That is the task

before us. When we describe, analyze, and interpret religions, we come to a better understanding of that protean force, religion, within this world. In that way we make better sense not of ourselves alone but of others. A principal motive of understanding religions is to overcome that dislike of the unlike that makes for hatred and war. But how are we to learn to describe, analyze, and interpret what is different from ourselves? In the humanistic study of religions, we seek those intellectually sound methods for description, analysis, and interpretation that permit us to see the other in ourselves, and ourselves in the other. These all provide examples of a shared existence. When the humanistic study of religions succeeds, the alien seems less strange. Then, too, the self seems more strange. The alien is within. It is when we understand that we remain perpetually outsiders in our own richly complex, astonishing traditions, strangers where we feel most at home, that the humanistic study of religions begins.

Jacob Neusner

Part One

Analysis
Judaism in Ancient Times

Introduction

Three points of analysis of a religion begin our work. Appropriately, the age subject to analysis is the one in which the religion under study took shape. We ask the most fundamental and indicative questions: how do we define a religion in its initial period? How do we discern the relationship between ideas held by framers of that religion and the social life of the community addressed by those ideas? How do we characterize and categorize the principal representatives of a religion, its religious leadership or virtuosi? Inquiry into the social relevance of religion and comparative study of the types of leaders of a religion—these present the analytical points at which the work starts. It is difficult to think of more fundamental or more suggestive problems in the study of a religion than the two analytical ones before us.

Before we follow the analysis of this section, however, we had best step back and describe the principal literary sources, religious history and myth, encompassed in the formation of Judaism. We deal with ancient times, roughly marked off by the formation of ancient Israel on the one side, and the end of antiquity with the rise of Islam on the other, from a considerable time before 1,000 B.C.E. (Before the Common Era, corresponding to B.C.) to about 600 C.E. (Common Era, corresponding to

1

A.D.). During that long period, there were many Judaisms, that is, cogent ways of life and world views addressed to Israel, the Jewish people, in the name of God. The one that endured, called rabbinic Judaism, Talmudic Judaism, or just "Judaism" reached the form in which we know it in the second half of those sixteen centuries, having taken shape and reached its present form from the end of the second century B.C.E. to the end of the sixth century C.E., that is, during a period of about eight hundred years.

Judaism in the form in which it has endured for the past two thousand years locates its roots in remote antiquity. But Judaism is not the religion solely or principally described in the records of ancient Israel called by Christians "the Old Testament" and called by Jews "the Torah," or "Tanakh" (from the three constituents, Torah, revealed law, Nebiim, prophets, and Ketubim, writings), or called by some, "the Hebrew Scriptures." Stated simply, Judaism rests upon the foundations of the revelation of God to Moses at Sinai contained in the Hebrew Scriptures, just as (but no more, and no less, firmly than) Christianity rests upon the foundations of that same revelation. While Christianity looks upon the Hebrew Scriptures as the Old Testament, preparatory to the New Testament, completion and fulfillment of the old, Judaism has a different, but comparable, conception. It posits the belief in two Torahs, not an old one and a new one, but a written one and an oral one, both of them equally old, both revealed by God to Moses at Sinai. The Hebrew Scriptures constitute the written Torah. The oral Torah is that other, complementary revelation handed on, as the name makes clear, not in written form but through memory, from one set of religious authorities to the next. The oral Torah ultimately was written down as well, and in the writings of the ancient rabbis of the Mishnah and the two Talmuds formed around the Mishnah the oral Torah endures. The Mishnah and its associated literature, therefore, constitute for Judaism the equivalent of the New Testament for Christianity.

But the Mishnah, for its part, is quite different from the Scriptures. It is a six-part code of law, aimed at showing how the principal parts of the life of Israel, the Jewish people, may be made holy. Covering holiness in agriculture, holiness in the passage of the seasons and the Sabbath, holiness in the life of the family, holiness in all matters of civil law and government, holiness in the Temple, and holiness in connection with food and drink, both in the Temple and elsewhere, the Mishnah is a vast document. It is made much larger still by the two Talmuds, one created in the Land of Israel, the other in Babylonia, which take up the Mishnah and explain and apply its teachings and laws. And the ancient Scriptures lived on in yet a second way, for the rabbis who created and applied the laws of the oral Torah, the Mishnah, also read the written Torah, the Scriptures, and extensively commented on it. Their explanations of the written Torah

are contained in compilations called *midrashim* (singular: *midrash*), in-
quiries into, and exegeses of, the scriptural writings. Judaism, then, is the
religion of the two Torahs, written and oral, revealed by God to Moses at
Sinai and ultimately reaching us in the form given to the two Torahs by the
rabbis of late antiquity, from the early centuries before the Common Era
to the early centuries afterward. Conventional dates would be from Ezra,
ca. 500 B.C.E., to the sixth century C.E. But these are mere conventions.

While this book takes up a different problem from the narrative description of the history of Judaism, the reader will want to have in mind a
picture of that early history, along with some dates from ancient times. I
suppose the first date should be the creation of the world. But then the last
date will have to be the end of time. For Israel's history begins, in the
biblical narrative, with the creation of the world and ends with the redemption of humankind and the conclusion of history. The Jews traced
their origin to Abraham, who migrated from Mesopotamia and became a
sojourner in the land of Canaan (the present-day land of Israel). That
migration was given religious significance: Abraham left the gods of this
world—idols and no-gods—to serve the Lord, Creator of heaven and
earth. His descendants, Isaac and Jacob, were bearers of the promise God
had made to Abraham that, through him, the families of man would bless
themselves and that Abraham would be the father of a great people.
Jacob, called Israel, went down to Egypt in the time of famine, when his
son Joseph served Pharaoh, and there his children multiplied. A Pharaoh
arose who did not know Joseph; he oppressed the children of Israel until
they cried out to the God of their fathers. God sent Moses to redeem
Israel from the bondage of Egypt—to bring them through the wilderness
to the Promised Land.

So goes the biblical legend. It has been adopted by many peoples.
Jews see it not only as a spiritual paradigm but as a personal, concrete
history, the family history of Israel after the flesh. The history of Israel
probably ceases to be legend with Moses. But the shift from legends to
relatively secure historical facts makes little theological difference. Great
events called forth, and continue to call forth, a singular two-part response among Jews: first, to provide a written record of those events;
second, to reflect on their meaning.

In retrospect, we see that the great event of the Exodus from Egypt
produced the Mosaic revelation. The monarchy of King David, several
centuries afterward, so shaped the Israelite imagination as to produce
histories, psalms, and, above all, the messianic hope attached to the
Davidic line. The destruction of the northern part of the kingdom, the ten
tribes of Israel, in 722 B.C. provoked prophecy. The end of the southern
kingdom, Judea—that is, the destruction of its city and the Temple of
Jerusalem in 586 B.C., and the exile of Judeans (Jews or Yehudim) to

Babylonia—resulted in the formation of much of the Hebrew Bible as we know it. The conquest of Jerusalem by the Romans in 70 c.e. led to the foundation of classical, rabbinic Judaism under the leadership of Yohanan ben Zakkai and other great rabbis. The Moslem conquest of the Middle East in 640 afterward renewed the philosophical and mystical inquiry. The advent of modern times—marked by the political emancipation of Western European Jewry, the destruction of European Jewry, and the creation of the State of Israel—this, too, has had important religious consequences.

The fate of the Jewish people and the faith of Judaism thus were forever bound up with one another. One became a Jew—that is, part of the Jewish people—not through ethnic or territorial assimilation but through profession of faith in one God and adoption of the laws of the Torah. Professing that faith and practicing those laws make a person into a Judaist, a part of the community of Judaism.

The beginning of Israel-the-people marked the appearance not only of a new group but also of an entirely new religious ideal—monotheism. To understand what was new in the biblical legacy, one must know what was old. Biblical writers invariably misrepresented paganism, calling it the worship of wood and stone, of dumb idols—that is, fetishism. What was actually central to paganism was the deification of worldly phenomena (not the simple carving of idols), the view that all manifestations of nature are aspects of a mysterious supernatural vitality. Israel began with the affirmation that God is transcendent over creation. God created the world and is wholly different from it. He has no myth, no birth. He is not subject to nature, to anything above himself, to any primordial reality. He is sovereign, and there is no realm beyond him.

Moses transformed the liberation of slaves into the birth of a nation, the birth of a nation into the creation of a new faith. He did so by pronouncing the redemption to be the work of the supreme God who revealed his will through the liberation from Egyptian slavery. The Lord further made a covenant at Sinai, a contract, that Israel should be his people and he should be their God, that Israel should do his will and he should protect and defend them. That will was both universal and specific. Some of the commandments concerned only Israel; others, including the respect for the sanctity of life, marriage, property, and justice, pertained to everyone. Ethics applied to the entire nation. A new moral category, the people, was created, which bore ethical and legal responsibilities beyond those that earlier pertained to individuals.

The creation of the monarchy, ca. 1000 b.c.e., a political event, called forth prophecy of religious significance. The king was not to be deified; he, too, was not God but was subject to the law of God. When political and military disasters produced social disintegration, prophets came forward as apostles of God, emphasizing the primacy of morality. What was new was the conviction that the cult had no intrinsic value. God demanded justice, mercy, and loving-kindness. History was decided, not by force, but by the moral condition of the people. Idolatry, a religious matter, and social corruption, a moral one—these were the predominating facts in the shaping of the people's political destiny. The prophets looked forward to the end of days, when God would make himself known to the nations as he was now known to Israel. Thus history was seen as a succession of events that were not meaningless but pointed toward a goal, the fulfillment of the divine, moral law. Through prophecy, Israelite religion created the notion of a single, all-encompassing, universal history of mankind.

The destruction of Jerusalem in 586 B.C.E. produced a crisis of faith, because ordinary folk supposed that the god of the conquerors had conquered the God of Israel. Israelite prophets saw matters otherwise. Israel had been punished for her sins, and it was God who had carried out the punishment. God was not conquered but vindicated. The pagans were merely his instruments. God could, moreover, be served anywhere, not only in the holy and promised Land of Israel. Israel in Babylonian exile continued the cult of the Lord through worship, psalms, and festivals; the synagogue, a place where God was worshiped without sacrifice, took shape. The Sabbath became Israel's sanctuary, the seventh day of rest and sanctification for God. When, for political reasons, the Persians chose to restore Jewry to Palestine and many returned (ca. 500 B.C.E.), the Jews were not surprised, for they had been led by prophecy to expect that with expiation of sin through suffering and atonement God would once more show mercy and bring them homeward. The prophets' message was authenticated by historical events.

In the early years of the Second Temple (ca. 450 B.C.E.), Ezra, the priest-scribe, came from Babylonia to Palestine and brought with him the Torah-book, the collection of ancient scrolls of law, prophecy, and narrative. Jews resolved to make the Torah the basis of national life. The Torah was publicly read on New Year's Day in 444 B.C.E., and those assembled pledged to keep it. Along with the canonical Scriptures, oral traditions, explanations, instructions on how to keep the law, and exegeses of the Scriptures were needed to apply the law to changing conditions of everyday life. A period of creative interpretation of the written Torah began, one that has yet to come to conclusion in the history of Judaism. From that time forward, the history of Judaism became the history of the interpretation of the Torah and its message for each successive age.

The next great event in the history of the Jews was the destruction of the Second Temple in 70 C.E. A political and military event, its religious consequences were drawn by great rabbis of the age. These rabbis, heirs

of the tradition of oral interpretation and instruction in Torah and the
continuators of the prophets of old, taught that the God of Israel could still
be served by the Jewish people. They had not been abandoned by God but
had once more been chastised. The rabbis taught that, by obedience to
Torah, Israel would again be restored to its land.

Once again a historical event produced a major religious revolution in
the life of Judaism. That revolution is embodied in the pages of the Pales-
tinean and Babylonian Talmuds, compendia of Judaic law, lore, and theology produced by the rabbis of the Land of Israel and Babylonia, on the
basis of the ancient oral tradition, and finally edited in the fifth and sixth
centuries C.E. Once and for all, the rabbis defined "being Jewish" in
terms of universally applicable laws, that might be kept by Jews living in
every civilization. Wherever Jews might go, they could serve God through
prayer, study of Torah, practice of the commandments, and acts of
loving-kindness. All Jews were able to study. No clerical class was
required—only learned men. So rabbis took the priests' place as teachers of
the people. The Jews thus formed a commonwealth, living in conformity
with the laws of various governments but in addition carrying out their own
Torah. It was a commonwealth founded on religious belief, a holy community whose membership was defined by obedience to laws believed
given at Sinai and interpreted and applied by rabbinical sages to each
circumstance of daily life.

That in brief is the religion of ancient times subject to analysis in the
following two papers. What we want to inquire into is, first (Chapter 1), the
relationship between the ideas framed by the rabbis of the Mishnah and
the social and historical situation of the Jews of their own day, the first
two centuries C.E. Second (Chapter 2), we inquire into the nature of the
religious leadership demanded by the myth of the two Torahs and how
that type of religious leadership reveals the inner character and definition
of the religion and holy community led by the rabbis.

                                                                J. N.

One

Religion and Society

The Case of Ancient Judaism

Jacob Neusner

One route toward the comparison of religions is laid out by forming questions to be addressed equally to them all. Yet a question must constitute more than a quest for inchoate information. To be interesting, it must phrase a thesis, propose an explanation for why we find a given phenomenon in one set of circumstances and not in some other. In the analysis of the relationship between a religion and the larger social setting of that religion, Max Weber is a preeminent figure, a model in both shaping and answering questions, proposing, testing, and refining theories. In describing the interplay between, on the one side, the modes of thought and the characteristic way in which intellectual exercises were framed and worked out in ancient Judaism and, on the other side, the social situation of ancient Israel in the Holy Land of the later first and second centuries, I therefore revert to Max Weber. He forms the bridge between the discussion which follows and parallel discussions to be generated in describing other religious traditions in their social settings. His question applies equally everywhere: how do religious ideas relate to the way in which a society works?

There are two points of interest today in Weber's thought, one which serves to define my problem, and one which shows the way in which I propose to solve it. First, Weber's interest in the relation between social stratification and religious ideas presents an enduring perspective for the analysis of the place of religion in society and of the relationship between religion and society. Second, Weber's mode of formulating ideal types for the purposes of analysis provides a model for how we may think about the castes, professions, and classes of society and the religious ideas they hold. The former is the fundamental issue. If we ask about whether we may discern congruence between the religious ideas to be assigned to a given group, described in gross terms as an ideal type, in ancient Israelite society, and the class status of that group, we use a mode of thought shaped by Weber in the analysis of a question raised by Weber.

It is in that sense alone that I revisit Weber. I do not propose to enrich the vast literature of interpretation of his writings, let alone discuss the enduring or transient value of his work on ancient Judaism, which is important only in the study of Weber. I shall simply take the road laid out by Weber, in order to cross frontiers of problems of interpretation not known to the world of learning in the time of Weber's *Ancient Judaism*. My purpose, stated simply, is to explore the paramount theme of Weber's great work, as expressed by Reinhard Bendix:

> In order to understand the stability and dynamics of a society we should attempt to understand these efforts in relation to the ideas and values that are prevalent in the society; or, conversely, for every given idea or value that we observe we should seek out the status group whose material and ideal way of life it tends to enhance. Thus, Weber approached the study of religious ideas in terms of their relevance for collective actions, and specially in terms of the social processes whereby the inspirations of a few become the convictions of the many (Reinhard Bendix, *Max Weber. An Intellectual Portrait* [New York, 1962: Doubleday], p. 259).

The question, then, is how to relate the religious ideas held by an important group of Jews in the later first and second centuries to the social world imagined by that group.

The group under discussion is that handful of sages who, from before 70, through the period between the second war against Rome, in 132–135, and down to the end of the second century, worked out the principal themes of Israelite life and law and produced the Mishnah, their systematic account of the way in which Israel, the Jewish people in the Holy Land, should construct its life.* Taking up, in succession, the holiness of the Land, the proper conduct of cult and home on holy days, the holiness

---

* Weber's formulation of the problem—the relationship of religious ideas to the group which held them—justifies our concentrating on the Mishnah. First, we assume only that the Mishnah speaks for its authorities, with no presuppositions, at this point, about their prospective audience. Second, since the Mishnah, to begin with, is a collective document, carefully effacing the signs of individual authorship or authority, we are

of family life with special reference to the transfer of women from the father's house to the husband's bed, the stable conduct of civil life, the conduct of the cult on ordinary days, and the bounds of holiness in a world of cultic uncleanness, the Mishnah designed the formative categories of reality and designated their contents.

My work is to generalize about fundamental religious perspectives and collective actions. Now it is not difficult to take up one teaching or another within that law code and speculate about who may have said it, for what material or ideal purpose, and as an expression of which social status or context. But that sort of unsystematic and unmethodical speculation is hardly worthy of the question presented to us by Max Weber, because in the end the answers are beside the point. We wish to ask how and why "the inspirations of a few"—the sages of the document under discussion and the people who stand behind the document—become "the convictions of the many." For that purpose, episodic speculation on discrete sayings is not really pertinent, even if it *were* to be subject to the controls and tests of verification and falsification.

Rather I wish to turn to a more fundamental matter, which is the mode of thought of the group as a whole. That mode of thought is revealed, in particular, in the way in which questions are formulated. For what is significant is the asking; what is revealing is how people define what they wish to know. If we may discover the key to the system by which questions are generated and by which the logic for forming and answering those questions is made to appear to be self-evident, and if we may then relate that mode of logic and inquiry to its social setting, then I believe we may claim to speak to that program of thought laid forth by Weber in his effort "to analyze the relation between social stratification and religious ideas" (Bendix, p. 258). In this regard, individual ideas, let alone the ideas of individual thinkers, are not important. The great classical historian, Harold Cherniss, says, "The historian is concerned to comprehend the individuality of a work of art only in order that he may eliminate it and so extract for use as historical evidence those elements which are not the creation of the author" (Harold Cherniss, "The Biographical Fashion in Literary Criticism," in *University of California Publications in Classical Philology*, ed. J T. Allen, W. H. Alexander, and G. M. Calhoun, 12 no. 15, pp. 279–80). We must do the same. That is, we are not helped to know the ideas of individuals or even the concrete and specific doctrines of the document. We wish, rather, to eliminate not only individuality but also all specificity. So we turn to what is most general. That is, as I said,

justified in deeming it to speak for a group. Third, as we shall see, the Mishnah most certainly is a corpus of religious conceptions, framed, in some measure, to be sure, through the medium of civil law. So it would be wrong to suppose that at hand is an exercise in treating a book as a religious community. Within the framework of Weber's paradigm, the Mishnah constitutes an ideal program for description and analysis of one suggestive aspect of the relationship between religion and society.

we want to discover the systemic motive behind asking a question, the power which generates and defines both problems and the logic by which they will be solved.

The issues which occupy the Mishnah's philosophical mode of forming ideas and defining questions to be taken up will be seen to emerge from the social circumstances of the people of Israel in the Land of Israel. Specifically, the Mishnah's systematic preoccupation with sorting out uncertainties, with pointing up and resolving points of conflict, and with bringing into alignment contradictory principles, corresponds in thought to the confusion and doubt which then disordered Israelite social existence in the aftermath of defeat and catastrophe. In every line the Mishnah both expresses the issue of confusion in the wake of the end of the old mode of ordering life above and below, and also imposes order by sorting out confused matters. The Mishnaic message is that Israel's will is decisive. What the Israelite proposes is what disposes of questions, resolves conflict, settles doubt. Everything depends upon Israelite will, whether this thing of which we speak be expressed in terms of wish, intention, attitude, hope, conception, idea, aspiration, or other words which speak of parts of the whole entity. So the medium is a sequence of problems of conflict and confusion, and the message is that things are what you will them to be. At a time of deep despair and doubt such as the later first and second centuries, this appeal to the heart and mind of Israel penetrated to the depths of the dilemma.

The Mishnah in Its Social Setting

The Mishnah presents a "Judaism," that is, a coherent world view and comprehensive way of living. It is a world view which speaks of transcendent things, a way of life expressive of the supernatural meaning of what is done, a heightened and deepened perception of the sanctification of Israel in deed and in deliberation. Sanctification means two things: first, distinguishing Israel in all its dimensions from the world in all its ways; second, establishing the stability, order, regularity, predictability, and reliability of Israel at moments and in contexts of danger, meaning instability, disorder, irregularity, uncertainty, and betrayal. Each topic of the Mishnah's system of Judaism as a whole takes up a critical and indispensable moment or context of social being. Through what is said in regard to each of the Mishnah's principal topics, what the system as a whole wishes to declare is fully expressed. Yet if the parts both severally and jointly give the message of the whole, the whole cannot exist without all of the parts, so well-joined and carefully crafted are they all.

Let us review the divisions, starting with Agriculture. The critical issue in economic life, which means in farming, is in two parts. First,

Israel, as tenant on God's Holy Land, maintains the property in the ways God requires, keeping the rules which mark the Land and its crops as holy. Second, at the hour at which the sanctification of the Land comes to form a critical mass, namely, in the ripened crops, comes the moment ponderous with danger and heightened holiness. Israel's will so affects the crops as to mark a part of them as holy, the rest of them as available for common use. The human will is determinative in the process of sanctification. Second, what happens in the Land at certain times, at "appointed times," marks off spaces of the Land as holy in yet another way. The center of the Land and the focus of its sanctification is the Temple. There the produce of the Land is received and given back to God, the One who created and sanctified the Land. At these unusual moments of sanctification, the inhabitants of the Land in their social being in villages enter a state of spatial sanctification. This is expressed in two ways. First, the Temple itself observes and expresses the special, recurring holy time. Second, the villages of the Land are brought into alignment with the Temple, forming a complement and completion to the Temple's sacred being. The advent of the appointed times precipitates a spatial reordering of the Land, so that the boundaries of the sacred are matched and mirrored in village and in Temple. At the heightened holiness marked by these moments of appointed times, therefore, the occasion for an effective sanctification is worked out. Like the harvest, the advent of an appointed time, a pilgrim festival, also a sacred season, is made to express that regular, orderly, and predictable sort of sanctification for Israel which the system as a whole seeks.

If for a moment we bypass the next two divisions, we come to the counterpart of the divisions of Agriculture and Appointed Times, that is, Holy Things and Purities. These divisions deal with the everyday and the ordinary, as against the special moments of harvest, on the one side, and special time or season, on the other. The Temple, the locus of continuous, as against special, sanctification, is conducted in a wholly routine and trustworthy, punctilious manner. The one thing which may unsettle matters is the intention and will of the human actor. The division of Holy Things generates its companion, the one on cultic cleanness, Purities. The relationship between the two is like that between Agriculture and Appointed Times, the former locative, the latter utopian, the former dealing with the fields, the latter with the interplay between fields and altar. Here too, once we speak of the one place of the Temple, we address, too, the cleanness which pertains to every place. A system of cleanness, taking into account what imparts uncleanness and how this is done, what is subject to uncleanness, and how that state is overcome—that system is fully expressed, once more, in response to the participation of the human will. Without the wish and act of a human being, the system does not function. It is inert. Sources of uncleanness, which come naturally and not by volition, and modes of purification, which work naturally and not by human intervention, remain inert until human will has imparted susceptibility to uncleanness, that is, introduced into the system that food and drink, bed, pot, chair, and pan, which to begin with form the focus of the system. The movement from sanctification to uncleanness takes place when human will and work precipitate it.

The middle divisions, the third and fourth, on Women (family law) and Damages (civil law), finally, take their place in the structure of the whole by showing the congruence, within the larger framework of sanctification through regularity and the perfection of social order, of human concerns of family and farm, politics and workaday transactions among ordinary people. For without attending to these matters, the Mishnah's system does not encompass what, at its foundations, it is meant to comprehend and order. What is at issue is fully cogent with the rest. In the case of women, attention focuses upon the point of disorder marked by the transfer of that disordering anomaly, woman, from the regular status provided by one man, to the equally trustworthy status provided by another. That is the point at which the Mishnah's interests are aroused: once more, predictably, the moment of disorder. In the case of damages, there are two important concerns. First, there is the paramount interest in preventing, so far as possible, the disorderly rise of one person and fall of another, and in sustaining the status quo of the economy of the household Israel, the holy society in perfect stasis. Second, there is the necessary concomitant in the provision of a system of political institutions to carry out the laws which preserve the balance and steady state of persons.

The divisions which take up topics of concrete and material concern, the formation and dissolution of families and the transfer of property in that connection, the transactions, both through torts and through commerce, which lead to exchanges of property and the potential dislocation of the state of families in society, are both locative and utopian. They deal with the concrete locations in which people make their lives, household and street and field, the sexual and commercial exchanges of a given village. But they pertain to the life of all Israel, both in the Land and otherwise. These two divisions, together with the household ones of Appointed Times, constitute the sole opening outward toward the life of utopian Israel, that diaspora in the far reaches of the ancient world. This community from the Mishnah's perspective is not merely in exile but unaccounted for; it is simply outside the system, for the Mishnah declines to recognize and take it into account. Israelites who dwell in the land of (unclean) death instead of in the Land simply fall outside of the realm and range of (holy) life.

Now if we ask ourselves about the sponsorship and source of special interest in the topics just now reviewed, we come up with obvious answers.

So far as the Mishnah is a document about the holiness of Israel in its Land, it expresses the conception of sanctification and theory of its mode which will have been shaped among those to whom the Temple and its technology of joining Heaven and Holy Land through the sacred place defined the core of being—I mean among the caste of the priests.

So far as the Mishnah takes up the way in which transactions are conducted among ordinary folk and takes the position that it is through documents that transactions are embodied and expressed (surely the position of the relevant tractates on both Women and Damages), the Mishnah expresses what is self-evident to scribes. Just as, to the priest, there is a correspondence between the table of the Lord in the Temple and the locus of the divinity in the heavens, so, to the scribe, there is a correspondence between the documentary expression of the human will on earth, in writs of all sorts, in the orderly provision of courts for the predictable and just disposition of exchanges of persons and property, and Heaven's judgment of these same matters. When a woman becomes sanctified to a particular man on earth, through the appropriate document governing the transfer of her person and property, in heaven as well the woman is deemed truly sanctified to that man. A violation of the writ therefore is not merely a crime. It is a sin. That is why the Temple rite involving the wife accused of adultery is integral to the system of the division of Women.

So there are these two social groups. But they are not symmetrical with one another. For one is the priestly caste, and the other is the scribal profession. We know, moreover, that in time to come, the profession would become a focus of sanctification too. The scribe would be transformed into the rabbi, locus of the holy through what he knew, just as the priest had been, and would remain, locus of the holy through what he could claim for genealogy. The tractates of special interest to scribes-become-rabbis and to their governance of Israelite society, those of Women and Damages, together with certain others particularly relevant to utopian Israel beyond the system of the Land—those tractates would grow and grow. Others would remain essentially as they were with the closure of the Mishnah. So we must notice that the Mishnah, for its part, speaks about the program of topics important to the priests. It does so in the persona of the scribes, speaking through their voice and in their manner.

Now what we do not find is astonishing in the light of these observations. It is sustained and serious attention to the matter of the caste of the priests and of the profession of the scribes. True, scattered through the tractates are exercises, occasionally important exercises, on the genealogy of the priestly caste, their marital obligations and duties, as well as on the things priests do and do not do in the cult, in collecting and eating their sanctified food, and other topics of keen interest to priests. Indeed, it would be no exaggeration to say that the Mishnah's system, seen whole, is not a great deal more than a handbook of how the priestly caste wished to design its life in Israel and the world. And this is what makes amazing the fact that in the fundamental structure of the document, its organization into divisions and tractates, there is no place for a division of the Priesthood. There is no room even for a complete tractate on the rules of the priesthood, except, as we have seen, for the pervasive way of life of the priestly caste, which is everywhere. This absence of sustained attention to the priesthood is striking, when we compare the way in which the Priestly Code in Leviticus, chapters 1 through 15, spells out its triplet of concerns: the priesthood, the cult, the matter of cultic cleanness. Since we have divisions for the cult and for cleanness at Holy Things and Purities, we are struck by the absence of a parallel to the third division.

We must, moreover, be equally suprised that, for a document so rich in the importance lent to petty matters of how a writ is folded and where the witnesses sign, so obsessed with the making of long lists and the organization of all knowledge into neat piles of symmetrically arranged words, the scribes who know how to make lists and match words nowhere come to the fore. They speak through the document. But they stand behind the curtains. They write the script, arrange the sets, design the costumes, situate the players in their place on the stage, raise the curtain—and play no role at all. We have no division or tractate on such matters as how a person becomes a scribe, how a scribe conducts his work, who forms the center of the scribal profession and how authority is gained therein, the rights and place of the scribe in the system of governance through courts, the organization and conduct of schools or circles of masters and disciples through which the scribal arts are taught and perpetuated. This absence of even minimal information on the way in which the scribal profession takes shape and does its work is stunning, when we realize that, within a brief generation, the Mishnah as a whole would fall into the hands of scribes, called rabbis,* both in the Land of Israel and in Babylonia. These rabbis would make of the Mishnah exactly what they wished. The makers of the Mishnah, the priests and the scribes who provided content and form, substance and style, therefore, turn out to have omitted all reference to actors, when laying out the world which is their play.

The metaphor of the theater for the economy of Israel, the household

---

* But the title "rabbi" cannot be thought particular to those who served as judges and administrators in small-claims courts and as scribes and authorities in the Jewish communities, called "rabbis" in the Talmudic literature and afterward. The title is clearly prior to its particularization in the institutions of the Talmudic community.

of Holy Land and people, space and time, cult and home, leads to yet another perspective. When we look out upon the vast drama portrayed by the Mishnah, lacking as it does an account of the one who wrote the book, and the one about whom the book was written, we notice yet one more missing component. In the fundamental and generative structure of the Mishnah, we find no account of that other necessary constituent: the audience. To whom the document speaks is never specified. What group ("class") generates the Mishnah's problems is not at issue. True, it is taken for granted that the world of the Mishnah expresses the sanctified being of Israel in general. So the Mishnah speaks about the generality of Israel, the people. But to whom, within Israel, the Mishnah addresses itself, and what groups are expected to want to know what the Mishnah has to say, are matters which never come to full expression.

Yet there can be no doubt of the answer to the question. The building block of Mishnaic discourse, the circumstance addressed whenever the issues of concrete society and material transactions are taken up, is the householder and his context. The Mishnah knows all sorts of economic activities. But for the Mishnah the center and focus of interest lie in the village. The village is made up of households, each a unit of production in farming. The households are constructed by, and around, the householder, father of an extended family, including his sons and their wives and children, his servants, his slaves, the craftsmen to whom he entrusts tasks he does not choose to do. The concerns of householders are in transactions in land. Their measurement of value is expressed in acreage of top, middle, and bottom grade. Through real estate critical transactions are worked out. The marriage settlement depends upon real property. Civil penalties are exacted through payment of real property. The principal transactions to be taken up are those of the householder who owns beasts which do damage or suffer it; who harvests his crops and must set aside and so by his own word and deed sanctify them for use by the castes scheduled from on high; who uses or sells his crops and feeds his family: and who, if he is fortunate, will acquire still more land. It is to householders that the Mishnah is addressed: the pivot of society and its bulwark, the units of production of which the village is composed, the corporate component of the society of Israel in the limits of the village and the land. The householder, as I said, is the building block of the house of Israel, of its *economy* in the classic sense of the word.

So, to revert to the metaphor which has served us well, the great proscenium constructed by the Mishnah now looms before us. Its arch is the canopy of heaven. Its stage is the Holy Land of Israel, corresponding to Heaven. Its actors are the holy people of Israel. Its events are the drama of unfolding time and common transactions, appointed times and holy events. Yet in this grand design we look in vain for the three principal participants: the audience, the actors, and the playwright. So we must ask why.

The reason is not difficult to discover, when we recall that, after all, what the Mishnah really wants is for nothing to happen. The Mishnah presents a tableau, a wax museum, a diorama. It portrays a world fully perfected and so wholly at rest. The one thing the Mishnah does not want to tell us about is change—how things come to be, or cease to be, what they are. That is why there can be no sustained attention to the caste of the priesthood and its rules, the scribal profession and its constitution, the class of householders and its interests. The Mishnah's pretense is that all of these have come to rest. They compose a world in stasis, perfect and complete, made holy because it is complete and perfect. It is an economy—again in the classic sense of the word—awaiting the divine *act* of sanctification which, as at the creation of the world, would set the seal of holy rest upon an again-complete creation, just as in the beginning. There is no place for the actors when what is besought is no action whatsoever but only perfection, which is unchanging. There is room only for a description of how things are: the present tense, the sequence of completed statements and static problems. All the action lies within, in how these statements are made. Once they come to full expression, with nothing left to say, there also is nothing left to do, no need for actors, whether scribes, priests, or householders.

We have now to ask how the several perspectives joined in the Mishnah do coalesce; what that single message is which brings them all together, and how that message forms a powerful, if transient, catalyst for the social groups which hold it—these questions define the task of portraying the Judaism for which the Mishnah is the whole evidence. Integral to that task, to be sure, is an account of why, for the moment, the catalyst could serve, as it clearly did, to join together diverse agents, to mingle, mix, indeed unite, for a fleeting moment, social elements quite unlike one another, indeed not even capable of serving as analogies for one another.

One of the paramount, recurring exercises of the Mishnaic thinkers is to give an account of how things which are different from one another become part of one another, that is, the problem of mixtures. This problem of mixtures will be in many dimensions, involving cases of doubt; cases of shared traits and distinctive ones; cases of confusion of essentially distinct elements and components; and numerous other concrete instances of successful and of unsuccessful, complete and partial catalysis. If I had to choose one prevailing motif of Mishnaic thought, it would be this: this joining together of categories which are distinct, the distinguishing among those which are confused. The Mishnaic mode of thought is to bring together principles and to show both how they conflict and how the conflict is resolved; to deal with gray areas and to lay down principles for disposing of cases of doubt; to take up the analysis of entities into their component parts and the catalysis of distinct substances into a single entity; to analyze the whole, to synthesize the parts. The motive force behind the Mishnah's intellectual program of cases and examples, the thing the authorship of the Mishnah wants to do with all of the facts it has in its hand, is described within this inquiry into mixtures. There are several reasons for this deeply typical, intellectual concern with confusion and order.

For, after all, the basic mode of thought of the priests who made up the priestly creation-legend (Gen. 1:1–2:4a) is that creation is effected through the orderly formation of each thing after its kind and through correct location of each in its place. The persistent quest of the Mishnaic sub-systems is for stasis, order, the appropriate situation of all things.

A recurrent theme in the philosophical tradition of Greco-Roman antiquity, current in the time of the Mishnah's formative intellectual processes, is the nature of mixtures,* the interpenetration of distinct substances and their qualities, the juxtaposition of incomparables. The types of mixture were themselves organized in a taxonomy: a mechanical composition, in which the components remain essentially unchanged, a total fusion, in which all particles are changed and lose their individual properties, and, in between, a mixture proper, in which there is a blending. So, concern for keeping things straight and in their place is part of the priestly heritage, and it also is familiar to the philosophical context in which scribes can have had their being. Nor will the householders have proved disinterested in the notion of well-marked borders and stable and dependable frontiers between different things. What was to be fenced in and fenced out hardly requires specification.

And yet, however tradition and circumstances may have dictated this point of interest in mixtures and their properties, in sorting out what is confused and finding a proper place for everything, I think there is still another reason for the recurrence of a single type of exercise and a uniform mode of thought. It is the social foundation for the intellectual exercise which is the Mishnah and its Judaism. In my view the very condition of Israel, standing, at the end of the second century, on the outer limits of its own history, at the frontiers among diverse peoples, on both sides of every boundary, whether political or cultural or intellectual—it is the condition of Israel itself which attracted attention to this matter of sorting things out. Let me say this emphatically: *The concern for the catalyst which joins what is originally distinct, the powerful attraction of problems of confusion and chaos on the one side, and order and form on the other—these form the generative problematic of the Mishnah as a system*

* I refer to S. Sambursky, *The Physics of the Stoics.*

because they express in intellectual form the very nature and essential being of Israel in its social condition at that particular moment in Israel's history. It is therefore the profound congruence of the intellectual program and the social and historical realities taken up and worked out by that intellectual program, which accounts for the power of the Mishnah to define the subsequent history of Judaism. That is why the inspirations of the few would become, in time, the convictions of the many. This program is what Weber's questions generate for answers.

The Mishnah's Methods of Thought

Now that the tributaries to the Mishnah have been specified, we have to turn to those traits of style and substance in which the Mishnah vastly exceeds the flood of its tributaries, becomes far more than the sum of its parts. The Mishnah in no way presents itself as a document of class, caste, or profession. It is something different. The difference comes to complete statement in the two dimensions which mark the measure of any work of intellect: style and substance, mode of thought, medium of expression, and message. These have now to be specified with full attention to recurrent patterns to be discerned among the myriad of detailed rules, problems, and exercises of which the Mishnah is composed.*

Let us take up, first of all, the matter of style. The Mishnah's paramount literary trait is its emphasis on disputes about the law. Nearly all disputes, which dominate the rhetoric of the Mishnah, derive from bringing diverse legal principles into formal juxtaposition and substantive conflict. So we may say that the Mishnah as a whole is an exercise in the application to a given case, through practical reason, of several distinct and conflicting principles of law. In this context, it follows, the Mishnah is a protracted inquiry into the intersection of principles. It maps out the gray areas of the law delimited by such margins of confusion. An example of this type of "mixture" of legal principles comes in the conflict of two distinct bodies of the law. But gray areas are discerned not only through mechanical juxtaposition, making up a conundrum of distinct principles of law. On the contrary, the Mishnaic philosophers are at their best when they force into conflict laws which, to begin with, scarcely intersect. This they do, for example, by inventing cases in which the secondary implications of one law are brought into conflict with the secondary implications of some other. Finally, nothing will so instantly trigger the imagination of the Mishnah's exegetical minds as matters of ambiguity. A species of the genus of gray areas of the law is the excluded middle, that

---

* Documentation for the general statements made in this section will be found in my *Judaism: The Evidence of the Mishnah* (Chicago: The University of Chicago Press, 1981).

is, that creature or substance which appears to fall between two distinct and definitive categories. The Mishnah's framers time and again allude to such an entity, because it forms the excluded middle which inevitably will attract attention and demand categorization. There are types of recurrent middles among both human beings and animals as well as vegetables. Indeed, the obsession with the excluded middle leads the Mishnah to invent its own examples, which have then to be analyzed into their definitive components and situated in their appropriate category. What this does is to leave no area lacking in an appropriate location, none to yield irresoluable doubt.

The purpose of identifying the excluded middle is to allow the lawyers to sort out distinct rules on the one side, and to demonstrate how they intersect without generating intolerable uncertainty on the other. For example, to explore the theory that an object can serve as either a utensil or a tent, that is, a place capable of spreading the uncleanness of a corpse under its roof, the framers of the Mishnah invent a "hive." This is sufficiently large so that it can be imagined to be either a utensil or a tent. When it is whole, it is the former; if it is broken, it is the latter. The location of the object, e.g., on the ground, off the ground, in a doorway, against a wall, and so on, will further shape the rules governing the cases (M. Ohalot 9:1–14). Again, to indicate the ambiguities lying at the frontiers, the topic of the status of Syria will come under repeated discussion. Syria is deemed not wholly sanctified, as is the Land of Israel, but also not wholly outside of the frame of Holy Land, as are all other countries. That is why to Syria apply some rules applicable to Holy Land, some rules applicable to secular land. In consequence, numerous points of ambiguity will be uncovered and explored (M. Shebiit 6:1–6).

Gray areas of the law in general, and the excluded middle in particular, cover the surface of the law. They fill up nearly every chapter of the Mishnah. But underneath the surface is an inquiry of profound and far-reaching range. It is into the metaphysical or philosophical issues of how things join together and how they do not, of synthesis and analysis, of fusion and union, connection, division, and disintegration. What we have in the recurrent study of the nature of mixtures, broadly construed, is a sustained philosophical treatise in the guise of an episodic exercise in ad hoc problem-solving. It is as if the cultic agenda, laid forth by the priests, the social agenda, defined by the confusing status and condition of Israel, and the program for right categorization of persons and things, set forth for the scribes to carry out, were all taken over and subsumed by the philosophers, who proposed to talk abstractly about what they deemed urgent, while using the concrete language and syntax of untrained minds. To put it differently, the framers of the Mishnah, in their reflection on the nature of mixtures in their various potentialities for formation

and dissolution, shape into hidden discourse on an encompassing philo-
sophical-physical problem of their own choosing, topics provided by
others.

In so doing, they phrased the critical question demanding attention
and response, the question in dimensions at once social, political,
metaphysical, cultural, and even linguistic, but above all historical: the
question of Israel, standing at the outer boundaries of a long history
now decisively done with. That same question of acculturation and assimilation, alienation and exile, which had confronted the sixth century
B.C. priests of the Priestly Code, was raised once more during the years
from 70 to 200. Now it is framed in terms of mechanical composition,
fusion, and something in between, mixture. But it is phrased in incredible
terms of a wildly irrelevant world of unseen things, of how we define the
place of the stem in the entity of the apple, the affect of the gravy upon the
meat, and the definitive power of a bit of linen in a fabric of wool. In
concrete form, the issues are close to comic. In abstract form, the answers speak of nothing of workaday meaning. In reality, at issue is Israel
in its Land, once the lines of structure which had emanated from the
Temple had been blurred and obliterated. It is in this emphasis upon
sorting out confused things that the Mishnah becomes truly Mishnaic,
distinct from modes and thought and perspective to be assigned to groups
represented in the document. To interpret the meaning of this emphasis,
we must again recall that the Priestly Code makes the point that a well-
ordered society on earth, with its center and point of reference at the
Temple altar, corresponds to a well-ordered canopy of heaven. Creation
comes to its climax at the perfect rest marked by completion and signify-
ing perfection and sanctification. Indeed, the creation myth represents as
the occasion for sanctification a perfected world at rest, with all things in
their rightful place. Now the Mishnah takes up this conviction, which is
located at the deepest structures of the metaphysic of the framers of the
Priestly Code and, therefore, of their earliest continuators and imitators in
the Mishnaic code. But the Mishnah does not frame the conviction that in
order is salvation through a myth of creation and a description of a cult of
precise and perfect order, such as is at Genesis 1:1–2:4a. True, the Mishnah imposes order upon the world through lines of structure emanating
from the cult. The verses of Scripture selected as authoritative leave no
alternative.

Yet, the Mishnah at its deepest layers, taking up the raw materials of
concern of priests and farmers and scribes, speaks that concern after the
manner of philosophers. That is to say, the framers of the Mishnah speak
of the physics of mixtures, conflicts of principles which must be sorted
out, areas of doubt generated by confusion. The detritus of a world seek-

ing order but suffering chaos is reduced to the construction of intellect. If, therefore, we wish to characterize the Mishnah when it is cogent and distinctive, we must point to this persistent and pervasive mode of thought. For the Mishnah takes up a vast corpus of facts and treats these facts, so to speak, "Mishnaically," that is, in a way distinctive to the Mishnah, predictable and typical of the Mishnah. That is what I mean when I refer to the style of the Mishnah: its manner of exegesis of a topic, its mode of thought about any subject, the sorts of perplexities which will precipitate the Mishnah's fertilizing flood of problem-making ingenuity. Confusion and conflict will trigger the Mishnah's power to control conflict by showing its limits, and, thus, the range of shared conviction too.

For by treating facts "Mishnaically," the Mishnah establishes boundaries around, and pathways through, confusion. It lays out roads to guide people by ranges of permissible doubt. Consequently, the Mishnah's mode of control over the chaos of conflicting principles, the confusion of doubt, the improbabilities of a world out of alignment, is to delimit and demarcate. By exploring the range of interstitial conflict through its ubiquitous disputes, the Mishnah keeps conflict under control. It so preserves that larger range of agreement, that pervasive and shared conviction, which is never expressed, which is always instantiated, and which, above all, is forever taken for granted. The Mishnah's deepest convictions about what lies beyond confusion and conflict are never spelled out; they lie in the preliminary, unstated exercise prior to the commencement of a sustained exercise of inquiry, a tractate. They are the things we know before we take up that exercise and study that tractate.

Now all of this vast complex of methods and styles, some of them intellectual, some of them literary and formal, may be captured in the Mishnah's treatment of its own, self-generated conflicts of principles, its search for gray areas of the law. It also may be clearly discerned in the Mishnah's sustained interest in those excluded middles it makes up for the purpose of showing the limits of the law, the confluence and conflict of laws. It further may be perceived in the Mishnah's recurrent exercise in the study of types of mixtures, the ways distinct components of an entity may be joined together, may be deemed separate from one another, may be shown to be fused, or may be shown to share some traits and not others. Finally, the Mishnah's power to sort out matters of confusion will be clearly visible in its repeated statement of the principles by which cases of doubt are to be resolved. A survey of these four modes of thought thus shows us one side of the distinctive and typical character of the Mishnah, when the Mishnah transcends the program of facts, forms, and favored perspectives of its tributaries. We now turn to the side of substance. What causes and resolves confusion and chaos is the power of the Israelite's will. As is said in the context of measurements for minimum quantities to be subject to uncleanness, "All accords with the measure of the man" (M. Kelim 17:11).

The Mishnah's principle message is that Israelite man is at the center of creation, the head of all creatures upon earth, corresponding to God in heaven, in whose image man is made. The way in which the Mishnah makes this simple and fundamental statement is to impute power to the Israelite to inaugurate and initiate those corresponding processes, sanctification and uncleanness, which play so critical a role in the Mishnah's account of reality. The will of man, expressed through the deed of man, is the active power in the world. Will and deed—these constitute those actors of creation which work upon neutral realms, subject to either sanctification or uncleanness: the Temple and table, the field and family, the altar and hearth, woman, time, space, transactions in the material world and in the world above as well. An object, a substance, a transaction, even a phrase or a sentence, is inert but may be made holy when the interplay of the will and deed of man arouses and generates its potential to be sanctified. Each may be treated as ordinary or (where relevant) may be made unclean by neglect of the will and inattentive act of man. Just as the entire system of uncleanness and holiness awaits the intervention of man, which imparts the capacity to become unclean upon what was formerly inert, or which removes the capacity to impart cleanness from what was formerly in its natural and puissant condition, so in the other ranges of reality man is at the center on earth, just as is God in heaven. Man is counterpart and partner in creation, in that, like God, he has power over the status and condition of creation, putting everything in its proper place, calling everything by its rightful name.

So, stated briefly, the question taken up by the Mishnah is, What can a man do? And the answer laid down by the Mishnah is, Man, through will and deed, is master of this world, the measure of all things. Since, when the Mishnah thinks of man, it means the Israelite, who is the subject and actor of its system, the statement is clear. This man is Israel, who can do what he wills. In the aftermath of the two wars, in 66–73 and 132–35, the message of the Mishnah cannot have proved more pertinent—or poignant and tragic. The principal message of the Mishnah is that the will of man affects the material reality of the world and governs the working of those forces, visible or not, which express and effect the sanctification of creation and of Israel alike. This message comes to the surface in countless ways. At the outset a simple example of the supernatural power of man's intention suffices to show the basic power of the Israelite's will to change concrete, tangible facts. The power of the human will is nowhere more effective than in the cult, where, under certain circumstances, what a person is thinking is more important than what he does. The basic point is that if an animal is designated for a given purpose, but the priest prepares the animal with the thought in mind that the beast serves some other sacrificial purpose, then, in some instances, in particular involving a sin offering and a Passover on the fourteenth of Nisan, the sacrifice is ruined. In this matter of preparation of the animal, moreover, are involved the deeds of slaughtering the beast, collecting, conveying, and tossing the blood on the altar, that is, the principal priestly deeds of sacrifice. Again, if the priest has in mind, when doing these deeds, to offer up the parts to be offered up on the altar, or to eat the parts to be eaten by the priest, in some location other than the proper one (the altar, the courtyard, respectively), or at some time other than the requisite one (the next few hours), the rite is spoiled, the meat must be thrown out. Now that is the case, even if the priest did not do what he was thinking of doing. Here again we have a testimony to the fundamental importance imputed to what a person is thinking, even over what he actually does, in critical aspects of the holy life (M. Zebahim 1:1–4:6, Menahot 1:1–4:5).

Once man wants something, a system of the law begins to function. Intention has the power, in particular, to initiate the processes of sanctification. So the moment at which something becomes sacred and so falls under a range of severe penalties for misappropriation, or requires a range of strict modes of attentiveness and protection for the preservation of cleanness, is defined by the human will. Stated simply: at the center of the Mishnaic system is the notion that man has the power to inaugurate the work of sanctification, and the Mishnaic system states and restates that power. This assessment of the positive power of the human will begins with the matter of uncleanness, one antonym of sanctification or holiness. Man alone has the power to inaugurate the system of uncleanness.

From the power of man to introduce an object or substance into the processes of uncleanness, we turn to the corresponding power of man to sanctify an object or a substance. This is a much more subtle matter, but it also is more striking. It is the act of designation by a human being which "activates" that holiness inherent in crops from which no tithes have yet been set aside and removed. Once the human being has designated what is holy within the larger crop, then that designated portion of the crop gathers within itself the formerly diffused holiness and becomes holy, set aside for the use and benefit of the priest to whom it is given. So it is the interplay between the will of the farmer, who owns the crop, and the sanctity inherent in the whole batch of the crop itself, which is required for the processes of sanctification to work themselves out.

In addition to the power to initiate the process of sanctification and the system of uncleanness and cleanness, man has the power, through the working of his will, to differentiate one thing from another. The fundamental category into which an entity, which may be this or that, is to be placed is decided by the human will for that entity. Man exercises the power of categorization, and so ends confusion. Once more, the consequence will be that, what man decides, Heaven confirms or ratifies. Once man determines that something falls into one category and not another, the interest of Heaven is provoked. Then misuse of that thing invokes Heavenly penalties. So man's will has the capacity so to work as to engage the ratifying power of Heaven. Let us take up first of all the most striking example, the deed itself. It would be difficult to doubt that what one does determines the effect of what one does. But that position is rejected. The very valence and result of a deed depend, to begin with, on one's prior intent. The intent which leads a person to do a deed governs the culpability of the deed. There is no intrinsic weight to the deed itself. Human will not only is definitive. It also provides the criterion for differentiation in cases of uncertainty or doubt. This is an overriding fact. That is why I insisted earlier that the principal range of questions addressed by the Mishnah—areas of doubt and uncertainty about status or taxonomy—provokes an encompassing response. This response, it now is clear, in the deep conviction of the Mishnaic law, present at the deepest structures of the law, is that what man wills or thinks decides all issues of taxonomy.

The characteristic mode of thought of the Mishnah is, then, to try to sort things out, exploring the limits of conflict and the range of consensus. The one thing which the Mishnah's framers predictably want to know concerns what falls between two established categories or rules, the gray area of the law, the excluded middle among entities, whether persons, places, or things. This obsession with the liminal or marginal comes to its climax and fulfillment in the remarkably wide-ranging inquiry into the nature of mixtures, whether these are mixtures of substances in a concrete framework or of principles and rules in an abstract one. So the question is fully phrased by both the style of the Mishnaic discourse and its rhetoric. It then is fully answered. The question of how we know what something is, the way in which we assign to its proper frame and category what crosses the lines between categories, is settled by what Israelite man wants, thinks, hopes, believes, and how he so acts as to indicate his attitude. With the question properly phrased in the style and mode of Mishnaic thought and discourse, the answer is not difficult to express. What makes the difference, what sets things into their proper category and resolves those gray areas of confusion and conflict formed when simple principles intersect and produce dispute, is man's will. Israel's despair or hope is the definitive and differentiating criterion.

The Convictions of the Many

Passionate concern for order and stability, for sorting things out and resolving confusion, ambiguity, and doubt—these may well characterize the mind of priests, scribes, and householders. The priests, after all, emerge from a tradition of sanctification achieved through the perfection of the order of creation—that is the theology of their creation myth. The scribes, with their concern for the correspondence between what they do on earth and what is accorded approval and confirmation in Heaven, likewise carry forward that interest in form and order characteristic of a profession of their kind. But if I had to choose that single group for whom the system speaks, it would be neither of these. We noted at the outset that the scribe and the priest are noteworthy by their absence from the fundamental structure and organization of the Mishnah's documents. By contrast, the householder forms the focus of two of the six divisions, those devoted to civil law and family. Let us then reflect for a moment on the ways in which the householder will have found the Mishnah's principal modes of concern congruent with his own program. We speak now of the householder in a courtyard, for he is the subject of most predicates. He is the proprietor of an estate, however modest, however little. He also is a landholder in the fields, an employer with a legitimate claim against lazy or unreliable workers, the head of a family, and the manager of a small but self-contained farm. He is someone who gives over his property to craftsmen for their skilled labor but is not a craftsman himself. He also is someone with a keen interest in assessing and collecting damages done to his herds and flocks, or in paying what he must for what his beasts do. The Mishnah speaks for someone who deems thievery to be the paltry, petty thievery ("Oh! the servants!") of watchmen of an orchard and herdsmen of a flock, and for a landowner constantly involved in transactions in real property.

The Mishnah's class-perspective, described merely from its topics and problems, is that of the undercapitalized and overextended upper-class farmer, who has no appreciation whatsoever for the interests of those with liquid capital and no understanding of the role of trading in commodity futures. This landed proprietor of an estate of some size sees a bushel of grain as a measure of value. But he does not concede that, in the provision of supplies and sustenance through the year, from one harvest to the next, lies a kind of increase no less productive than the increase of the fields and the herd. The Mishnah is the voice of the head of the household, the pillar of society, the model of the community, the arbiter and mediator of the goods of this world, fair, just, honorable, above all, reliable.

The Mishnah therefore is the voice of the Israelite landholding, proprietary class (compare *Soviet Views of Talmudic Judaism. Five Papers by Yu. A. Solodukho in English Translation,* edited with a commentary by this writer [Leiden, 1973: E. J. Brill]). Its problems are the problems of the landowner, the householder, as I said, the Mishnah's basic and recurrent subject for nearly all predicates. Its perspectives are his. Its sense of what is just and fair expresses his sense of the givenness and cosmic rightness of the present condition of society. Earth matches Heaven. The Mishnah's hope for Heaven and its claim on earth, to earth, corresponding to the supernatural basis for the natural world, bespeak the imagination of the surviving Israelite burgherdom of the mid-second-century Land of Israel—people deeply tired of war and its dislocation, profoundly distrustful of messiahs and their dangerous promises. These are men of substance and means, however modest, aching for a stable and predictable world in which to tend their crops and herds, feed their families and workers, keep to the natural rhythms of the seasons and the lunar cycles, and, in all, live out their lives within strong and secure boundaries, on earth and in Heaven.

Now when we turn away from the Mishnah's imagined world to the actual context of the Israelite community after the destruction of the Temple in 70 and still later after Bar Kokhba, we are able to discern what it is that the Mishnah's sages have for raw materials, the slime they have for mortar, the bricks they have for building. The archaeological evidence of the later second and third centuries reveals a thriving Israelite community in Galilee and surrounding regions, a community well able to construct for itself synagogues of considerable aesthetic ambition, to sustain and support an internal government and the appurtenances of an abundant life. What that means is that, while the south was permanently lost, the north remained essentially intact. Indeed, it would be on the sturdy and secure foundations of that stable community of the northern part of the Land of Israel that Israelite life for the next three or four hundred years—a very long time—would be constructed.

So when the Mishnah's sages cast their eyes out on the surviving Israelite world, their gaze must have rested upon that thing which had endured, and would continue to endure, beyond the unimaginable catastrophe brought on by Bar Kokhba and his disruptive messianic adventure. Extant and enduring was a world of responsible, solid farmers and their slaves and dependents, the men and women upon the backs of whom the Israelite world would now have come to rest. They, their children, slaves, dependents could yet make a world to endure, if only they could keep what they had, pretty much as they had it—no more, but also no less. Theirs was not a society aimed at aggrandizement. They wanted no more than to preserve what had survived out of the disorderly past. That is why the Mishnah is not a system respectful of increase. It asks only that what is to be, is to be. The Mishnah seeks the perfection of a world at rest, the precondition of that seal of creation's perfection sanctified on the seventh day of Creation and perpetually sanctified by the seventh day of Creation.

But if the philosophers of Israelite society refer to a real world, a world in being, the values of which were susceptible of protection and preservation, the boudaries of which were readily discerned, they also defied that real world. They speak of location but have none. For Israelite settlements in the Land then were certainly not contiguous. There was no polity resting on a homogeneous social basis. All Israel had was villages, on a speckled map of villages of many peoples. There was no Israelite nation, in full charge of its lands or Land, standing upon contiguous and essentially united territories. This locative polity is built upon utopia: no one place. The ultimate act of will is forming a locative system in no particular place, speaking nowhere about somewhere, concretely specifying utopia. This is done—in context—because Israel wills it.

At the end, Weber's problem points the way for further inquiry: how do the inspirations of a few become the convictions of the many? For, we observe, while the Mishnah came into the world as the law-book of a class of scribes and small-claims-court judges, it in time to come formed the faith and piety of the many of Israel, the Jews at large, the workers and craftsmen. And these, it must be emphasized, were not landholders and farmers. They were in the main landless craftsmen and workers, but they took over this book of landholders and farmers and accepted it as the other half, the oral half, of the whole Torah of God to Moses at Mount Sinai.

That is to say, in somewhat less mythological terms, the Mishnah began with some one group, in fact with a caste, a class, and a profession. But it very rapidly came to form the heart and center of the imaginative life and concrete politics, law, and society of a remarkably diverse set of groups, that is, the Jewish people as a whole. So the really interesting question, when we move from the account of Israelite religion and society in the first and second centuries, represented by the Mishnah, to religion and society in the third and fourth centuries, represented by the Talmuds, and in the fifth and later centuries, represented by the Midrashim, is how the Mishnah was transformed in social context from one thing into something else. If, as I said at the outset, we locate "the status group whose material and ideal way of life a given idea or value tends to enhance," then we must ask why that same idea or value served, as it did, to enhance a far wider and more encompassing group within Israelite society. We must investigate how it came about that, in time to come, Judaism, the world view and way of life resting upon the Scriptures and upon the Mishnah and in due course upon the Talmuds, came to constitute the world view and way of life of nearly all Israel.

For the difficult question before us is the truly historical one: the question of change, of why things begin in one place but move onward, and of how we may account for what happens. The weak point of sociology of religion, in Weber's powerful formulation, emerges from its strong point. If we begin by asking about the relevance of religious ideas to collective actions, we must proceed to wonder about the continuing relevance of religious ideas within a changing collectivity and context. If, as Bendix says, Weber emphasizes the issue of how a given idea or value enhances the way of life of a "status-group," then we must wonder why that given idea or value succeeds in maintaining its own freestanding, ongoing life among and for entirely other status-groups and types of social groups. The history of Judaism from the formation of the Mishnah onward through the next four centuries, amply documented as that period is, provides one important arena for inquiry into yet another constituent of Weber's grand program.

Two

Storytelling and Holy Man

The Case of Ancient Judaism

William Scott Green

The attempt to describe the religious virtuosi of
ancient Judaism must begin not with the rabbis
themselves, their personalities, responsibilities, or
beliefs, but with the sources that tell us about them.
This strategy has an obvious epistemological virtue
in any exercise of historical research, but here it
carries a particular pertinence. Whatever else we
think we know about ancient rabbis, we certainly
know that some of them, at different times, produced texts. Virtually all our information about
these figures comes from documents formulated,
written, and redacted within the rabbinic movement. With few exceptions, these texts, fashioned
and molded by rabbis, constitute the material remains of rabbinic Judaism; they are the primary
evidence for its existence. To base a description of
rabbinic leadership solely on the content of rabbinic
literature is to deny the materiality of the texts and
thereby to overlook important data about rabbinic
culture. It is to read the texts as if they were not
there. Since a precise understanding of rabbinic
textual constructions provides the foundation and
justification for all other inferences from the texts, a
prerequisite to any historical reconstruction of ancient rabbis is a delineation of the textual facts of
the literature they made.

Rabbinic literature is made up of documents
dated from the third century to early medieval times

that treat two broad subjects: *halakhah* (rabbinic praxis, the way of doing things) and the interpretation of Scripture. The documents consist of large numbers of distinct, usually self-contained passages of varying length and character grouped in patterns of thematic, topical, or scriptural arrangement. These pericopae may be brief halakhic or exegetical dicta, somewhat elaborated discourses composed of the arguments and opinions of several rabbis on a halakhic problem, or narratives about rabbis or, less often, about biblical characters. The stories about rabbis are always about unrelated events; the literature is devoid of biography or hagiography.

Most rabbinic documents are unattributed works; all in fact are anonymous; and all comprise significant numbers of unassigned pericopae. Rabbinic literature has no authors. No document claims to be the writing of an individual rabbi in his own words, and all contain the ostensible sayings of, and stories about, many rabbis, usually of several generations. Selected to suit the purposes of compilers and redactors, the documents' components are not pristine and natural. They have been revised and reformulated in the processes of transmission and redaction, with the consequence that the *ipsissima verba* of any rabbi are beyond recovery. Rabbinic literature is severely edited, anonymous, and collective.

Rabbinic documents do not introduce or explain themselves to their readers, and they provide no easy access for tyros and noninitiates. The literature as a whole, especially its halakhic content, presupposes not only considerable information but also codes for interpretation. Its terse and formulaic syntactic constructions and its lean and disciplined vocabulary constitute a scholastic shorthand. Even the most elementary halakhic statement presumes a tacit dimension of rabbinic knowledge, attitudes, behaviors, and motivations. Rabbinic literature virtually ignores the world beyond its own preoccupations. Its documents obscure their origins by neglecting the events that led to their formation, and they report remarkably little about ordinary Jews or non-Jews. This insularity is reinforced by the nearly total absence of external witness to rabbinic religion, culture, and society. The documents present the restricted discourse of a small number of men who appear primarily engaged in observing, discussing, and analysing ideas, opinions, and behaviors, sometimes those recounted in Scripture, but most often those of one another. Rabbinic writing addresses rabbinic specialists; it is a parochial literature wholly obsessed with itself.

The work before us is to develop a strategy of reading these faceless and self-enclosed texts that will yield a critical description of the men they claim to represent, to devise a mode of inquiry that will sunder their seemingly impenetrable facade. This labor requires reflection on the activity of text-making and on the materiality of the texts themselves.

Groups and individuals constitute themselves in society not only through their speech and behavior but also through the production of material works. In the case of literate groups, this means the making of texts. The texts establish the group's identity, objectify its existence, consolidate its picture of reality, and codify the discourse that gives the group its distinctive character. The priestly and Pharisaic struggles to control the form and content of what has become "Scripture" in Judaism, the obsession with the production and protection of texts at Qumran, and the Marcionite controversy, for instance, testify to the importance of text-making in the histories of early Judaism and Christianity. The production of a text, like that of any cultural artifact, is a social activity. Producers of texts draw on socially acquired linguistic, literate, and literary skills and are informed by a tacit awareness of the socially embedded behavioral conventions, cognitive capacities, and aesthetic traits and preferences of their actual or expected audience. The texts produced by literate groups are intricate cultural constructions, and the elements and syntactical frameworks of textual constructions lend whatever significance to their substance a controlled analysis can discern. The form of such texts governs and contrains the presentation of their substance and is as much a part of their production as is their content.

The technical knowledge presupposed by most of rabbinic literature shows that rabbis produced their texts not for the world at large, nor for strangers and outsiders (and, therefore, certainly not for us), but for themselves. In the texts, selected reports of the opinions, arguments, and activities of generations of rabbis are encased in anonymous, synchronic, and rhetorically disciplined frameworks. It follows that the documents' picture of the world and of the rabbis themselves necessarily is over-determined, manipulated, and incomplete. Rabbinic editors offer no comprehensive and nuanced report, no mirror image of their colleagues and precursors. They produce instead a vision of their world as they understood it, their world as they construed it, and, therefore, their world as they imagined it and described it to themselves. With language as their principal representational tool, the producers of rabbinic documents create the world they reveal. Rabbinic literature thus emerges not, as so many have assumed, as an arcane, unsystematic, yet essentially neutral and inerrant record of "what actually happened" in rabbinic antiquity, but rather as an enormous labor of intellect and imagination that codifies a particular Jewish conception of reality in a distinctive mode of discourse that both derives from and generates that conception.

Rabbinic documents are formally discontinuous with, not imitative of, earlier Jewish writing, and they exhibit all the signs of deliberately and consciously wrought literary products, of strategic and willful literary choice. No mere vehicles for the passive receipt and transmission of what precedes them, these texts manifest rabbinism's cultural vitality and sense of originality. Since rabbis are their intended audience, they emerge as a principal mode of rabbinic self-representation. The construction of rabbinic documents, their genre(s), their discursive style and practice, and their rhetorical tropes constitute the primary data we know rabbis made in their own way and for themselves. Rabbinic discourse, the way of talking, thinking, and knowing delimited by the material forms rabbis devised for their literature, is palpable evidence of their culture. Attention to the rabbinic literary strategy for mapping the world and representing rabbis to themselves can open a path to understanding the men whose experience made such writing plausible.

The enormous and variegated rabbinic literary output and our still primitive knowledge of most documents reduce to folly attempts to characterize all of rabbinic literature with a single adjective. Nevertheless, the documents from which any description of ancient rabbis must be drawn—the Mishnah, the Tosefta, the earlier nonhomiletical midrashic collections, and the two *gemarot*—do share some common formal traits. These are most easily identified in the Mishnah, the only rabbinic document to be analyzed as an autonomous composition,[1] but they have broader applicability.

Like most rabbinic literature, the Mishnah is an anonymous document composed of brief, discrete passages or cognitive units that address halakhic topics. These units have been arranged into series, each of which treats and elaborates a particular halakhic theme. The largest of these thematic catalogues, the tractates of the Mishnah, contain subtractates, smaller series of passages on subtopics of the tractate's larger subject. Throughout the Mishnah, the discrete units of the tractates and subtractates are neither chronologically nor biographically aligned, nor, in general, are they formally linked to one another. The Mishnah exemplifies the list genre, and the absence of formal links among units suggests a rhetorical strategy of parataxis. That is, although the subtractates and intermediary units of the Mishnah do develop particular themes or problems, each cognitive unit is formally independent and isolated. Each can be known and studied by itself, independent of its position in the present list. An internal Mishnaic witness, the measurable, if not excessive, number of units that appear in more than one tractate, makes this conclusion plausible.[2]

These same traits are evident, mutatis mutandis, in the other documents from which our information about ancient rabbis derives. To be sure, the argumentation characteristic of the pericopae (*sugyot*) in the Babylonian and Palestinian *gemarot* is more elaborated and sustained than anything in the Mishnah or the Tosefta, and the study of the formation of these pericopae poses a special and interesting problem in the study of

Talmudic literature.[3] But the two Talmuds follow the Mishnah's arrangement, and the relations among their *sugyot* resembles that among the
Mishnah's cognitive units. The intra-Talmudic index (*masoret ha-shas*)
along the outer side of each page of *gemara* reveals a sizable number of
independent units, or parts of them, that have been used in different
tractates, *sugyot,* and halakhic contexts. The midrashic collections consist largely of lists of autonomous exegetical comments attached to and
arranged in the order of the verses of the biblical book being interpreted.
The ubiquitous use in these texts of the disjunctive device *davar ʾaḥer*
("another thing") to distinguish one comment from another, provides
palpable evidence of parataxis. Even the later, homiletic *midrashim,*
alleged to be coherent compositions, exhibit in their prologues the rabbinic penchant for paratactic lists.[4]

The configuration of rabbinic documents thus places each cognitive
unit in a formal relation of equivalence to all others. No single halakhic
dictum, exegesis, or idea (or document, for that matter) dominates all
others. None is subordinate, none formally set off as the epitome of all
wisdom and truth. Rather, all stand, as it were, next to one another in a
relation of mutuality and exquisite tension. For this reason rabbinic
documents read as if suspended in space, moving towards no literary or
cognitive conclusion. Many of them even lack formal beginnings and
endings. The paratactic construction of rabbinic documents makes their
generative conceptions and foundational principles seem recondite and
rabbinism's structure of ideas seem intractable and elusive. Even such
devotees as E. E. Urbach point to the literature's failure to provide "a
systematic treatment of... beliefs and opinions" and its "lack of con-
sistency and system."[5] This claim for the prevalence of paratatic con-
strution in rabbinic literature does not condemn its documents as chaotic, inchoate, or unsystematic. Rather, it calls attention to the absence of
explicit formal hierarchy and documentary hypotaxis as a deliberate literary and rhetorical strategy that both reflects and shapes the way rabbinic
Judaism sees, knows about, and experiences the world.

These substantive and literary traits all inform the presentation of
persons in rabbinic documents and make the construction of portraits of
ancient rabbis extremely problematic. The sources at best provide the
barest hint of the relations between rabbis and the nonrabbinic social and
economic world, and they thus block our perception of the rabbis at work
in society. A truly critical analysis of rabbinic religious leadership becomes difficult, for without evidence of followers little of certainty can be
said about leaders. The absence of biography obscures evidence of family
lineage, local origin, economic status, and other marks of social
identification. Indeed, rabbinic masters are never introduced, and their
patronymic surnames, though known in most cases, are sparingly applied.

In the documents rabbis simply appear from nowhere, speaking and arguing as if everyone knows who they are. The absence of biography, however, hardly exhausts the problem. The picture of rabbis offered by their texts is exceedingly fragmented. The dicta and opinions assigned to, and the stories told about, any given master are nowhere collected under his name but are scattered throughout the documents, often in different versions that serve the varied purposes of compilers and redactors. In the texts rabbis routinely appear in disagreement with one another, but the tradents (those who transmit sayings) and editors who report the disputes tend not to resolve them. The conflicting opinions remain in endless juxtaposition. This strategy of representation leaves the relative importance of the opinions uninflected. It thereby suppresses evidence of authority, domination, and power among the disputants and makes all rabbis appear as equals.

Rabbinic literature is largely indifferent to the presentation of distinctive individuality. No document pays homage to a particular rabbi; none celebrates one man's virtue, reflects his thoughts, or recounts his deeds. The sources offer no museum of well-rounded rabbinic portraits, only a gallery of partial sketches and disjointed images. Rabbinic literature presents its protagonists paratactically, in pieces. It is a literature of contention without victors, in which the sense of separate existences is minimal. This massive labor of homogeneity suggests that devotion to individual masters played little role in the motivations of the men who made up the texts. In all of the literature no rabbi emerges as central, dominant, or determinative; none appears to symbolize, guide, or shape rabbinic destiny. No rabbinic texts claims to be the product of the life, career, or inner struggle of a single great man. Rather, the men appear as products of the sources.

No doubt, individual rabbis achieved importance, decisively shaped rabbinic culture, and affected the lives of their contemporaries. No doubt, stories about rabbis are not wholly fabrications and falsehoods, literary inventions grounded in no historical reality. But, whatever their origin, the segments of rabbinic lives thought worthy of narration and transmission appear in their present form for purposes other than hero worship, dedication to a particular master, or a desire to recount and preserve the past.

A representative narrative illustrates these problems. The story, which appears in the Mishnah, Tractate Rosh HaShanah 2:8–9, reads:

> A. Rabban Gamaliel had pictures of the shapes of the moon on a tablet and on the wall of his upper chamber, which he would show to untrained observers and say, "Did you see it like this or like that?"

B. It happened that two came and said, "We saw it in the east in the morning and in the west in the evening."

C. Said R. Yohanan b. Nuri, "They are false witnesses."

D. When they came to Yavneh, Rabban Gamaliel accepted them.

E. And again two came and said, "We saw it at its [expected] time, but on the next night it did not appear."

F. And Rabban Gamaliel accepted them.

G. Said R. Dosa b. Harkinas, "They are false witnesses.

H. "How can they testify that a woman has given birth when the next day her belly is between her teeth?"

I. R. Joshua said to him, "I approve your words."

J. Rabban Gamaliel sent a message to him: "I decree that you shall come before me with your staff and your money on the day that falls as the Day of Atonement according to your reckoning."

K. R. Aqiba went and found him upset.

L. He said to him, "I am able to learn that whatever Rabban Gamaliel has done is done,

M. "as it is written, *These are the appointed seasons of the Lord, the holy assemblies which you shall proclaim* (Leviticus 23:4). Whether in their time or not in their time, I have no other appointed seasons but these."

N. He came to R. Dosa b. Harkinas.

O. He said to him, "If we come to judge the court of Rabban Gamaliel, we will have to judge each and every court that has stood from the days of Moses until now,

P. "as it is written, *Moses went up with Aaron, Nadav, and seventy of the elders of Israel* (Exodus 24:9). And why were the names of the elders not made explicit? Rather, it is to teach that each and every [group of] three who stood as a court over Israel, lo, they are like the court of Moses."

Q. And he took his staff and his money in his hand and went to Yavneh on the day that fell as the Day of Atonement according to his reckoning.

R. Rabban Gamaliel stood up and kissed him on the head.

S. He said to him, "Come in peace, my master and my disciple—my master in wisdom, and my disciple, since you have accepted my words."

This account is particularly useful since it reports an alleged historical event with political consequences for the rabbinic movement. It also treats an issue crucial in the history of Judaism, the determination of the sacred calendar after the destruction of the Jerusalem temple.

In Judaism the yearly calendar is calculated according to the sun, but the months, and therefore the dates of the annual holy days, are determined by the appearance of the moon. Before the fall of the Jerusalem temple in A.D. 70, the priests proclaimed the sacred times of the year. In the aftermath of the temple's destruction, the new rabbinic movement appropriated that priestly task to itself. This story reports a conflict on this issue between Gamaliel II, the patriarch and ostensible leader of the rabbis at Yavneh, and two other Yavnean masters, Dosa b. Harkinas and Joshua b. Hananiah.

The story, as well edited as any in rabbinic literature, can be divided into three substantively related but formally unintegrated segments, A, B–D, and E–S. A sets the stage and supplies the halakhic topic of the pericope, the examination of witnesses about the appearance of the new moon. B–D is a brief prelude to the longer account at E–S. In B–D Gamaliel examines two witnesses and accepts their testimony, presumably for the beginning of a new month, despite the objection of Yohanan b. Nuri. In the barrenness of B–D, so typical of rabbinic narratives, we are told the rationale neither for Yohanan b. Nuri's judgment nor for Gamaliel's rejection of it. The opinions simply are juxtaposed without being brought into explicit interaction.

At issue in both B–D and E–I is the correct evaluation of testimony about the new moon. Gamaliel accepts even irregular testimony. Yohanan b. Nuri and Dosa b. Harkinas oppose such practice and are supplied with identical language. At no point in either B–D or E–I does anyone deny or even question the patriarch's authority to proclaim the dates of festivals. The addition of Joshua's comment at I does not change matters; the issue still is not who decides but how one decides. At J this matter is dropped, never to be resolved, and the focus of concern abruptly shifts to the question of patriarchal authority. The issue is not who is right but who is in charge. Gamaliel commands Joshua to violate what the latter regards as the correct Day of Atonement.

Aqiba's appearance at K–M is a surprise. He plays no role in the disagreement, and his apparent support of the patriarch on this matter conflicts with the testimony of Mishnah Rosh HaShanah 1:6, in which he attempts to prevent witnesses from testifying before him. K–M obviously is an intrusion into the narrative.

According to N, Joshua goes to Dosa. The identity of the speaker at O–P is unclear, but H. Albeck supposes it to be Dosa.[6] This reading is questionable since the ruling against Gamaliel is attributed to Dosa, not Joshua. Q–S complete the narrative. The actor at Q must be Joshua, for the language at Q is identical to that of J. At R–S Gamaliel appears the magnanimous victor.

The uncertain identity of the speaker at O calls attention to Joshua's place in the story. His name and words appear only once, at I, where he affirms Dosa's judgment. After that, he becomes an invisible figure whose presence is never made explicit. Talmudic literature contains many accounts of Joshua's opposition to Gamaliel, the most famous of which tells of Gamaliel's deposition from the patriarchate. In such cases Joshua typically propounds his own opinion, which is reported in his own name. His role here, then, is highly unusual, and this suggests that his name has been inserted into an earlier account of a Gamaliel-Dosa dispute. Dosa b. Harkinas is an obscure figure who appears only eleven times in the Mishnah. At Mishnah Ketuvot 13:1–2, however, he sides with priestly authority in civil matters, and after A.D. 70 he may have represented priestly claims in religious matters as well. If so, then the earlier account on which this version is based, something like E–G, J, and Q, would have been a straightforward story about Gamaliel's dominance of the priestly party after 70. If this be the case, then the addition of Joshua and Aqiba to the account has preserved the plot of the original, something difficult to alter if the earlier version were well known, but the addition has dramatically redirected the implications of the plot. This analysis, which is necessarily speculative because of the nature of the sources, shows the difficulty of constructing the historical background of rabbinic texts. Even if accurate, it does not explain what the narrative is about. Let us return to the story in its present form and read it as a whole.

In a conventional narrative about Gamaliel, G would precede F, on the model of B–D. The reversal of those elements here establishes that the point at issue is Gamaliel's ruling. At G Dosa demurs, and the graphic imagery supplied at H, a common rabbinic expression, adds bite to his judgment. Gamaliel cannot be right. At I Joshua endorses Dosa's view, to be made the object of Gamaliel's displeasure at J. The point of J is clear; Gamaliel's decree is a blatant exercise of authority. At K Aqiba enters to find Joshua "upset." Rabbinic stories normally eschew such nonessential detail, so the description of Joshua's mood is uncharacteristic. Its presence here highlights the dispute and fixes the context for Joshua's action at the end of the story. Aqiba supports Gamaliel at L–M with the exegesis of Leviticus 23:4, but he endorses Gamaliel's position as patriarch, not his opinion. Indeed, the exegesis at M makes clear that Gamaliel is wrong. If the appointed seasons were observed "in their time," that is, properly, there would be no reason to apply the verse. Aqiba takes the verse to mean that Israel's appointed seasons are only those proclaimed by human agency, and since Gamaliel is the recognized leader of the rabbis what he "has done is done," whether or not it conforms to the times revealed by nature. Aqiba's conclusion is presented as the result of intellection; it is something he has been "able to learn."

N–P contains the exchange between Joshua and Dosa, but the identity of the speaker is unclear. In the flow of the narrative the words at O–P make better sense if said by Joshua than to him. Since at K–L Aqiba "went" and "said," N–O ought to read likewise. Joshua, therefore, goes to Dosa to withdraw his support and offer his reasons. His rationale and the exegesis of Exodus 24:9 assume the existence of a line of rabbinic courts that extends back to Moses. If the decision of one court can be held open to question, then so can the decisions of all courts—a procedure that would undermine the coherence and credibility of rabbinic (self-) government. The issue in O–P, then, is the welfare of the rabbinic movement, not the correctness of Gamaliel's opinion.

At Q–S Joshua goes to Gamaliel in apparent submission and is received with generosity. Gamaliel rises to greet him, a gesture of respect, and welcomes him warmly. But the words of greeting assigned to him blunt the effect of his victory. Joshua is both "master" and "disciple," at best an ambiguous status. By calling Joshua his "master in wisdom" (in the story's context a clear reference only to the halakhic conflict between them), Gamaliel implicitly acknowledges the error of his own decision. Joshua is Gamaliel's "disciple" by virtue of his acceptance of the latter's words, but the exegesis at O–P leaves no doubt that Joshua's "discipleship" is voluntary, motivated neither by fear of nor personal devotion to Gamaliel, nor by regard for his halakhic acumen, but by a concern for the solidarity of rabbinic collectivity.

In the end it is not clear who has won. Joshua and Gamaliel are both "master" and "disciple" to one another, a relation that blurs any hierarchy. Gamaliel's position remains intact, but his authority results from Joshua's refusal to judge his court, not from Gamaliel's qualities of intellect, charisma, or power. Indeed, it could be argued that the real hero of the narrative is Joshua, and secondarily Aqiba. It is Joshua who is able to suppress his correct opinion for the sake of the collective welfare, and it is Aqiba who calls the matter to his attention.[7]

Although doubtless grounded in some event of conflict between the new Yavnean patriarch and other rabbis, the story actually says little about it. We do not know where or when the conflict took place, and we are told nothing of its broader social, religious, or political ramifications. Indeed, its very presence in the Mishnah, in the midst of legal rulings and disputations, suggests that rabbinic authorities did not want such consequences as part of their record. The protagonists appear in a skeletal and paratactic narrative framework that allows characters to be added to the story without altering the plot. They speak in clipped, truncated phrases that may indicate what they think but expose nothing of why they think it. The motives, passions, reasons, and principles that make the conflict possible are wholly obscured. Finally, from J onwards the protagonists are identified by pronouns whose antecedents are not clear. As readers we cannot be certain who speaks and who listens, but this ambiguity obstructs neither the story's progress nor its intelligibility. At one level, then, although the narrative includes the names of Gamaliel, Dosa, Aqiba and Joshua, it really is about no one in particular. Its images consequently tell us less about life as lived than about life as imagined.

But if this story tells us little about history as we would like to know it, it does reveal much about the contours and values of rabbinic culture and religion. It portrays rabbis as heirs and, for their own time, equivalents of Moses. To judge one of their courts is, of necessity, to judge the court of Moses. Rabbis, not God, fix the boundaries of sacred time, and he has "no other appointed seasons but these." The story exposes a powerful recognition that the rabbis are creating something new in their culture, something they, not God, are responsible to maintain. The persistence of that creation depends on the voluntary cooperation and mutuality of numbers of rabbis and can be destroyed by contrary attitudes and behaviors. In such a context no rabbi can appear to dominate others, and disputes among rabbis must be resolved without humiliation to any party. In this narrative, the medium for such resolution is the exercise of intellect. Joshua changes his mind neither because he fears Gamaliel's power nor because he respects the person of Aqiba. He does so because of the exegesis Aqiba has "learned." In idealized rabbinic life it is through the discipline of "learning" that the sharp and projecting edges of individuality and ego are blunted, controlled, and directed in pursuit of some larger goal.

The attempt to describe the rabbis of antiquity yields a result disappointing for conventional history but fruitful for the study of culture. The virtual anonymity of persons in rabbinic literature reveals a powerful cultural disinclination, perhaps an incapacity, to construe rabbinic culture and religion as the work of powerful individuals. It is as if, when they came to put their story down on paper, rabbis could not bring themselves to tell it, and therefore were unable to imagine it, in terms of themselves. In rabbinic documents there is no place for the expression of private ego, no room for the imposing, charismatic personality, and no occasion for the emergence of any single, great man who represents the fate and destiny of the many in his own life and person.

As we have seen, the content of rabbinic documents virtually certifies that they were produced for an internal audience. They are of rabbis, by rabbis, and for rabbis; they constitute a rabbinic conception of rabbinic culture, composed for itself and addressed to itself. Rabbinic texts present their contents, whether halakhic teaching or images of persons, in pieces, in fluid paratactic literary frameworks that exhibit little temporal dimension. Rabbinic discourse shields itself from intellectual penetration by others; it is the work of a group bounded and set apart. It would be derelict to claim that these texts existed in precisely their present form throughout rabbinic antiquity. The diachronic range of most documents indicates that their production is not contemporary with the events described and the persons depicted in their pages. But it also is gratuitous to argue that the present form of the texts is unrelated to or at variance with the ways their contents initially were composed, received, transmitted, and redacted. Rather, the generations of rabbis who produced, preserved, accepted, and believed the materials contained in rabbinic documents apparently found this mode of depicting reality credible. Unless we suppose all of rabbinic writing to be one massive literary artifice, we must assume that to some degree the texts reflect and conform to rabbinic experience of and in the world.

This proposition can be tested by a consideration of some aspects of rabbinic social life. Unfortunately, because of the character of the sources, our knowledge of the inner workings of rabbinic society is likely always to be fairly schematic. Rabbinic social life in Palestine after 200 remains substantially unexplored. But the data about Sasanian Babylonia and Roman Palestine before 200 have been critically analyzed, and some conclusions are possible. In a meticulous philological examination of academic terminology in the Babylonian Talmud, David Goodblatt has shown that Babylonian rabbinic instruction was effected through disciple-circles rather than schools.[8] Rabbinic disciples apparently did not attend institutions with corporate identities but clustered around individual masters whom they served, at least in part, as apprentice lawyers. Rabbinic disciples could change teachers either for intellectual or personal reasons. Masters could be abusive and demanding, and some had acquired special expertise in particular subjects. Martin Goodman's work on Roman Palestine suggests that the model of disciple-circles applies there as well.[9]

The picture of a network of relatively autonomous disciple-circles suggests that in order to attract students rabbis had to be figures of forceful personality and distinctive individuality. But the very possibility that students could change teachers at will, the apparent movement of disciples among masters, implies a system of social relations in which all rabbis theoretically were equivalent to one another. In a world of face-to-face relationships in which rabbis had to compete with one another for students, no master could fail to be aware of his colleagues' skills, and none could escape public scrutiny within the movement. In such a system individual claims to special power and authority are easily refuted and rendered fragile.

Hints that the realities of rabbinic social life restrained rabbinic claims to special power and encouraged the literary suppression of individuality also appear in the rabbis' treatment of themselves as miracle-workers. During the first two centuries, charismatic types who claimed miraculous powers were antithetical to and played little role in rabbinism. God could perform miracles, but rabbis could not. By the middle of the third century that picture had changed, and miracle-power became a conventional component in the rabbinical dossier.[10] This shift corresponds to a general development among religious virtuosi in the late Roman world. The third century is witness to the emergence of a class of charismatic individuals, holy men, "friends of God," who claim a special power, an intimate relation with the divine, that definitively sets them off from other men.[11] In late antique Christianity and paganism this claim accompanies a vigorous expression of individuality and is recounted in individual lives, in the literary portraiture of hagiography. In rabbinism, however, miracle-working does not generate hagiography and appears not to have had the socially disruptive effects it did in pagan and Christian manifestations.

This difference, rabbinism's failure to adopt the pagan and Christian model and portray itself to itself in terms of great and powerful individuals, is partly a function of the social system sketched above. But it also is a consequence of the distinctly intellectual character of the rabbinic enterprise. Whatever personal traits, whatever magnetism or charisma, a rabbi possessed, his standing and credibility within the rabbinic movement initially depended on his learning. Rabbinical status derived not from the exercise of mysterious and arbitrary divine favor but from the result of intellectual labor. Whatever else being a rabbi meant, it meant the publicly demonstrable mastery of a considerable body of Scripture and halakhic material. Rabbis did not hide from one another in the desert, nor did they seclude themselves behind cloister walls. The evidence of the sources suggests that they lived in a world of persistent mutual scrutiny, a world of continual evaluation and judgment. In such a world rabbis could not help but be aware of their mortality and could not possibly maintain the illusion of special power, at least, and especially, among themselves.

The rabbis of antiquity constituted a recognized group of intellectual specialists in ancient Jewish society. But despite their claims to control Israel's destiny, they lacked the political power to direct their society or to enforce the myriad *halakot* and scriptural interpretations they believed held the key to its redemption. Their literature's manifest lack of interest in that society suggests its reciprocal lack of interest in them. In the absence of real power, rabbis exerted what influence they could but devoted themselves primarily to forging their own collective identity. The bulk of their literature is recondite and insular, bespeaking the shared privacy of the initiated. Its obsession with detailed scriptural exegesis and halakhic disputation means that rabbis needed each other as an audience. Their sense of social credibility and group membership, therefore, in large measure depended on how they treated one another. To alienate a colleague by arrogance, humiliation, or claims to special power was to risk losing an audience and consigning the work of collective identity to fail-

ure. Peter Brown's observations about the *philotimia* of Antonine city life
could apply with equal force to the rabbis of antiquity.

> Elites tend to maintain a set of strong invisible boundaries, which
> mark firm upward limits to the aspirations of individuals, and to direct
> the aspirations of their members to forms of achievement that could
> potentially be shared by all other members of the peer group. In a peer
> group, therefore, forms of individual achievement, like wealth, are
> there to be spent, not hoarded. Those who accumulate too much to
> themselves are cut down to size in no uncertain manner, if not by the
> envy of their fellows, then, at least by the ineluctable envy of
> death . . . Men committed to constant competition within a "model of
> parity" are not likely to allow any one of their peers to draw heavily on
> sources of power and prestige over which they have no control. Ap-
> peals to the other world as a source of special status had to be kept
> within strictly conventional limits if they were to be acceptable.[12]

All these values are manifested in the formal traits of rabbinic literature and in the narrative we examined above. That story is neither a report
of a historical event "as it actually happened" nor an account about
Gamaliel, Joshua, Dosa, or Aqiba as individuals. Rather, it is an idealized
model of rabbinic behavior, a culturally determined construction of how
rabbinic society ought to operate. The search for the rabbis of antiquity,
then, suggests a degree of conformity among the ways rabbis lived with
one another, imagined one another, and represented one another in their
literature. It leads not into the lives and careers of great men but into a
self-absorbed community of intellectuals who competed with each other
but needed each other and strove to maintain at least the illusion of each
other's dignity.[13]

Notes

1. See Jacob Neusner, *Judaism: The Evidence of the Mishnah* (Chicago, 1981).

2. This description is based on ibid., and is abbreviated from my "Reading the Writing
of Rabbinism: Toward an Interpretation of Rabbinic Literature," *Journal of the American
Academy of Religion* (forthcoming).

3. See David Goodblatt, "The Babylonian Talmud," in J. Neusner, ed., *The Study of
Ancient Judaism* (New York, 1981), 2:120–99. In the same volume, see Baruch M. Bokser,
"An Annotated Bibliographical Guide to the Study of the Palestinian Talmud," pp. 1–119.

4. Martin Jaffee, "The Midrashic Proem," in W. S. Green, ed., *Approaches to Ancient
Judaism* V (Chico, forthcoming).

5. E. E. Urbach, *The Sages: Their Concepts and Beliefs,* trans. Israel Abrahams
(Jerusalem, 1975), p. 4.

6. H. Albeck, *Shishah Sidré Mishnah, Seder Moʿed* (Jerusalem–Tel-Aviv, 1958), p.
317.

7. For somewhat different analyses of this passage, see Shamai Kanter, *Rabban
Gamaliel II: The Legal Traditions* (Chico, 1980), pp. 107–11, and my *The Traditions of
Joshua ben Hananiah* (Leiden, 1981), pp. 116–19.

8. David M. Goodblatt, *Rabbinic Instruction in Sasanian Babylonia* (Leiden, 1975).

9. Martin Goodman, *State and Society in Roman Palestine: 120–200* (Totowa, N.J., forthcoming).

10. See Jacob Neusner, *A History of the Jews in Babylonia* (Leiden, 1969), 4:334–69, and my "Palestinian Holy Men: Charismatic Leadership and Rabbinic Tradition," in W. Haase and H. Temporini, eds., *Aufstieg und Niedergang der Römischen Welt* (Berlin, 1979), 19.2, pp. 619–47.

11. Peter Brown, *The Making of Late Antiquity* (Cambridge and London, 1978).

12. Ibid., p. 35.

13. My thanks are due to Professors Fitz John Porter Poole, Gary G. Porton, Eugene D. Genovese, Elizabeth Fox-Genovese, Geza Vermes, and Martin Goodman for insights I could not have gained on my own and for helping to develop the theoretical aspects of this problem.

Part Two

Description
Judaism in Medieval and Modern Times

Introduction

To describe a religion we assemble facts about this and that to form an intelligible pattern. To do so we ask simple and basic questions, capable of address to a variety of religions. Such questions by definition must focus attention upon fundamental matters, such as, for any one or several religions, these: the nature of worship; the experience of mysticism; the life of piety and the interplay between more pious and less pious people; and the place and activity, within a religious community, of the more thoughtful, or intellectual, folk. These are the topics before us. The facts selected by the several authors are so shaped as to present, out of Judaism, a coherent account of one example of the place of worship, mysticism, piety and its ethics, and intellect, in the life of a religion. In this way we deal with the three fundamental ways in which a religious believer receives and works out the religious life: in heart and soul, emotions and inner life, through worship, mystical experience, and piety; in the formation of and participation in a social group, through shared and common patterns of piety and faith; and in the life of the mind, through intelligible discourse about the religious world and intellectually accessible reflection upon religious experience. The period under discussion runs from ancient into modern times. We do not recognize much of a break for the conventional divisions of Western history into ancient, medieval, and modern. As I shall explain, Judaism has been continuous, its history unbroken, from its formation in the first and second centuries C.E. to the beginning of the present century. Its symbolic structure has proved stable and enduring. Its legal and theological conceptions have constantly expanded and unfolded in terms of their own inner logic and dynamic and have remained essentially intact. Its institutions—leadership, law, modes of organization—have continued coherent, cogent, and consistent from beginnings onward. Judaism's paramount place within the life of the Jewish nation or people has remained definitive and indicative. Let me amplify this striking fact.

In the period under discussion in this section, from the end of Talmudic times, that is, the sixth century C.E., down to the end of the nineteenth century, there is no important break in Judaism as a way of life and world view. What we conventionally call "ancient" and "medieval" Judaism are continuous. The Hebrew Scriptures and the Talmud—"the whole Torah of Moses our rabbi"—shaped in late antiquity, continued through medieval and modern times to impose the fundamental definition of Judaism. Accordingly, the temporal continuum over which Talmudic Judaism has endured is not to be divided up into diverse, essentially distinct segments, ancient, medieval, and modern. The "classical period" of Judaism ran from well before the end of the first century into the nineteenth century.

This is an amazingly long time for something so volatile as a religion to have remained, as Judaism did, essentially stable, that is, to have endured without profound shifts in symbolic structure, ritual life, or modes of social organization for the religious community. The Judaism which predominated during that long period and which has continued to flourish in the nineteenth and twentieth centuries bears a number of names: *rabbinic* because of the nature of its principal authorities, who are rabbis; *Talmudic* because of the name of its chief authoritative document after the Hebrew Scriptures, which is the Talmud; *classical* because of its basic quality of endurance and prominence; or, simply, *Judaism* because no other important alternative was explored by Jews.

What provided the stability and essential cogency of rabbinic Judaism during the long period of its predominance was the capacity of rabbinic Judaism—its modes of thought, its definitions of faith, worship, and the right way to live life—to take into itself and to turn into a support and a buttress for its own system a wide variety of separate and distinct modes of belief and thought. Of striking importance were the philosophical movement and the mystical one. Both put forward alien ideas through modes of thought themselves quite distinct from those of rabbinic Judaism. Philosophers of Judaism raised a range of questions and dealt with those questions in ways essentially separate from the established and accepted rabbinic ways of thinking about religious issues. But all of the philosophers of Judaism lived in accord with the rabbinic way of life. All of them were entirely literate in the Talmud and related literature. Many of the greatest philosophers also were great Talmudists. The same is to be said of the mystics. Their ideas about the inner character of God, their quest for a fully realized experience of union with the presence of God in the world, their particular doctrines, with no basis in the Talmudic literature produced by the early rabbis, and their intense spirituality were all thoroughly "rabbinized"—that is, brought into conformity with the lessons and way of life taught by the Talmud. In the end, rabbinic Judaism received extraordinary reinforcement from the spiritual resources generated by the mystic quest. Both philosophy and mysticism thus found their way into the center of rabbinic Judaism. Both of them were shaped by minds that, to begin with, were infused with the content and spirit of rabbinic Judaism.

From the destruction of the Second Temple to the beginning of the nineteenth century—nearly nineteen hundred years—Jews lived among two great civilizations, Islam and Christendom, but under their own law and within their own community. They did not seek to be integrated with "the nations" but to endure as a singular people among them. We can hardly reduce to a few generalizations the complex facts of their history and culture. The religious events of those long centuries likewise cannot be summarized in a brief catalogue: mysticism, philosophy, study of the law through Talmudic commentary, logical codification, the issuing of concrete decisions. To the outside world, Jewish history was the tale of persecution and massacre, degradation and restriction to despised occupations, then riot and expulsion, and the discovery of new homes elsewhere. To the medieval Jew, such dates as 1290, when Jews were expelled from England; 1309, when the same took place in France; 1391, when the great and flourishing communities of Spain were overtaken by destruction; 1492, when the Jews were expelled from Christian Spain; 1648, when Polish Jews were massacred in vast numbers—such dates marked times for penitence and reaffirmation of the Torah. It is only in modern times that other than religious consequences have been drawn from cataclysmic historical events. Because Judaism had developed prophecy and rabbinic leadership, it was able to overcome the disasters of 586 B.C.E. and 70 C.E. The challenge of modern times comes not only from the outside but also from within: the nurture of new religious leadership for Jews facing a world of new values and ideals.

J. N.

Three

Religion and Worship
The Case of Judaism

Richard S. Sarason

When Friedrich Heiler, late Professor of Comparative History of Religions at Marburg, wrote in his influential cross-cultural study of prayer that "prayer is the central phenomenon of religion, the very hearthstone of all piety,"[1] a major problem with comparative studies of religion was illustrated. Although Heiler's statement accurately reflects some forms of Western Christianity, it may not hold true for all forms of Christianity at all times, and it certainly does not obtain as a categorical statement about all religious cultures (including Judaism, as this chapter will argue). The problem is one of perspective. In the past, most comparative studies of religions have been undertaken, explicitly or implicitly, from the perspective of that religion—Christianity—to which the others were to be compared. The way of carving up reality that is self-evident within the broad Christian frame of reference—categories of analysis, conceptual schemes, vocabulary—has been superimposed uncritically on the data of other religious cultures, and the result has been a strange conceptual hybrid frequently unrecognizable to adherents of the other traditions.[2] This study attempts to lay a basis for more careful and methodologically self-conscious comparative work in all areas while concentrating, for purposes of illustration, on a single area: the description and interpretation of worship and religion in Judaism.

Meaningful comparative work requires first and foremost a valid context of interpretation. It is impossible to understand one element in a religious culture—worship, in our case—in isolation from the larger system of meanings which *is* that culture, and which gives that element its particular significance. Cogent comparison must necessarily be contextual comparison. As Jacob Neusner has repeatedly insisted, "The comparison of details of one system against those of some other by itself produces no insight. It yields no heuristic result, either for the meaning of the detail shared in common or for the description and interpretation of the several systems which share it.... For each detail is significant only in the specific context established by all details."[3] This is why an account of worship (or any other phenomenon) in Judaism must begin with, and constantly refer back to, an account of Judaic religion as the larger network of cultural meanings in which that phenomenon becomes meaningful. Accordingly, I shall defer discussing worship in Judaism until I have clarified the context of its interpretation.

To describe succinctly a religious-cultural tradition as rich, old, and complex as Judaism obviously entails certain additional methodological difficulties. There is no such thing as an abstract "essence" of Judaism, only a synchronic and diachronic variety of historical "Judaisms." It is possible, nonetheless, to identify a common set of symbols and generative problematics, or points of structural tension, which are shared among these various "Judaisms," particularly among variations of rabbinic Judaism, that form which has come to predominate since the second century c.e. I shall attempt here to characterize these commonalities, recognizing all the while that the term "Judaism" (or "Hinduism" or "Christianity") remains problematic.

All historical forms of Judaism have been preeminently concerned with problems of meaning, order, and justice in the world (usually, with their apparent lack). Traditional Judaic religious culture is radically teleological, obsessed with order and ordering—presumably because the actual social context of Judaism has invariably been experienced by Jews as disorderly and chaotic.[4] Judaism fiercely asserts that everything ultimately is meaningful and purposive, since all reality has been created and patterned by a single, purposive divine intelligence. Herein lies the functional significance of Judaic monotheism. The universe is a cosmos—an ordered system—in which both the social order (that over which man can exercise some direct control) and the natural and supernatural orders (that over which human control, prima facie, is more tenuous or nonexistent) form a seamless whole. All is directed by a transcendent deity who enters into direct contact with man through revelation. The central, generative symbol in Judaism, and particularly in rabbinic Judaism, is Torah, God's revealed will to the people Israel. Torah is the bridgehead between the

Jew and ultimate reality, because it is the divinely revealed blueprint of that reality. In Torah, God also reveals laws and norms for the social order and for the conduct of everyday life. There is, thus, both a cognitive and a normative element in Torah: it is to be both studied and practiced. Torah study puts the Jew in touch with the revealed mind of God and hence with "the way things really are," affording a series of explanations and meanings for the vicissitudes of individual and group life. Observance of God's norms as laid forth in the Torah, on the other hand, is perceived by the Jew as an act of bringing his own will—and the collective purpose of Jewish society—into compliance with the will of God, such that human actions and behavior will be in harmony with "the way things really are." Such conformity to the divine will must invariably lead to this-worldly welfare and ultimate salvation for the individual, and messianic redemption (and vindication) for the group. In the language of cultural anthropology, Torah in Judaism mandates and expresses both a world view and a corresponding way of life (ethos).[5] In terms of that ethos, the Jew sees his relationship to deity (which in all forms of Judaism excepting philosophical reflection is construed to some degree anthropomorphically and anthropopathically) as one of a subject or servant to a king or master (sometimes also as a son to a father or a wife to a husband). God has singled out the Jewish people to receive his Torah; it is the Jews' duty in joy and gratitude to obey. In rabbinic Judaism, Torah is defined inclusively; it consists of Scripture *and* rabbinic traditions preserved in the Mishnah, Talmud, and all subsequent rabbinic writings (quintessentially a literature of commentary and supercommentary). For the rabbis, as scholastics, Torah study constitutes the salvific activity par excellence.

One further aspect of rabbinic Judaism that will prove crucial to our analysis of worship is a function of its historical circumstances. Although there were pre-70 antecedents, rabbinic Judaism developed most fully after, and through wrestling with the consequences of, the destruction of the Second Temple in 70 C.E. The statutory form of worship in Judaism before 70 was not prayer but bloody sacrifice performed in ceremonial silence. The sacrificial cult was viewed as eternally mandated in the Torah itself. Through offering up daily sacrifices at the appropriate times, the Jewish people contributed to the maintenance of the cosmic order. Restitution and atonement for social or cultic infractions of that order could be made only through the shedding of blood, the life-force. The destruction of this system of world-maintenance, communication, and restitution was obviously a devastating blow to the traditional Judaic world view. Rabbinic Judaism, significantly, preserves the morphology of the defunct Temple cult—its concern for order, punctiliousness, and repetition—and applies it metaphorically to the daily life of the Jewish people and the individual Jew. While the sacrifices cannot now be performed, they can be evoked and performed symbolically in word and deed, through study, observance, and prayer, as we shall see. The individual Jew, scrupulously performing God's commandments every day, is like the priest in the Temple, scrupulously performing the daily sacrifices. Rabbinic Judaism structurally may be viewed as a kind of surrogate Temple cult.

From this brief account of what I conceive to be the basic symbols, structures, and concerns of rabbinic Judaism, it should already be clear that worship in Judaism—how man relates to and approaches deity—is considerably more inclusive than prayer alone. The central ontological and epistemological role assigned to Torah as the primary intermediary between man and God—as the vehicle through which each approaches the other—suggests that Torah study will be a major mode of divine worship in Judaism, and such in fact is the case. Significantly, Torah study constitutes a major part of statutory synagogue worship. A section of the Torah (the Pentateuch) is read publicly in the synagogue from an archaic scroll every Sabbath morning and afternoon, twice during the week, and on every festival. Sections of the prophetic books follow the Torah reading on Sabbaths and festivals, while other scriptural books also are read on the festivals. It is not uncommon in traditional synagogues today to see the Torah-reader "davvening," or "praying" the text, viz., accompanying his intonation of the words with the same constant swaying or bowing motions that are used when praying—a sign that both activities are construed as "worshiping before the Lord." The very architecture of the synagogue testifies to the importance of Torah study as worship.[6] A synagogue comprises simply rows of seats with a large table in the midst of the congregation, at which the Torah scroll is read. The sightlines converge on an ark at the center of the front wall, which faces eastward in the direction of Jerusalem and the destroyed sanctuary. In the ark are housed several Torah scrolls, each clothed in a mantle and decorated with silver ornaments. Above the ark is a continually burning flame (*ner tamid*). Both the flame (light) and the ark containing the Torah scrolls (enlightenment) symbolize the presence of God, and all worshipful activity is performed facing the ark. The reading from the Torah on Sabbath mornings is preceded and followed by a magisterial procession of the scroll through the congregation, at which time the Torah is venerated as a holy object and kissed by devout worshipers (though never directly touched, as a sign of respect for its holiness). The symbolism here is manifest: the Torah is God's emissary.

In addition to the reading from the scrolls, Torah study and recitation of scriptural passages are part of daily worship services. A major rubric of the morning and evening services, called *Qeriat Shema* (the recitation of the *Shema*, "Hear O Israel"), consists simply in the recitation of three scriptural passages (Deut. 6:4–9, Deut. 11:13–21, Num. 15:37–41), which

affirm basic elements of the Judaic world view: God's unity and providence, and the cosmic-moralistic significance of obeying (or disobeying)
his commandments. So, too, the daily morning service begins with the
ritual study of passages from Scripture, Mishnah, and Talmud, preceded
by a benediction thanking God for his gift of the Torah, and for sanctifying
Israel through the commandment of Torah study.[7]

It is highly significant that the bulk of the scriptural and Talmudic
passages routinely studied (or "prayed") in the synagogue as part of
statutory worship deal with the sacrificial cult, and specifically with those
sacrifices which were to be offered at that very time when the worshiper
was reciting the passages.[8] Some of these are followed by prayers for the
restoration of the Temple cult.[9] Here is a clear indication that study is
viewed in rabbinic Judaism not simply as a mode of worship but as a
surrogate mode of worship for the now-defunct Temple cult. While the
divinely ordained sacrifices cannot presently be offered up, they can be
conjured up in imagination, and these conjurings can be reified through
spoken words. "And we will offer up the bullocks of our lips" (Hos. 14:3)
is a verse often quoted to express this idea: the Jew prays that his words
of study and prayer may be acceptable to God *as if* the word were
the deed. This is most evident on the Day of Atonement—the occasion of
the cultic expiatory rite par excellence—when the synagogue service includes a lengthy, dramatic, and totally unique scenario of the Temple
rites, which the worshiper relives through recitation and study.[10] Appropriate descriptions of the day's cultic offerings also are read from the
Torah scroll on each of the festivals. And symbolically, the Torah-reading
desk in the synagogue takes the place of the sacrificial altar in the Temple.

The fundamental notion that words may substitute for deeds and that
study can be a surrogate for sacrifice is not, however, confined in rabbinic
Judaism to the locus of the synagogue. It permeates (and in some sense
justifies) the entire culture. Fully two-thirds of the Mishnah, the earliest
rabbinic document (edited c. 200 C.E.), is devoted to a minute analysis and
imaginative description of cultic activities and concerns—a powerful and
stubborn act of conjuring 130 years after the fact! Study of this material
and its subsequent elaborations is deemed especially meritorious in rabbinic culture. Indeed, for the rabbis, study (particularly of the Talmud)
remains the preferred mode of worship and the chief salvific activity, by
virtue of which one earns his portion in the world to come.[11] The simple
Jew prays, but the rabbi studies.[12]

Torah study, of course, is not the only mode of worship in rabbinic
Judaism. In my characterization of Judaic religion, I noted that Torah
generates two sorts of activities: study and observance. The second activity, observance of God's revealed norms, is also an important and ubiquitous form of worship that is frequently overlooked in discussions of this

topic. The Judaic cultural ideal, an ideal of piety, is that all of life should be a continuous act of divine worship. "I have set the Lord before me always" (Ps. 16:8) is frequently inscribed over the ark in synagogues and often cited in medieval halakhic and ethical tracts.[13] The Jew's chief joy in life is to serve his or her Creator. This idea finds classic expression in the opening sentence of Joseph Karo's authoritative compendium of Jewish law and custom, the *Shulḥan Arukh* (Set Table, from the sixteenth century): "One should arise in the morning with the strength of a lion to worship/serve one's Creator." This sets the tone for all of one's waking activities. The Hebrew word *abodah* used by Karo means both "worship" and "service" and is the standard term for the activity of the Temple cult.

Perpetual service in one's daily life—joyful obedience to God's norms and attunement of one's own will to that of the Creator of the universe—is perhaps the ultimate form of worship in Judaism. Man is to be ever mindful of God and to behave accordingly. A series of benedictions is prescribed by the rabbis to be recited before performing God's commandments (*mitsvot*), before and after eating a meal, upon beholding some particularly impressive or strange natural phenomenon, etc.[14] These benedictions both express and guarantee the Jew's perpetual awareness that everything experienced or enjoyed comes from God, and that all actions are performed before God. Traditional Judaic piety is God-intoxicated; nothing a Jew does is unrelated to divine service. Herein is the morphology of the Temple cult applied metaphorically to the totality of the individual Jew's life and the social life of the community. Divine paradigms, as laid forth by the rabbis, regulate every human activity. But this ritualization of daily life is experienced subjectively as living in harmony with the cosmic order of things, and as grateful submission to the divine will. Thus the Jew in all his daily activities is constantly worshiping God, and his very life—as well as the collective life of Israel—constitutes a perpetual offering.

A third mode of worship in Judaism, besides the study and living out of God's Torah, is, of course, prayer. I have purposely deferred a discussion of prayer to this point in order more fully to clarify its context in Judaic religious culture. It should be clear now why Heiler's categorical statement that "prayer is the central phenomenon of religion" simply does not hold true about traditional Judaism. To be sure, prayer is an important mode of Judaic worship and piety (more important in some forms of Judaism than in others), but the central and generative phenomenon of rabbinic Judaism is to be located in Torah, and most forms of rabbinic piety relate back to Torah. Having elaborated this point, we may now proceed to discuss the meaning(s) of prayer as worship in Judaism.

The most important and distinctive Judaic prayer-activity is the statutory communal worship service in the synagogue, which takes place three times daily, with additional services on Sabbaths and festivals. The primary significance and logic of this structure is evident from its timing, form, and the rules governing it: daily statutory prayer in rabbinic Judaism is the most explicit surrogate for the daily sacrifices of the Temple cult. A Talmudic dictum states that "the statutory prayers were established to correspond to the [times of the] daily offerings in the Temple" (b. Berakhot 26b). Whatever may be the historical accuracy of this statement, it indicates that at a certain point some rabbis conceived the timing and structure of daily prayer-worship to be derivative from the daily Temple rites. The common designations of various services in fact bear this out. *Minhah,* the designation for the afternoon service, is the standard name for the afternoon sacrifice. *Musaf,* the additional service on Sabbaths and festivals, is the term for the additional sacrifice on these occasions. *Shaharit,* the morning service, takes place at the time of the offering of the morning *tamid,* or "regular" daily sacrifice in the Temple.[15] *Ne'ilah,* the closing service on the Day of Atonement, takes its name from the closing of the gates of the Temple compound at the end of the day.

Besides recapitulating the daily time-clock of the cult, the synagogue prayer service also carries forward the cultic seasonal calendar, the *mahzor hashanah* ("cycle of the year," which is also the designation for the synagogue's holiday prayer book). The biblical festivals are marked by special prayer services in the synagogue, as are the agricultural seasons of the year in the Land of Israel by prayers for rain and dew. Significantly, many of the cult's nonsacrificial activities are still performed in the synagogue, where they are accompanied by prayers. On the New Year, the ram's horn (*shofar*), which was blown in the Temple, is blown in the synagogue. During Sukkot, the autumn harvest festival, prayers for rain are offered while the congregation in a solemn procession circles seven times around the Torah-reading desk (instead of the Temple's sacrificial altar), waving the festival bouquet of myrtle, willow, and palm branches (*lulab*) and citron (*etrog*). Although priests are not required in order to conduct a prayer service, the ancient priestly prerogatives are preserved. During the additional service on all festivals (and, in the State of Israel today, on every Sabbath), the priests bless the congregation with the biblical priestly benediction (Num. 6:24–26), which, according to the Mishnah (Tamid 7:2), was recited daily in the Temple at the conclusion of the morning sacrifice. A priest and a Levite are the first persons called upon to recite benedictions when the Torah is read in the synagogue.

The formal requirements for synagogue prayer services and the rules governing prayer also relate to its function as a surrogate Temple cult. In the same manner as the sacrificial cult, the prayer service is a communal rite. It is offered up on behalf of the Jewish people as a collective entity.

This basic notion underlies the formal demand for a quorum (*minyan*) of ten adult males in order to hold a service: ten is the smallest number of persons deemed to constitute a community that can "stand for" the entire people. If a Jew is unable for some reason to pray in a congregation, he is obliged to offer his private prayer at the same hour at which the community is praying. Similarly, the prayers are phrased in the first-person plural ("we") instead of the singular ("I"). The individual is thereby enjoined (and, through repeated exposure to the rabbinic prayer book, learns) to see himself and his individual needs as part of the larger collective—just as the sight of numerous fellow worshipers attending the sacrifices once stimulated a sense of community among the worshipers.[16] As in the Temple precincts, so in the traditional synagogue during services, there is a strict separation of men and women, though for somewhat different reasons. In the Temple, cultic purity was the paramount concern, while the synagogue rule is justified as an attempt to forestall any lewd thoughts (on the part of males) during prayer—ultimately a concern for purity as well. The women's gallery in an Orthodox synagogue is called the *'ezrat hanashim,* "the court of women," the same designation used in the Temple precincts.

The statutory prayer service, like the Temple cult, is heavily regulated. Rabbinic rules govern the manner, attitude, and form in which all the prayers are recited, as well as the actions and gestures which are to accompany them—when the worshiper is to stand, to sit, to bow, etc. The wording of the prayers is fixed, although this was not always the case, as will be noted below.[17] The rabbinic prayer book itself is called the *siddur,* "order" of prayer, and the order prescribed must be followed precisely for a Jew to have fulfilled the obligation of daily worship. Numerous medieval halakhic compendia spell out in detail the liturgical order of the year. But, as I have previously suggested, it would be incorrect to view the rabbinic regulation of prayer in isolation from the structure of Judaism as a whole, and it is not so understood by traditional Jews. The rules governing prayer are simply a subset of the rules governing all of Jewish life, and a reflection of the culture's preoccupation with order and system. In the *Shulḥan Arukh,* the classic restatement of Jewish norms, the rules of prayer are laid forth, appropriately, in the division entitled *'Oraḥ Ḥayyim,* "The Way of Life," which reverently chronicles the paradigms of Jewish living-as-worship, from sunup to sundown through weekdays, Sabbaths, and festivals.

Thus far, I have tried to show how the cultic meanings of the statutory prayer service in rabbinic Judaism may be deciphered from its immanent formal structures and governing rules. But there are also numerous dicta in rabbinic literature which make this point explicitly, while shedding further light on the ethos that undergirds it. For example, an early rabbinic exegetical text juxtaposes the basic notions of study and prayer as cultic surrogates in a comment on Deuteronomy 11:13, "To love the Lord your God and to serve Him [la*abdo*] with all your heart":

> To serve Him: This refers to study . . . and just as the service of the Temple altar is called *abodah,* so is study called *abodah.* Another interpretation: *To serve Him:* This refers to prayer. You may retort, "How do you know that this refers to prayer? Perhaps it refers to the Temple service." But Scripture continues, [*to serve Him*] *with all you heart and all your soul.* Is there a sacrifice (*abodah*) performed [literally] in the heart?! Yet Scripture explicitly says, *To serve Him* (*la*abdo*). This can only mean prayer (*Sifre Deuteronomy* 41, ed. Finkelstein, pp. 87–88; cf. b. Taanit 2a).

Prayer here is called "the worship/service of the heart," analogous to the Temple cult, but internalized in the heart of the individual Jew who can now perform it anywhere. Study also is deemed analogous to the cult; the two interpretations of the biblical verse are left side by side, as if complementing rather than contradicting one another. A later homily also indicates how prayer was viewed as a cultic surrogate:

> Said Rabbi Isaac: At this time we have neither prophet nor priest, neither sacrifice nor Temple nor altar. What is it that can make atonement for us, even though the Temple has been destroyed? The only thing that we have left is prayer (*Tanḥuma, Wayishlaḥ* 9).[18]

Significantly, the cultic analogy is applied not only to the statutory prayers but also to the benedictions recited before eating:

> Our Rabbis have taught: It is forbidden for a man to enjoy anything of this world without first reciting a benediction; and one who enjoys anything of this world without first reciting a benediction has, as it were, committed sacrilege (b. Berakhot 35a).

Expressed here is the fundamental cultic notion that the world—and particularly the Land of Israel and all produce of the Land—is God's property, from which man benefits on divine sufferance, and only after having desacralized or redeemed the item in question. The cultic gifts to God (through his agents, the priests) of the firstfruits, firstborn of the flock, and tithes release the rest of the crop and flock for human use. The benedictions before eating, we are told here, accomplish the same purpose by offering up *words* of acknowledgment and gratitude to God. The lack of such acknowledgment is the equivalent of cultic sacrilege, that is, misappropriation for personal use of God's property.[19]

Having amply demonstrated that rabbinic statutory prayer-worship is viewed as a cultic surrogate, we must now ask why this should be the case. We ask, in other words, what it is about prayer in particular that

makes it an appropriate substitute for bloody sacrifice as a vehicle for
world-maintenance and expiation. The answer to this question surely has
to do with alternative symbolic modes of power. The power of sacrifice lies
in the symbolic shedding of blood, the very life-force, which is returned to
the source of that life-force in a timely act. In expiatory sacrifices, the
blood of the animal symbolically may substitute for the blood of the
offending human, or may effect purification for him.[20] Prayer (as well as
study), on the other hand, is made up solely of words and gestures. Yet
the underlying conviction is that these, too, have symbolic, causal
efficacy. The sympathetic and creative power of the word is a firmly
rooted notion in traditional Judaic culture. In the first creation-story in
Genesis, the world is created through the power of God's word. In rabbinic exegesis, this powerful word is associated with Torah. The central
symbolic importance in rabbinic culture of Torah—perceived as divine
words transmitted to man—suggests just how powerful words may become in this culture. Prayer-as-worship is simply a further example of the
larger resymbolizing process which takes place in Judaism in the wake of
the destruction of the Temple, in which words come to substitute for
deeds, and symbolic deeds for more literal deeds. To the extent that the
Jews' direct control over their lives and fortunes decreased after 70, their
attempts at symbolic control increased.

Given this larger structure, it should not be surprising that there has
always been a theurgic element in Judaic prayer, though, to be sure, this
element is more pronounced in some forms of Judaism than in others, and
it is balanced by nontheurgic elements, as we shall see below. Prayer as
theurgy is an attempt mechanistically to coerce the divine will and over-
laps with magic. If the proper words are recited at the proper time in the
correct manner and with the correct intention, they must necessarily be
efficacious. Perhaps the most notable reinterpretation of Judaic prayer
with a pronounced theurgic element is that of sixteenth-century Lurianic
Kabbalah. In this system, the entirety of rabbinic Judaism becomes a
corpus symbolicum for larger cosmic processes occurring within the
Godhead itself. Judaic man lies at the center of the system, for through
proper action and intention he can work vast cosmic redemptions and
restore God himself to his primal unity. Prayer in this context becomes a
potent means of effecting cosmic redemption. The words lose their literal
meanings and become symbols for aspects of the Godhead. But as cosmic
symbols, the words must be properly recited with correct intentions, and
without any alterations or deletions, or great harm is liable to result. It is
hardly coincidental that, historically, the major attempts to fix precisely
the wordings of the prayers in Judaism have come from mystical-pietistic
movements with pronounced theurgic tendencies.[21]

Balancing the urge to control is the desire to submit (and, sometimes, thereby to control). The theurgic element in Judaic prayer is balanced by, and in constant tension with, a more submissive (but no less insistent) "dialogic" element. Deity is conceived in personalistic terms; one of God's attributes is that he "hearkens to prayer" and can thereby be influenced. Statutory prayer becomes part of an ongoing dialogue with one's Creator and Master. It is noteworthy that the *Tefillah*, the "Prayer" par excellence in Judaism, which is recited three times daily and constitutes the basic cultic surrogate, is primarily a petitionary prayer. What is offered up to God in place of sacrifices is not simply a formal, mechanistic litany but petitions of heartfelt content. The worshiper prays for the material welfare of the Jewish people (among whom he includes himself)—for healing, sustenance, and a good crop—and for those traits of mind and character which his culture prizes—wisdom, discernment, the ability to return to God's ways—as well as for messianic restoration of his people to their land and their appointed place in the scheme of things. He prays with the hope or assurance (the ambiguity is instructive) that his prayers will be answered. Rabbinic literature is replete with discussions on the etiquette of prayer, which both shapes and expresses personal piety. These discussions indicate how the personal relationship between the worshiper and God is to be conceived, and what sort of posture thereby becomes appropriate in addressing God. The predominant metaphorical relationship in Judaic prayer, as indicated above, is that of a servant to a king or master. The appropriate posture therefore is one of supplication. This posture is spelled out in the Talmud's post facto attempt to rationalize the structure of the *Tefillah*, which begins with three benedictions of praise and concludes with one of thanksgiving and acknowledgment:

> In the opening benedictions, the worshiper is like a servant who recites praises before his master; in the intermediate benedictions, he is like a servant who requests a favor from his master; in the concluding benedictions, he is like a servant who has received a favor from his master and takes his leave (b. Berakhot 34a).[22]

This posture in fact is acted out in the worshiper's stance and gestures as he recites the *Tefillah*. The prayer is recited standing, facing the ark (since one stands when addressing a king). At the outset and conclusion of the first benediction of praise, the worshiper bows slightly in the direction of the ark. He bows again at the words, "We acknowledge You, O Lord our God," in the benediction of thanksgiving/acknowledgment. At the very end of the *Tefillah*, he steps backward three paces, while bowing slightly with each step (leaving the king's presence). Some pious Jews bow repeatedly during the recitation of the *Tefillah*.

A suppliant does not control his master, except insofar as his compliance with the master's wishes may move the master to accede to his requests. Both aspects of this posture are relevant to the understanding of Judaic petitionary prayer. Still, a supplication may not always be answered. There are, in fact, certain kinds of personal petitions which rabbinic Judaism deems from the outset to be worthless, because they violate "reasonable" canons of what may be expected from God's providential activity. Thus, a man whose wife is pregnant should not pray to God for a boy, since the sex of the child, though yet unknown, has already been determined and even God cannot change it. Similarly, one who hears sounds of wailing as he approaches his town should not pray to God that they do not come from his house—since whatever calamity may have occurred has already taken place, and God cannot change the results (Mishnah Berakhot 9:3). Implicit in prayer as supplication, therefore, is a didactic as well as an instrumental function. One learns the proper way of approaching God (etiquette, piety) and of conceiving the relationship so that the results of one's petitioning—positive or negative—may be properly interpreted within the rabbinic world view, and so that one's behavior may be in conformity with God's norms.

The dialectical tensions in Judaic prayer which we have noted thus far—between theurgy and supplication, between the attitude of control and the attitude of submission—overlap with, and correspond to, yet another tension: between fixity/formalism and spontaneity/inwardness. The cultic understanding of Jewish prayer tends to favor fixity, regularity, and the importance of precision and proper form. (It should be clear by now that we do not deal here with a formalism for formalism's sake but with a basic ontological stance which undergirds this understanding.) But prayer as an act of personal piety and relatedness to God, or as an act of supplication, additionally requires intentionality, inwardness, concentration, and some spontaneity. A Mishnaic dictum already warns, "When you pray [the *Tefillah*], do not make your Prayer a matter of fixed routine, but an entreaty for mercy and grace before the Omnipresent One, praised be He" (Abot 2:13). The Talmud offers several interpretations of what is meant in the Mishnah by "fixity" (*qebaʿ*): (1) "anyone who recites his Prayer as if it were a burden to him"; (2) "anyone who does not recite his Prayer in the language of entreaty"; (3) "anyone who is unable to insert in it something new [each time]" (b. Berakhot 29b). Statutory prayer, though regular, must not become routine. The act of worship is an act of direct communication with God as well as an act of piety, and must be intended and experienced as such. Initially, the exact wording of the prayers was not fixed, only the topics and their order and general form. As fixity came to be the norm, additional prayers and hymns were composed in order to "insert something new." So, too, as the performance of the *mitsvot* and the recitation of the prayers became routine, various pietistic movements arose demanding inwardness and intense concentration on the inner meaning of the *mitsvot* and the prayers. The various medieval *musar* (ethical-pietistic) tracts all demand proper *kavannah* (intentionality, inwardness) in prayer. The major eighteenth-century revivalist movement known as Polish Hasidism put special emphasis on proper inwardness and enthusiasm in prayer, since this serves as a major vehicle for the mystic's ultimate goal of ecstatic *devekut,* the experience of adhesion or attachment to God.[23]

The tension in Judaic prayer between fixity and spontaneity—between externalization and internalization—has been an ongoing and generative one precisely because the significance of prayer in Judaism is overdetermined.[24] Prayer simultaneously bears a number of meanings the ontological bases of which ultimately conflict with each other: communal cultic surrogate *and* locus of individual piety, theurgic-magical *and* petitionary, activist *and* quietistic-contemplative, etc. Historians of religion must do justice to all these aspects, and to the structural tensions among them, if we aim at a fully ramified description and interpretation of prayer (let alone of worship) in Judaism.

I have attempted in this article to lay out the major lines of structure for a nuanced understanding of Judaic worship in the total context of Judaic religious culture. We have seen that Judaic worship extends far beyond the activity of prayer to include study and, ultimately, every waking activity of the pious Jew, all of whose acts are to be performed in the acknowledgment of God's kingship.[25] I have indicated that the reasons for this are to be sought in the fundamental ontological structures of Judaism, which are metaphorically transferred after 70 from the defunct Temple cult to the ongoing daily life of the people Israel, and in the centrality of Torah (divinely revealed norms and words) in Judaic religion. We have also seen that Judaic prayer—one kind of worship in Judaism—is itself a complex and overdetermined phenomenon, the tensions in which derive from a variety of sometimes contradictory motifs and concerns in Judaic religious tradition. It is this kind of richly textured, thoroughly contextualized "thick description"[26] that students of comparative religion must necessarily seek out if their enterprise is validly to be furthered.

Notes

1. Friedrich Heiler, *Prayer: A Study in the History and Psychology of Religion* [*Das Gebet: Eine religionsgeschichtliche und religionspsychologische Untersuchung,* Munich, 1918], trans. and ed. by Samuel McComb with the assistance of J. Edgar Park (New York: Oxford, 1932), p. xiii. Heiler follows this statement with a series of citations on prayer from noted scholars and theologians, all of which decidedly reflect the cultural perspective of nineteenth-century European (particularly German) Christianity. Thus, Adolf Deissmann: "religion, wherever it is alive in man, is prayer" (p. xiii), and Samuel Eck: prayer is "the

essential and characteristic expression of the religious consciousness" (p. xiv). Particularly invidious to sound comparative work has been the kind of naive evolutionism and Christian (usually Protestant) triumphalism reflected in the following categorical pronouncements: "Nothing reveals to us better the moral worth and the spiritual dignity of a form of worship than the kind of prayer it puts on the lips of its adherents" (Auguste Sabatier, p. xvi); "Prayer is a perfectly accurate instrument for grading the religious life of the soul. Did one only know how a man prays, and what he prays about, one would be able to see how much religion that man has. . . . What [the soul in prayer] has to say shows quite distinctly how rich or poor it is" (K. Girgensohn, pp. xv–xvi); "There is no part of the religious service of mankind that so clearly reveals the various views of the divine nature held by the different races at the different stages of their development . . . as the formulas of prayer" (L. R. Farnell, p. xvi). Though Heiler's work is over sixty years old, it remains the classic work on this topic, and therefore I have seen fit to address it here.

2. This complaint is frequently voiced in the study of Islam and the religious traditions of the Far East. It is equally applicable to many studies on Judaism.

3. Jacob Neusner, *A History of the Mishnaic Law of Purities. Part XXII. The Mishnaic System of Uncleanness* (Leiden: Brill, 1977), pp. 11–12. Neusner continues there: "The logic and structure of a system for purposes of comparison are to be set up against those of some other. In such a way comparison permits us to see systems whole and in perspective. Details of systems, when brought into juxtaposition with one another, by contrast produce chaos, on the one side, and a false sense of significance where there is none, on the other" (p. 13). The concept of "system" may be problematic for the historian, who is painfully aware of contingency and change, but it is heuristically useful in speaking about the interrelatedness of cultural meanings.

4. To mention a few salient (and relevant) examples: the religious world view expressed in the finally redacted Torah and prophetic literature must be interpreted against the backdrop of the calamitous destruction of the First Temple in 586 B.C.E.; late Second Commonwealth messianism and apocalypticism respond to the perceived humiliations of Hellenistic and Greco-Roman hegemony in the Land of Israel; early rabbinism follows upon the second destruction in 70 C.E.; Lurianic Kabbalah responds imaginatively to issues made salient by the expulsion of the Jews from Iberia in the 1490s; Zionism arises in the context of the problems of post-Emancipation European anti-Semitism; and contemporary Judaism sees itself challenged to respond to the twin traumas represented by the memory of the Holocaust and the reality of a Jewish state in the Land of Israel under seige.

5. The terminology is that of Clifford Geertz, "Religion As A Cultural System," in Michael Banton, ed., *Anthropological Approaches to the Study of Religion* (London: Tavistock, 1966), pp. 1–46; reprinted in Geertz, *The Interpretation of Cultures* (New York: Basic Books, 1973), pp. 87–125.

6. The origins of the synagogue as an institution are unclear, but the public reading of the Torah has always been one of its major functions, and possibly (at least in the Land of Israel) its exclusive original function. The earliest Palestinian synagogue inscription uncovered to date (the so-called Theodotus inscription, in Greek, from the second half of the first century B.C.E.) mentions the building of "this synagogue for the reading of the Law and for the teaching of the Commandments," but says nothing about communal prayer. See Hershel Shanks, *Judaism in Stone: The Archaeology of Ancient Synagogues* (New York: Harper, 1979), pp. 17–19.

7. See Philip Birnbaum, ed., *Daily Prayer Book* (New York: Hebrew Publishing Co., 1949), pp. 13–16.

8. See ibid., pp. 27–42 (daily morning service).

9. Cf. the following prayer inserted between the recitation of Exodus 30:17–21 (cultic purification) and Numbers 28:1–8 (the daily burnt-offering): "May it be Your will, Lord our

God and God of our fathers, to have mercy on us and pardon all our sins, iniquities, and transgressions; and rebuild the Temple speedily in our days, that we may offer before You the daily burnt-offerings to atone for us, as You have written in Your Torah through Moses Your servant, as it is said: [here follows Num. 28:1–8]," Birnbaum, p. 28.

10. See Philip Birnbaum, ed., *High Holyday Prayer Book* (New York: Hebrew Publishing Co., 1951), pp. 811–30.

11. There are in the Talmud occasional expressions of tension between the values of study and prayer. Cf. the following pair of stories in b. Shabbat 10a: "(1) Raba saw R. Hamnuna prolonging his Prayer [viz., his praying of the *Tefillah*, the petitionary prayer par excellence in Judaism, on which see below]. He [Raba] said, 'They abandon eternal life and occupy themselves with temporal, ephemeral life.' But he [Hamnuna] held that the time for prayer is distinct from the time for Torah-study. (2) R. Jeremiah was sitting before R. Zera and they were engaged in study. As it was growing late for the Prayer, R. Jeremiah was hurrying. R. Zera applied to him the verse, *He who turns away from hearing Torah, even his prayer is an abomination* (Prov. 28:9)." In the first story, the petitionary prayer deals with temporal needs, while Torah-study earns one his place in the world to come, for it deals with the revealed mind of God. The saying here attributed to Raba occurs in three other passages in the Talmud (b. Shab. 33b, b. Beṣah 15b, b. Taanit 21a), where the conflict is not between study and prayer but between study and attending to needs of this-worldly sustenance, which ultimately is the conflict here as well. In none of these passages is this saying left to stand as the last word; it either is rejected as an extreme position or (as here) is taken issue with. The second story is more straightforward in its conclusion, but it may also be understood as a case of bad manners. I have benefited from a discussion of the issues here with my colleague Eugene Mihaly.

12. Historically, there have been rebellions in Jewish society against this rabbinic cultural ideal and against the social elitism which it fostered. The most noteworthy of these rebellions is the eighteenth-century "revival movement" known as Polish Hasidism. The Hasidim asserted that fervent and joyful prayer was a preferred mode of worship and piety to the rabbis' Torah-study. On Hasidism, see Gershom Scholem, *Major Trends in Jewish Mysticism* (New York: Schocken, 1954), pp. 325–50. On the Hasidic elevation of prayer over study, and the innovation which this represented in the traditional Judaic scheme of values, see Louis Jacobs, *Hasidic Prayer* (New York: Schocken, 1972), pp. 17–21.

13. Moses Isserles, the major European commentator on the classic sixteenth-century compendium of Jewish law, the *Shulḥan Arukh*, begins his commentary by citing this verse, which he amplifies by stating that man is constantly in the presence of God and should behave accordingly.

14. See Birnbaum, *Daily*, pp. 759–73 (benedictions after meals), and 773–78 (various benedictions).

15. Only *maʿarib*, the evening service, presented a problem to the rabbinic commentators, since there was no evening sacrifice in the Temple. The standard explanation in the Talmud (b. Berakhot 26b) is that the evening service corresponds to the offering at nightfall of the limbs of the burnt-offerings and the fat of the other offerings which had not been wholly consumed on the altar by evening. Historically, it is clear that some sort of daily prayer existed before the destruction of the Temple in 70, though its exact nature cannot be determined from the extant sources. After the Temple's destruction, prayer took on the additional meanings described here (or these became intensified) and became an area of progressively more detailed rabbinic concern.

16. Cf. Joseph Heinemann, *Prayer In the Talmud: Forms and Patterns*, English version by Richard S. Sarason (Berlin: de Gruyter, 1977), pp. 14–16. Heinemann points to a significant difference between the Temple cult and the synagogue service. In the cult, the individual worshiper's participation was vicarious. He brought occasional offerings (though

not the daily *tamid* offering), but the priest performed the sacrificial rites while the worshiper stood as a bystander (so much the more so in the case of women). In the synagogue, however, the individual Jew is an active participant, himself (and herself) reciting all the prayers (which, in the case of the *Tefillah*, are then repeated on behalf of everyone by the prayer leader). "The people themselves become both the performers and the bearers of the divine service" (p. 14). The significance of this phenomenon, I think, lies less in the democratization of the service, as Heinemann would have it (and which, in his formulation, carries modern, anachronistic overtones), than in the fact that the cult here is metaphorically carried forward in the daily life of Israelite society, and that this is a classic illustration of the larger morphological shift that occurs in Judaism after 70.

17. Even when the wording was not fixed, the topics and order of the prayers were carefully laid down by the rabbis. This is the situation reflected in the Mishnah and the Talmuds. See Heinemann, chap. 2.

18. See the additional passages cited in ibid., pp. 14–21.

19. See further on this issue, Baruch M. Bokser, "'Ma‘al and Blessings over Food: Rabbinic Transformation of Cultic Terminology and Alternative Modes of Piety," *Journal of Biblical Literature* (forthcoming).

20. On the system of meanings in the cultic rites, see Baruch A. Levine, *In the Presence of the Lord* (Leiden: Brill, 1974), Jacob Milgrom, *Cult and Conscience* (Leiden: Brill, 1976), and Herbert Chanan Brichto, "On Slaughter and Sacrifice, Blood and Atonement," in *Hebrew Union College Annual* 47 (1976): 19–55.

21. Twelfth-century German Hasidism and sixteenth-century Lurianic Kabbalah have had the most pronounced impact on the shape of Jewish liturgy in this regard. On both, see Scholem, *Jewish Mysticism*, pp. 80–118, 344–86. On German Hasidism, see Ivan Marcus, *Piety and Society: The Jewish Pietists of Medieval Germany* (Leiden: Brill, 1981). In the earlier Jewish "throne-mysticism" (*merkabah*)—a form of Hellenistic astral mysticism—elaborate prayer-formulas were used instrumentally, as means of achieving an ecstatic, visionary state, but theurgic elements also were present. See Scholem, *Jewish Mysticism*, pp. 40–79, and his *Jewish Gnosticism, Merkabah Mysticism, and Talmudic Tradition* (New York: Jewish Theological Seminary, 1960), especially pp. 75–83. Other attempts to fix the wording of the liturgy and its rules have had more to do with temporal than cosmic power. The attempt made at the beginning of the Islamic period by the heads of the Babylonian rabbinical academies (*geonim*) should be viewed as part of their larger attempt to establish Babylonian hegemony over the far-flung Jewish communities of the Islamic empire (including those in the Land of Israel). See Lawrence Hoffman, *The Canonization of the Synagogue Service* (Notre Dame: University of Notre Dame Press, 1979), and Salo W. Baron, *A Social and Religious History of the Jews*, 7 (New York: Columbia, 1958), pp. 62–134. My colleague Jakob J. Petuchowski has repeatedly pointed out that the (relatively) final fixing of the wording of the prayers was due less to any historical or ideological dynamic within Judaism than to the fortuitous invention of moveable type.

22. For an interesting discussion of various styles of addressing God in Jewish petitionary prayer, see Heinemann, *Prayer in the Talmud*, pp. 193–217, 243–50. Heinemann notes correctly that the posture of a humble suppliant is by no means ubiquitous in Jewish prayer. Some of these prayers are highly importunate.

23. Hasidic prayer, like that of some earlier mystical and pietistic movements in Judaism, is basically contemplative in character. Here, as in theurgic prayer, the literal sense of the petitions is abandoned. But, in Hasidism, the prayers become vehicles for self-annihilation and self-transcendence through *devekut* rather than symbols for cosmic processes. The ultimate processes are internal-psychological rather than external-cosmic, as in Lurianic Kabbalah. On the contemplative and quietistic aims of Hasidic prayer, see Jacobs, *Hasidic Prayer*, and Rivka Schatz Uffenheimer, *Hasidism as Mysticism: Quietistic*

Elements in Eighteenth-Century Hasidic Thought [Hebrew] (Jerusalem: Magnes, 1968), pp. 54–110, 129–47. Cf. also the useful typologies of Judaic prayer suggested by Shalom Rosenberg, "Prayer and Jewish Thought—Directions and Problems," in Gabriel Hayyim Cohen, ed., *Jewish Prayer: Continuity and Innovation* [Hebrew] (Jerusalem: Kedem, 1978), pp. 85–130.

24. On the dialectical tension between fixity and spontaneity in Jewish prayer, see Jakob J. Petuchowski, *Understanding Jewish Prayer* (New York: KTAV, 1972), pp. 3–16.

25. Significantly, in the modern period among nontraditionalist Jews, Judaic worship has in fact been confined to prayer—a situation which reflects the internalization by Jews of the modern Protestant religious ethos expressed by Heiler at the outset of this chapter. The modernization of Judaism and its simultaneous acculturation to the Western Christian definition of religion have both concentrated religious activity almost exclusively in the synagogue and emphasized prayer as the quintessential act of worship and religiosity. The modern reform of the Jewish worship-service reflects a fundamental shift in world view and ethos. Precisely those "static" aspects of Judaic worship—regularity, repetition, formal precision—which carry forward the ontology of the Temple cult have been discarded in favor of spontaneity, innovation, and dynamism, all components of the ontology of modernity.

26. The term is that of Clifford Geertz, "Thick Description: Toward An Interpretive Theory of Culture," in *The Interpretation of Cultures*, pp. 3–30.

Four

Religion and Mysticism
The Case of Judaism

Arthur Green

1

Judaism is a religious tradition that has been studied, both by its practitioners from within and by observers from without, for a great many centuries. Despite this fact, our view of Judaism has changed radically within the past hundred or even fifty years. This transformation is due in no small part to the rediscovery and reintegration of Jewish mysticism into our picture of the whole. All those definitions of Judaism so popular in the nineteenth and early twentieth centuries, whether by "essential spirit," by a few "irreducible principles," or as "ethical monotheistic nationhood" meet their match as they confront the great variety of evidence that research into Jewish mysticism has unearthed.

The term "mysticism" in the history of religions has been victim of a frequent murkiness of definition, one that, as some would say, is appropriate to its subject matter. Our problem in speaking of *Jewish* mysticism is an especially delicate one. Take the most narrow and precise definitions of the subject currently available in the intellectual marketplace (mysticism as an utter absorption within and identification with the deity), and we have very little about which we can write. With a few notable exceptions, such formulas are lacking in the canon of Jewish spiritual writings. Indeed this lack has misled some serious scholars of comparative mysticism to dismiss Judaism, seeing it as the most absolutely "Western" of all religions, in which the transcendence of God is so complete that the mystical spirit is simply unable to flourish. This judgment, as we shall see presently, is far from the truth. Take, on the other hand, a wide-ranging definition of mysticism (a religion of inner experience and intimacy with God), and we find that we can exclude very little of Judaism from our purview. Surely the Psalms are mystical by this definition, as are the prophets, the rabbis, and such differing later figures as Maimonides and Martin Buber. When the definition is this broad, we must question its usefulness: over against what other phenomena does mysticism, so defined, stand? What other phenomena does the definition help us to delineate? The answer is difficult, unless we resort to the old stereotypes about "true" or "inner" religion as opposed to "mere" priestly religion or devotion to legal forms. Such a distinction, totally alien to the Jewish experience, serves primarily to judge rather than to explain, and its prejudices are too obvious to require further comment.

In what sense is it, then, that we shall speak of "mysticism"? Let me propose, for our purposes, a working definition, one that takes a middle ground but seems to serve well the textual evidences of the Jewish sources. I shall speak here of mysticism as a religious outlook that: (1) seeks out inner experience of the divine, and to that end generally cultivates the life of inwardness; (2) longs to recover an original intimacy with God, the loss of which is essential to the ordinary human condition; and (3) involves itself with an esoteric lore that promises both to reveal the inner secrets of divinity and to provide access to the restoration of divine/ human intimacy.

Such a definition will perforce limit our consideration to Judaism as a postbiblical phenomenon, and this is quite intentional. Biblical religion (we speak here of the Hebrew Bible, but the statement would apply to the Christian Scriptures as well) is not yet fraught with the overwhelming sense of God's distance and the need to traverse it that is to so characterize later mystics. While the biblical God is indeed transcendent, he can and frequently does choose to manifest his presence quite directly within the human realm. This is true for the people of Israel collectively, in the wilderness shrine and then in the Temple, as well as for the prophets and heroes in their individual encounters with divinity. Though the God of Israel had been proclaimed universal and transcendent, biblical man still held fast to those legacies of earlier religion, both cultic and mantic, that allowed him to evoke the Presence. In this sense the essential rites were not esoteric, and no separate or "inner" reading of the traditions was needed in order to find their true meaning.

There is no single figure or document that we may describe as "typical" of the Jewish mystical tradition. In fact we are dealing not with a single tradition but with a variety of teachings, a wide range of personalities, and a complex series of historical phenomena that span some two thousand years. Mysticism, even within the scope of our definition, contains room for a broad spectrum of religious experiences and ways of conveying them. The case of Judaism should help us understand that no single doctrine or experiential typology can exhaust the mysticism of a particular tradition. On the contrary, religious types are cross-traditional, and this includes aspects of their mystical experiences. Though cultural limitations would likely prevent both from declaring so, a Hasidic master in his community might have more in common with a Sufi master than he would with an ancient Jewish apocalyptic visionary. To document this claim we shall turn, in the second part of this essay, to an examination of four very different literary sources found in Jewish mystics of various schools and times. But first some general remarks are in order, beginning with a brief historical mapping of these schools, so that the reader may have some temporal perspective in which to see the examples we shall offer.

From the first three or four centuries of the common era, the period when rabbinic Judaism itself was yet in formation, we have evidence of several sorts of mystical/occult activity, chiefly in the Land of Israel. These seem to have centered around mystical flights or inner "descents" into the divine throne room and visions of God as surrounded by his heavenly retinue. Such flights were induced by chants and incantations; the initiate was allowed to pass on to each succeeding stage of the journey only by possession of some secret knowledge, often the name of the angel who guarded that particular rung of the heavens. The documents that we have from these circles include accounts of the journey, ecstatic hymns, and descriptions of what appears to be an envisioned gigantic "body" of the Creator. There is much in this literature that is reminiscent of other late Hellenistic mysteries and the Gnostic circles that abounded in the later Roman empire, and an extensive scholarly literature exists on the subject of this "Jewish Gnosticism." We also possess a clearly magical literature that is closely related in date, form, and language to this mystical corpus. Here the angels and principalities are invoked not for permission to continue on the beatific journey but for some worldly good they can perform for the one who has the power of their secret names. In general it may be said that rigid distinctions between mysticism and magic, or even between magic and religion, once popular among historians of religion, are not borne out by the Jewish sources.

The sort of visionary mysticism we are discussing had a long history in Jewish circles. While its roots clearly go back to late antiquity (individual texts are extremely hard to date in this very slow-changing literature), we have evidence that it was still practiced in Mesopotamia in the tenth century C.E. Of its later history in the Near East we know little, but sources and traditions were imported to Europe, perhaps via Italy, in the tenth or eleventh century. Thence they were incorporated into a new sort of mystical pietism, one that flourished in the Jewish communities along the Rhine in the ensuing centuries. This movement of "German Hasidism" is surely related in type to the piety of the monastic reforms that characterized Franco-German Christianity in the same period. Outwardly the teaching was essentially a moralistic one, its achievement the promulgation of a religious folk-ethic that was to dominate Ashkenazic (northern European) Jewry for many centuries to come. The core of this revival was nurtured, however, by a speculative spirit, one that combined the older visionary traditions with early medieval philosophy to create an esoteric doctrine of its own. Unlike the earlier mystical sources, this tradition was an exegetical one, combing passages of Scripture in search of some hint as to their greater secret. Angels, demons, and the "Glory," a created form to be distinguished from God himself, were central subjects of these speculations. It is a certain aspect of this Glory, claim the pietists, which is the object of visionary experience, the ultimate reward for the life of righteousness. Thus, to say it all too briefly, are the moralistic, speculative, and visionary aspects of a mystical revival combined in the German Hasidic movement.

Toward the middle of the twelfth century, contemporaneous with the rise of this movement in northern Europe, there develops a parallel phenomenon, first in southern France along the Pyrenees, and then in northern Spain. This mystical movement among Spanish Jews, a bit later given the name "Kabbalah," was to become, from a doctrinal point of view, the major source for all later Jewish mysticism. It may be characterized as a symbolic-speculative movement, one that sought to pierce beyond the bounds of ordinary intellectual endeavor by the promulgation of a new symbolic language, one that was rooted, so the Kabbalists claimed, in realms of divine reality that were outside the reach of both philosophy and language. Their efforts centered around the ten *sefirot,* a series of symbol clusters that represented both the succeeding stages in the ongoing self-revelation of the hidden Godhead and the steps the adept might take (for their structure permeates all of reality, including the soul) in the attempt to return to him. By "symbol clusters" we mean that a group of well-known objects or realities are placed together and represent the same stage in the divine world. That "rung," itself inexpressible, is then understood by association with the symbols that represent it. One such aspect of divinity, for example, is that which might best be referred to as "Understanding/Mother/Womb/Palace/Jubilee/End/Persimmon/Upper Garden/World-to-Come/Repentance/Joy". A few other terms could be added to the list. For convenience, this aspect of divinity is called by the single name *binah* (understanding). The mystic was to contemplate the associations, seeing them both in the words of Scripture and in the happenings of human life. Such contemplation was to create a new attitude of mind, one in which the symbolic consciousness was to supplant ordinary thinking as the chief focus of the adept's mental life, leading him ever to rise higher, or penetrate more deeply, into a world of unending mystery.

The writings of the Kabbalists contain elements of both the visionary and the moralistic-pietistic strands, though both of these have now been subsumed within the greater theosophical or speculative interests of the Kabbalah. Visionary experience is surely possible, insofar as the Kabbalists are concerned, but its object is a lower "world" than that attained by constant and disciplined contemplation of the *sefirot,* and is thus of lesser value. The *Zohar,* the central work of the Spanish Kabbalah, has its own moralistic spirit and is quite filled with pious preachings, though these are generally original only insofar as they are interwoven with the speculative aspects of the work. Even among the Kabbalists of the thirteenth century, we should add, many of whom knew one another and were influenced by one another's work, there were many types. Some were poets, using the symbolic imagination to soar more freely than ordinary prose would have permitted; others were systematizers, commentators who sought to reread all of earlier Judaism in the Kabbalistic spirit, or apologists and fighters against rational philosophy. Some of course combined several of these elements, making their works rich sources of inspiration for centuries to come.

The next major revival of the Jewish mystical spirit took place in the sixteenth century, centered in a small circle in the Galilean town of Safed. Here gathered children of refugees who had fled Spain after the expulsion of 1492, along with Jews from several of the Near Eastern countries. In the self-contained environment of this small community, a revival took place in several areas of Jewish intellectual activity, most particularly in the cultivation of the spiritual life and the study of mysticism. Once again we see that very different types of mystical figures were present within the same small circle. There is a strong occultist strain in much of Safed mysticism, however, and it was to the most abstruse and often half-forgotten documents of earlier ages that these mystics looked for inspiration. It was here that the belief in reincarnation, long held by certain Kabbalists, took on great importance, as disciples claimed for their masters the ability to determine who each of the circle had been in his previous life on earth.

The dominant teaching to emerge from Safed was that of Isaac Luria (1534–72). His path, as preserved in the writings of his disciples, was one of infinitely detailed and refined meditations, in which the *sefirot* were replaced by a series of ever moving and changing configurations that made up the contemplative cosmos. Successive meditations on each stage of the emerging universe were to constitute collectively the rebuilding or "repair" of that universe; the theurgic aspect of Kabbalah, that which claimed an external effect for man's contemplative activity, was here much emphasized. This sense of a cosmos reestablished, the divine harmony restored by action in the meditative realm, was fully integrated with the ancient messianic imagery of Judaism and lent to mysticism a kind of redemptive urgency that it had not always known. The life of the individual contemplative or visionary was now bound up with the fate of the universe as a whole; his own strivings for God, the dream of Israel of being redeemed from exile, and the universal longing for the restored harmony of life before the Fall (or before Creation) were now joined together. It is no wonder that the Lurianic movement served as the religious impulse for the most widespread and devastating messianic movement in Jewish history, that which centered around Sabbatai Sevi in the mid- and late seventeenth century. The followers of the Sabbatian messiah created their own occultist doctrine, one in which Kabbalistic meditations and faith in the new messiah combined in the startling assertion that Sabbatai was himself a divine being, the kingship of God incarnate. The fact that certain of the Sabbatian leaders had themselves been educated as Catholics in Spain, where their families had remained as secret Jews in defiance of the Inquisition, surely had something to do with this surprising outgrowth of the Kabbalistic tradition.

Throughout their earlier history, the various mysticisms growing out of Judaism had been essentially elitist in character. The doctrines were difficult, the style of the sources abstruse, and circles that studied them always relatively small and restricted. While something of the mystics' spirit had, in each movement, penetrated into the wider society through liturgy, ascetic practice, or manner of thought, the true meaning of these innovations remained the secret of the few. For the broader populace, including many intellectuals, mystics were more to be revered than understood. From the sixteenth century on, however, this situation was dramatically altered. The revival in Safed caught the imagination of preachers and storytellers among Jews in both Europe and the Near East, and various popularized versions of Kabbalistic teaching and practice became widespread. This took place both before and after the Sabbatian episode, and multiform versions of the union between mystical devotion and messianic awakening are to be found, especially on the popular level. The seventeenth and eighteenth centuries, the period just preceding the advent of modernity and social emancipation in Jewish history, was the era in which mysticism had its greatest influence on the collective religious consciousness of Jewry.

A particular form of this popular mystical revivalism is that called

Hasidism (a name shared with several religious movements in Jewish history), as it developed in Russia and Poland toward the latter decades of the eighteenth century. Hasidism rejected the complex meditational exercises which earlier mystics had deemed necessary to effect redemption. It also tended to set aside the ascetic regimen and harsh view of human nature that had been its joint legacy from the Safed revival and the old Ashkenazic tradition. Instead it preached a more nearly pantheistic vision, one in which all things contained the presence of God; or, in a somewhat different formulation, nothing truly existed but God himself and all else was his external garb, hiding him from the unenlightened but dissolving in the face of true awareness. This essentially simple message was one of great power; Hasidism attracted more of a mass following than any similar movement in Jewish history, save possibly Sabbatianism in its first years. The religious teaching of Hasidism was borne by a series of charismatic leaders who were seen by their followers as current manifestations of the *zaddiq* ideal, that of the "righteous" or holy man, a figure with ancient roots in the folk imagination of Jewry. These *zaddiqim* were at once teachers of spiritual enlightenment, intercessors in prayer, and channels through which divine light and blessing were said to flow into the world. In the phenomenology of Hasidism it is impossible to separate these elements; here still, as in the earliest flowering of Jewish mysticism, the sublime and the quasi-magical remain bound together.

Such, in briefest outline, are the major historical dimensions within which our subject has existed. Countless individuals and substrata have here been neglected, of course, as have the various attempts to continue or reconstitute a Jewish mysticism in our own times. Our concern is with major movements on the historical scene, as well as with distinctive typologies of mystical life that are to be found within Judaism. Before we turn to the latter, however, there are a few general points about the place of mysticism within Jewish history that need to be made.

The endeavor that we have defined as mystical accompanies Judaism throughout the successive stages of its development. The religion of institutions, ceremonies, and law that so preoccupies the rabbis can in no period be fully separated from the life of the spirit that quickens it. From earliest rabbinic times, the names of such well-known teachers of exoteric Judaism as Yohanan ben Zakkai and Akiba are associated as well with the mystic lore of their time. While such associations are hard to prove for this early period, it is certainly the case that for such figures as Moses Nahmanides in medieval Spain and Joseph Caro in Safed that preoccupation with the law and insight into the mysteries went hand in hand. The same may be said of such Hasidic leaders as the rabbis of Gur and Lubavitch, who were considered legal authorities of the first rank, even by those who opposed their Hasidism. There were many others in Jewish history, including both the author of the *Zohar* and the Ba'al Shem Tov, the first central figure of latter-day Hasidism, whose energies were devoted wholly to the mystical/spiritual endeavor and who manifested a traditionally respectable, but not specialized, knowledge of the law. These too, however, lived wholly within the domain of legally sanctioned Jewish practice. The picture of mystics and rabbis at odds with one another reflects the exception rather than the rule in Jewish history.

But this tells only half the story. True, most mystics were traditionalists, and mysticism was used more than once in defense of traditional religious practice against some perceived threat. At the same time, there is a subtle shift of values that takes place as Judaism is given a mystical cast. The *will* of God, as manifest in the activist stance of a Judaism above all loyal to the commanding words of Torah, now must share center stage with the *being* or *presence* of God that the mystic seeks out or has come to know. The mediated quality of rabbinic religion, Israel related to God through Torah, has in a sense been inadequate to the needs of its most wholehearted devotees. From the mystic's point of view, claim as he may that all levels of the Torah's meaning are simultaneously valid and uncontradictory, it is clear that the *true* meaning, in some specially emphatic sense, is that of the secret tradition. In this sense it must be said that a certain ambivalence toward the exoteric tradition, despite great and sincere protestations of loyalty, accompanies Jewish mysticism through its history.

Whatever beliefs we may hold as to the ultimate oneness of mystical experience, the testimony of mystics as we find it is always colored by the particular cultural contexts within which they have lived. It is no surprise, then, to note that a great deal of Jewish esotericism is *intellectual* in nature. The object of the mystic's search, for most of the Kabbalistic sources, is the *knowledge* of God. True, this knowing is of an intimate, sometimes even unitive, character. But the highest states of mystical attachment and rapture remain closed before the one who does not know. This was already the case in the earliest visionary literature, where proper knowledge of an angel's name or a mysterious password was vital to surviving the heavenly journey. Kabbalah in the Middle Ages may be said to represent a maturation of this Gnostic stance, one in which the "secret" lore has taken on aspects of the search for wisdom and profundity. The highest triad of the *sefirot,* in a well-known Kabbalistic system, is that of *ḥokhmah, binah,* and *da'at,* or wisdom, understanding, and knowledge. Here the descent into the mystical realm is one of reaching out for ever more refined levels of mind, seeking that inner place where the mind of God will be joined to the most rarified human intellect. In this sense the Kabbalah is very much influenced by the contemplative vision of medieval philosophy; rather than speaking of mysticism and philosophy as two separate domains, as we often do, we might best think in terms of rational and esoteric traditions in the Middle Ages, the two seeking the same goal of intimate knowledge of God. Even for latter-day Hasidism, where a certain anti-intellectual strain is to be noted, *da'at,* or knowing awareness, remains crucial to the religious mind. Only the one who comes to know that all contains His presence can truly participate in the ecstatic worship that is the Hasidic community's hallmark. The transformation of mind, called for by many of the Kabbalistic and Hasidic masters, required, first, mind's highest cultivation.

This intellectual character is also manifest in the essential activity that we see preoccupying the Kabbalist, that of study and interpretation. Here the mystics remained fully within the value-system of the postrabbinic world, though using it to their own ends. Tremendous learning, and not only of the esoteric kind, is manifest in the major works of the Kabbalah, an effort that essentially involved a reinterpretation of the entire Jewish tradition, including the Bible itself, in a new spirit. No wonder then that the majority of mystical treatises take the form of commentaries, at least in the loosest sense of that word. Delving into the word of Scripture, seeking out the secret meanings God had hidden in it for the elect of times to come, is the contemplative exercise which the Jewish sources of all periods most widely attest.

2

Bearing these general remarks in mind, we turn now to an examination of four figures whom we find in the mystical literature of Judaism. Each of these ideal types is illustrated by a text, followed by some words of commentary. The sampler of sources offered here is taken from the widest range of sources, historically as well as typologically, and is fully intended to whet the reader's appetite for further study. Our types, the *heavenly voyager,* the *lover of God,* the *symbolmaker,* and the *holy man,* are to be found throughout the medieval and later literature. They are complementary rather than exclusive with respect to one another. Indeed, we could without great difficulty find texts from many a single Kabbalistic author that would illustrate all four.

The Heavenly Voyager

The literary sources of early Jewish visionary or *Merkavah* (literally "chariot") mysticism are a series of fragmentary accounts, preserved mostly in manuscripts through the ages, and edited by scholars only in the course of the past century. Some of these texts are very nearly incomprehensible, written in difficult and badly preserved code. Others

break off at crucial points, the voyager or author seemingly so overwhelmed by ecstasy that he loses the ability to speak; thus do the sources
seek to convey a sense of ineffability about that which they otherwise
describe in words. Only in a relatively few cases do we have whole accounts of such visions, recorded in a way that the reader can understand.
One of these more complete accounts is translated here. Its source is the
Merkavah Rabbah, composed possibly in the fourth or fifth century, and
printed in the collection *Merkavah Shelemah,* published in Jerusalem in
1921. The speaker, using the name of Rabbi Ishmael, has been transported
into the heavenly palaces:

Rabbi Ishmael recounted:
Sasgiel, angel of the countenance, said to me: "My beloved, be
seated in my bosom and I shall tell you what will become of Israel." I
sat in his bosom and he began to cry; tears flowed from his eyes and
fell down upon me. I addressed him: "My glorious brightness! Why
are you crying?" He responded: "Come, I shall bring you in and show
you what is in store for Israel, the holy people." He took me by the
hand and led me through chamber within chamber, secret place within
secret place, into the treasuries. There he took the account-books and
showed me written tales of woe, one worse than the other. I asked for
whom these were prescribed, and he said "For Israel." I responded:
"Israel can stand up to these." But he said: "Come tomorrow and I
will tell you of troubles yet worse than these." The next day he took
me through the secret places and the inner chambers and showed me
troubles more horrendous than the first. Many were to die, some by
sword and some by famine. Others were to be taken into captivity. I
said to him: "My glorious brightness! Have Israel sinned so badly?"
"Each day," he answered me, "new decrees are issued, more terrible
than these. But when Israel go into their synagogues and houses of
study to say 'Amen, May His great name be blessed,' we do not allow
the decrees to come forth from the innermost chambers."
As I left him, I heard a voice calling out in the Aramaic language,
saying: "O Temple, Temple for destruction, and palace for burning
fire! The joy of the king will be disgraced, his sons killed . . . * the vir-
gins despoiled. The pure altar will be defiled; the table set at the gates
of Jerusalem and the Holy Land will tremble."
When I heard this loud voice I was taken aback and silenced. I was
about to fall faint when Hadariel the angel came and restored my
spirit. He stood me up and asked me what had happened. I said to him:
"O glorious exalted one! Is there no redemption for Israel?" He replied: "Come, let me take you into the treasuries of consoling and salvation." There I saw groups of angels sitting and weaving garments of
salvation, fashioning crowns of life and fixing precious stones and
pearls into them. They were smelling fragrant spices and sweetening

* The text is here incomprehensible and probably corrupt.

wine for the righteous. I saw one crown finer than all the others; sun, moon, and the twelve constellations were all engraved in it. I asked: "O glorious exalted one! For whom are these crowns?" And he replied, "For Israel." "And for whom is that especially magnificent crown?" "For David, King of Israel." I said: "O glorious brightness! Show me his glory." "My beloved," he replied, "wait here three hours until David arrives, and then you will see his greatness." He grabbed hold of me and kept me in his bosom. "What do you see?" he asked me. I told him: "I see seven bolts of lightning, dancing about as one." "Hide your eyes," he said, "that you not be too shaken by these, which have come out to greet David."

Then all the wheels and Seraphim, the treasuries of snow and of hail, constellations, stars, angels, and fiery flames of heaven were aroused and proclaimed: "For the choirmaster, a Psalm of David." I heard a sound coming forth from Eden, calling out: "May the glory of God be forever!" And there was David, leading the procession, all the kings of his lineage walking behind him. Each had a crown on his head, but the crown of David outshone them all, its brilliance radiating from one end of the world to the other. When David arrived at the highest chamber of heaven, his throne was awaiting him: a throne of fire, five hundred miles high, and double that in width and breadth. Once David was seated on his throne, facing the throne of his Creator, all the kings of the house of David seated before him and all the kings of Israel standing behind him, he stood up and sang hymns and praises the like of which no ear has ever heard. Once he said: "May the Lord rule forever," Metatron and all his host recited: "Holy, Holy, Holy, is the Lord of Hosts." The holy beings called forth in praise: "Blessed is the glory of the Lord from His place!" The heavens called out: "May the Lord rule forever!" and all the kings of the House of David responded: "The Lord shall be King over all the earth!"

Happy is the eye that has seen it, happy the man who has merited this. Happy is his mother who received him, the breasts at which he nursed, the womb in which he grew. Happy is the Torah that he studied, the understanding he attained. Happy are the arms that have embraced him, the peace he has pursued. Happy is the eye that has seen him. Happy you, Ishmael, for you have merited this.

The report, though narrated in the name of a certain "Ishmael," is essentially anonymous. It is typical of these sources that they use a well-known rabbinic name, most often either Akiba or Ishmael, but these ascriptions are not to be taken literally. The concluding paragraph, typical of these sources in their complete form, represents a series of formulas ("happy" could as well be rendered "blessed") by which the ecstatic passion of the account itself is cooled down before the text is brought to a close.

Perhaps the most remarkable feature of these *merkavah* accounts is the way something of the intense experience is preserved in the telling of the tale. Here we have no mystic's complaint about the inadequacy of language or the impossibility of true communication. We are confronted rather with a skillful writer, one who has been able to recreate in his narrative the dramatic excitement and intense pace of ecstatic experience. It is impossible for us to know, of course, how wholly and literally such a narrative corresponds to a single inner event in the mystic's life and how much it may be embellished by the literary imagination. In dealing with such realms, however, attempts on our part to distinguish "experience," as though it could be fully isolated, from fantasy and imagination will not lead far. The mystic lives, writes, and "experiences" within a world that knows its own literary conventions and traditional figures of the imaginative fancy.

Indeed, the traditional character of this text is one that makes it of special interest. Sometimes it is thought that these *merkavah* experiences are of an entirely private sort, bearing no relation to the external world of historical reality. Here we see a visionary whose entire concern is historical, whose inward journey is wholly consumed by the question of Israel's collective fate. The consoling vision he receives is entirely within Jewish tradition: despite Israel's oppression in this world, the House of David lives on in heaven. Interestingly there is no specific mention of the Messiah here; it may be that David himself has taken on the messianic role, though that too remains unsaid. Many of the surrounding images of the vision, including the angels who weave garments for the righteous and the divine treasuries of snow and hail, are well attested in the Midrashic collections of rabbinic lore. The claim that evil decrees are averted each day by the power of Israel's "Amen, May His great name be blessed" is also typically rabbinic in form.

The combination of terror and ecstatic joy that characterizes this description, and the possibility of radical and instantaneous shifts from one of these emotions to the other, are also widely to be found in this literature. Another source describes the path one must traverse as running between fields of fire and fields of ice; the voyager must step carefully lest he be either burned or frozen. New dangers may appear at each stage of the vision, and it is only the voyager's divine protector who saves him from utter destruction. As danger passes, a new level of beatific vision is opened up, though that too may turn instantly into a nightmare if proper vigilance is not maintained.

The tradition of heavenly voyage literature is a long one in Jewish sources. Flourishing from the early centuries of the common era down into the early Middle Ages, it was mostly supplanted by the speculative mysticism of the Kabbalah. Even among Kabbalists, however, we find some continuation of this activity; the *Zohar* itself contains a significant body of visionary journey materials. Most famous among latter-day testaments to such experience is a letter written by the Ba'al Shem Tov in 1750, in which he describes an "ascent of the soul" that he had undertaken some three years earlier, during which he had held conversation with the Messiah and was given various secrets that he was sworn never fully to reveal.

The Lover of God

The motif of divine love, or of love and passionate longing as constituting the relationship between God and the human soul, is widely attested in mystical literature throughout the world. With mysticism defined as a "longing to recover an original intimacy," it is only to be expected that the language of human love, our great attempt to do the same, would cross our path.

Here the biblical legacy is particularly important to later Judaism. The love of man and wife as a metaphoric expression of God's covenant with Israel is well known to the prophets. The longing of the individual's heart for the nearness of God is a frequent motif in the Psalms, whence it becomes a major factor in both Jewish and Christian pieties. It is the Song of Songs, however, presented in seemingly secular form in the Bible, that is to become the central bearer of the great love-mysticisms in both of these traditions. Rooted in the cultic eroticism of the ancient Near East, the Song as found in the Bible has outwardly been stripped of its sacred context, this being too tied up with paganism and the cults of fertility to be tolerated by the biblical editors. But the old sense of sacrality about the Song persisted, and it was not coincidental that Akiba, in the second century, proclaimed it the "holy of holies" among the books of Scriptures. Both Judaism and Christianity embraced the Song as allegory, the one reading into it the love between God and the Community of Israel, the other hearing in it of the love between Christ and the Church.

The collective and historical reading of the Song dominated the Jewish exegesis of the early centuries. In medieval times, however, philosophers and Kabbalists alike were to offer other readings, some finding in the Song echoes of the love between God and the human soul, while others read it as recounting a love that takes place entirely within God, a sacred marriage within the divine world at which man could be but a devoted attendant. The latter tended to dominate in the Kabbalistic sources, where religious eroticism was given a new lease on life, though in the context of a highly guarded system of personal morality.

Discussions of the love of God are to be found in all the major moral treatises of medieval Jewry, beginning with Bahya's *Duties of the Hearts* in the eleventh century. They typically distinguish a "lower" love of God, one motivated by earthly rewards, or even the promise of paradise, from the "higher" or true love, one of pure and selfless devotion that knows no thought of reward. In later times these treatises were placed in a Kabbalistic context, and they were particularly important in the popular devotional literature that emerged from sixteenth-century Safed.

We have chosen to represent this aspect of Jewish mystical life with a poem by one of the leading figures of the Safed revival, Rabbi Eleazar Azikri (1533–1600). His well-known pietistic manual, *Sefer Haredim* (literally best translated as "Book of the Quakers," though of course without reference to the later Christian sect), was frequently reprinted and widely used. The poem, *Soul's Beloved,* is surely among the classics of mystical love poetry. The best testimony to its acceptance has been its frequent publication within the liturgy: the prayer books of most Near Eastern Jews offer it as a petition to be sung each morning, while the Hasidim of Eastern Europe assigned it to the Friday afternoon service, as an introduction to the Sabbath.

Soul's beloved, compassionate Father,
Draw Your servant to Your will.
Let him run, swift as a deer,
To kneel before Your majesty.
Sweeter is Your love to him
Than honey from the comb,
Than any taste of pleasure.

Glorious, radiant, cosmic light,
My soul is faint for love of You.
Heal her, I pray, O God,
Show to her Your splendrous glow.
Then will she be strengthened, cured,
Your maidservant forever.

O Faithful, may Your tender mercies
Reach Your son who loves You greatly.
In deepest longings has he sought
To gaze upon Your mighty splendor.
My God, my heart's delight,
Come quickly; be not hidden.

Reveal Yourself, my Dearest; spread over me
The shelter of Your peace.
Your presence lighting up the world,
We shall rejoice, exult in You.
Hurry, Lover, time has come,
Grant me Your grace
As You did of old.

The poem is not a Kabbalistic one in the specific sense; it does not refer to the *sefirot,* and the symbolic language of the Kabbalah is not to be found in it. It speaks directly to God, whose name, YHWH, is to be found in the opening letter of each stanza in the Hebrew. The metaphors it uses are remarkably accessible, familiar to anyone who has but the slightest experience, from reading or from personal encounter, with the reality of religious love.

We should note that the author seems to vacillate between the two central metaphors of personal relationship between God and Israel: that of father and child and that of lover and beloved. In the first and third stanzas the fatherhood of God is mentioned, and the voice of the poet is in the masculine gender. In the second stanza, the author speaks of his soul, using the feminine of *nefesh* as a way to heighten the erotic imagery, and to move from the language of father and faithful son to that of distant lover and lovesick bride. The third stanza, though returning to the masculine, continues the motif of lovesick longing, to a point where the metaphors are thoroughly commingled. By the final stanza father and son are no longer to be found, and the poem reveals itself to be one of passionate, sacred eros. This process, in which the intensity of erotic love first masks itself in filial form, is an accurate reflection of the ambiguity with which the love theme is treated in Jewish sources. Seemingly mindful of the biblical revulsion toward sacral eroticism in the pagan context, the public liturgy as compiled by the rabbis makes virtually no use of the sensual imagery that was part of its legacy. In those places where talk of love is to be found in the early liturgy, it is always carefully identified as the love of father and child or perhaps that of ruler and devoted subject. In the work of the ancient poets, however, whose *piyyutim* served as a quasi-esoteric counterpoint to the prose liturgy, it is the God and Israel of the allegorical Song of Songs who frequently come to the fore. The sense that such language, though proper, is best guarded for use by "the modest" is long established.

Soul's Beloved, however, does not belong to this genre of *piyyut.* Though accepted for liturgical usage, the poem has nothing in it to indicate that its primary meaning was other than private. With the exception of a single line in the last stanza, the poem is composed entirely in the singular, and its subject is the longing of a single soul for God, not that of the Community of Israel. Azikri's poem stands very much in the Spanish tradition of Hebrew poetry, one in which the expression of individual feeling, in sacred as well as "secular" contexts, was given a new legitimacy. The lover of God portrayed here is a lone seeker, having neither the comfort nor the conflict of feeling himself situated in or responsible to a religious community. The sense of the religious as essentially belonging to the private life of the individual and his inner relationship with God reflects medieval Judaism at its most universal, at its point of greatest similarity to contemporary Christianity or Islam. Indeed there is nothing in the poem, if we did not know its authorship and origin, that would tell us for certain that it was a Jewish and not a Christian or Sufi work.

Like its subject matter, the poem's language is remarkably accessible to the Hebrew reader of its (or almost any) day. It draws richly on both biblical and liturgical turns of phrase, placing it in the context of those writings most familiar to its intended readers. Azikri's goal, from a literary as well as a religious point of view, is one of exquisite simplicity—a goal precisely in line with the religious life he describes in his *Sefer Ḥaredim*.

The Symbol-Maker

The essential creative effort of the Kabbalists was, as we have indicated, devoted to promulgation of a new symbolic language. The Kabbalists thoroughly gleaned the earlier sources of Judaism, especially the Bible and the legendary portions of Talmud and Midrash, gathering together fragments of symbolic speech about matters divine and fashioning them into a coherent and systematic whole. Also interesting to them as a source of symbols, however, was their observance of everyday life. The *realia* of their times were joined together with biblical phrases and Talmudic legends, creating a symbolic edifice of tremendous power.

Our attempt here is to look in the laboratory, as it were, of the symbol-maker at work. The passage we choose is from the *Zohar*, and is to be seen as an extended meditation on the flame of a candle. Here we see the author, probably composing the passage by candlelight, looking at the object before him and allowing it to be transformed in his symbolic imagination. Rabbi Simeon, the speaker in this passage, is Rabbi Simeon ben Yohai, the chief speaker and alleged author of the *Zohar*. In fact he probably represents Rabbi Moses De Leon, the thirteenth-century Spanish Kabbalist who actually wrote the work but who saw himself as standing in special relationship with the soul of Rabbi Simeon.

> Rabbi Simeon began by citing two verses of Scripture: "The Lord your God is a consuming fire" (Deut. 4:24) and "You who cleave to the Lord your God are all alive today" (Deut. 4:4). This matter [how one can cleave to fire and live] has been discussed among the companions. Come and see: "the Lord your God is a consuming fire"; among the companions it is said that there is a fire that consumes fire. It consumes and destroys it, for one fire is stronger than the other. This has been established.
>
> But come and see. He who wants to understand the mystery of the holy union should look at the flame as it rises from a coal or a lighted candle. No flame can rise unless it is attached to some coarse matter. Come and see. There are two lights in the rising flame: one is a shining white light, the other is either black or blue. The white light is higher,

rising straight upward; beneath it, forming its seat, is the blue or black light. The white light hovers over it, and they are joined together as one. The black or blue light serves as the other's throne of glory. This is the mystery of the blue [thread in the fringed garment].

The blue-black flame is joined to that thing beneath it, binding it together with the white light. Sometimes the blue or black light turns red, but the white light above it never changes; it is forever white. The lower light does change: sometimes blue, sometimes black, sometimes red. It holds fast to both ends, to the white light above and to the burning substance beneath, ever consuming what comes its way. Whatever is joined to it is destroyed and devoured, for its path is one of destruction.

All annihilation and all death depend on this, as it devours all that is placed beneath it. The white light above, however, neither consumes nor destroys, nor does it change its light. For this reason Moses said "the Lord *your* God is a consuming fire"—indeed consuming, devouring all that comes its way. But he said "your God" rather than "our God," because Moses himself was in that white light above, the one that does not destroy.

Come and see: the blue flame could not be aroused to burn, to join itself to the white light, without Israel, those who cleave to it from below. Even though the way of that blue-black light is to destroy everything beneath it, Israel cleave to it and live. Therefore "you who cleave to the Lord your God are all alive today." Again, "your" God, and not "our" God; this is the blue-black light that devours all. But you cleave to it and yet you continue to live, you are "all alive today."

Above the white light is yet another light, an invisible light that surrounds it. There is sublime mystery here, and you will find it all in the rising flame. . . .

The mysterious aura of the passage is typical of the *Zohar,* a work of poetic imagination that should be read more as evocative verse than as discursive prose. The author has here taken a simple object, the burning candle, and has transformed it into a symbol of the divine universe and of the mystery of Israel's survival. There is an unspoken but strong association with the biblical tale of the burning bush, read by the much earlier rabbis as a symbol of Israel's survival amid the fires of destruction.

Here the Kabbalist speaks of three rungs of divinity as he perceives them in the burning candle. The highest rung, the God beyond all knowing, is represented by the glow that surrounds the top of the candle, the diffusion of light that cannot be seen. This is the most hidden and sublime mystery, that toward which the straight white flame is ever reaching, the Nothingness with which it seeks to unite. That white flame represents the world of the *sefirot,* the combined symbol-clusters that together constitute the personhood of God. Here they are focused together as a single flame, rising in collective purity toward that which is beyond.

The lower flame, out of which the white flame rises, is the *shekhinah,* the last of the ten *sefirot* and the symbolic presence of God in the lower world. She (the *shekhinah* symbols are mostly female) is at once black, for she has no light of her own, blue, for she is the holy color of sea and sky, and red, as judgment-fire is kindled through her and she stands as a judging, even punishing, monarch. The devouring and destroying female side of divinity is most surprising in the context of Judaism, though one who has studied the religions of India will surely find this side familiar.

It is through the *shekhinah,* God's manifest presence, that Israel is bound to him. Only Moses, the one with whom God spoke "face to face," has risen above this level, and is attached directly to the white light above. The miracle of Israel's existence, here in a striking reinterpretation of the burning bush image, is that they relate to this element in God that in all other cases would destroy and consume—yet they go on living. It is the consuming and passionate fire of God, rather than the destructive forces of earthly woes, that Israel survives. "Even though the Lord is a consuming fire," says Moses to Israel, "you who cleave to it remain alive this day."

The Holy Man

The figures of the *zaddiq* and the *hasid* (literally "righteous one" and "pious one") are well known throughout the religious literature of Judaism. Representing a somewhat different ideal than the normative rabbi or sage who stood as legal head of the community, these types embodied a living model of religious personality not wholly dependent on the traditions of learning that dominated the rabbinic role. Sometimes depicted as more extreme figures than the rather sober and responsible sage, *hasidim* could make demands of themselves that not all could follow but that few could fail to admire. *Hasid* and *zaddiq* fired the folk imagination of Jewry for many centuries. The Talmudic belief that no fewer than thirty-six (the figure is related to old astral speculations) righteous persons lived in each generation, and for their sake the world was sustained, was the basis of many a folktale in the medieval and later periods. Sometimes the figures claimed as members of these elect circles were anonymous holy men, no more than fleeting shadows in the sources of popular history. In other periods we have well-known historic personages, such as Judah the Hasid in medieval Germany or Isaac Luria in later Safed, serving as the bearers of this supranormative pietistic ideal.

It was only in Eastern European Hasidism, however, that the figure of the *zaddiq* became institutionalized. This Hasidism was a movement of popular piety that depended wholly upon the network of relationships between masters and disciples. It formed a world in which the presumed power to know men's souls and to intercede in their prayers was passed on by secret transmission from father to son or from teacher to leading disciple, a world in which the ordinary Jew participated chiefly by basking in his master's radiance. This charismatic revivalism, as it may be called, had both strengths and weaknesses; the spiritual and moral character of the climate created varied greatly with the quality of the person in whose hands leadership was so fully entrusted. The fact that Hasidism was, in its early days, a movement of great creativity and religious profundity stemmed almost wholly from the quality of those rabbis and preachers who were its first bearers.

Noteworthy amid this early group is the name of Rabbi Nahman of Bratslav (1772–1810), the great-grandson of the Ba'al Shem Tov and founder of the small but highly devoted sect of Bratslav Hasidim. A depressive person by nature, Nahman taught that true rejoicing in God, the goal of all religious life, could come only at the end of the most severe struggle. This message, combined with the unswerving loyalty he demanded of his disciples, meant that he was to lead but a small community of elite followers, unlike most of his contemporaries. Nahman was, however, blessed with unusual powers of expression, and many ideas recorded only clumsily in other Hasidic writings are presented with special grace and form in the Bratslav sources. The following are two passages from Nahman's collected teaching on the *ẓaddiq* and his disciples.

Know that there is a field, and in that field grow the most beautiful trees and grasses. The great beauty and grandeur of this field cannot be described; happy is the eye that has seen it.

These trees and grasses are holy souls that are growing there. And there are also a certain number of naked souls which wander about outside the field, waiting and longing for redemption, so that they can return to their place. Sometimes even a great soul, upon whom other souls depend, wanders outside the field and has great difficulty in returning. All of them are longing for the master of the field, who can concern himself with their redemption. Some souls require someone's death in order that they be redeemed, while others can be helped by acts of worship.

And he who wants to gird his loins, to enter the field as its master, has to be a very strong, brave, and wise man; a very great *ẓaddiq*. One has to be a person of the highest type in order to do this; sometimes the task can only be completed by one's own death. Even this [offering of one's life] requires a very great person; there are some great ones whose deaths would not even be sufficient. Only the very greatest of men could possibly accomplish the task within his own lifetime. How much suffering and hardship pass over him! But through his own greatness he transcends it all, tending to the field and its needs. When

he does succeed in bringing those souls in from the outside, it is good
to pray, for then prayer too is in its proper place.

This master of the field takes care of all the trees, watering them
and seeing that they grow, and doing whatever else needs to be done in
that field. He also must keep the trees far enough apart from one
another so that one does not crowd the other out. Sometimes you have
to show great distance to one who has become too close, so that one
does not deny the other. And know that these souls bear fruit when
they do the will of heaven. Then the eyes of the master light up, so that
he can see where he needs to see. This is the meaning of "the field of
seers" (Num. 23:14). But when they do not do the will of heaven, God
forbid, his eyes grow dark, and this is the meaning of "the field of
tears," for it is weeping that ruins one's vision. . . .

The second passage takes the form of a comment on the prophet
Elisha's final request as his master Elijah is about to be taken into the
heavens.

May your spirit be twofold upon me (2 Kings 2:9). . . . Know that it is
possible for a disciple to be greater than his master, even twice as
great. Nevertheless, it all comes about through his master's powers.
This is why Elisha said "your spirit": it was by Elijah's own spirit that
Elisha was given the double measure.

It is taught that the *zaddiq* has two spirits, one above and one
below. Thus Scripture says: "These are the generations of Noah,
Noah . . ." (Gen. 5:9): Noah above and Noah below; he had life above
and below. The life and spirit that remain above are indeed very great.

Disciples and *zaddiq* are of the same root, except that they depend upon him as do the branches upon the trunk. The tree trunk receives its nourishment from the root, and the branches are sustained
through the trunk. There are various qualities to all this: some disciples are like branches, others like leaves, and so forth. . . .

There are various kinds of disciples. But he who is really bound to
the *zaddiq*, as a branch is bound to the tree, will feel all the rises and
falls the *zaddiq* undergoes, even when he is not with the *zaddiq*. It is
proper for a disciple to feel within himself all the fluctuations of the
zaddiq, since he is bound to him as the branch is to the tree. For the
branches feel all the upward and downward motions that take place
within the tree. That is how they come to life and grow in the summer:
the tree draws its sustenance from the root, and, through certain inner
channels, causes the life-force to flow upward from it. In winter, when
the tree's moisture dries up and these channels are narrowed, the
branches also shrink, and shed their leaves. And he [the true disciple]
is bound to the *zaddiq* in this way, feeling all the inner ups and downs
of the *zaddiq*. . . .

It is not difficult to see from these passages why Hasidism was, and in
fact remains, so controversial a movement in the history of Judaism. The

degree of power the *zaddiq* is given over his disciples, particularly the sense that their relationship to the root is only through him, can be frightening to many. Such authority has indeed been misused frequently in the history of religion. On the other hand, these passages also show the tremendous sense of both awe and love with which the role of *zaddiq* is undertaken by one who treats it seriously. He must have no regard for his own life, realizing that he is but a channel through which others are to be sustained. Realizing that even by his death he may not succeed in accomplishing the great restoration of souls that is his dream, he undauntedly remains faithful to his task, as the gardener would not abandon his young plants or, perhaps more appropriately, as a loving father would not leave his children. The warm and affectionate parental metaphor through which Hasidism most often saw God as relating to his beloved children provided the model by which the master could similarly cherish and sustain his disciples.

Using a phrase they had inherited from the *Zohar,* the Hasidic sources describe the *zaddiq* as one who "holds fast to heaven and earth." Never turning aside from the mystic vision of union with the divine presence, the *zaddiq* was simultaneously to open himself to the demands and spiritual needs of ordinary Jews, however small-minded and profane these might seem to him. In joining together these two worlds in his own self, he was to serve as a channel, both for the flow of God's blessings upon his people and for the bringing of Israel's cry before the Throne of Glory. At his best, the *zaddiq* embodied a religious ideal that was heir to both the prophetic and mystical traditions, the religious charismatic made once again, like the prophets of old, a figure who could provide direction and meaning for the lives of those who would open themselves to his vision.

Though our four types do not exhaust the variety of mystical figures to be found within Judaism, they should suffice for the point we are seeking to understand: the range of mystical teachings and writings within a single tradition can be extremely broad, and the simple designation "Jewish mystic" (or Christian or Buddhist mystic) tells us rather little, from the phenomenological point of view, of what the inner life or devotional message of a particular figure may contain. The division of spiritual teachers according to the traditions that nurtured them will of course be helpful in certain ways: naturally the symbols and theological formulas employed by mystics who were taught the sources of classical Judaism will have much in common. But as the history of religions has shown us to look beyond the limits of individual traditions in other areas, so must we be willing to see the wide variety of mystical teachings present in a single tradition as testimony to the human search for a unitive truth that reaches beyond the divisions of our tribal and cultural boundaries.

What is it, then, that an encounter with Judaism may teach us about the mystical endeavor? The first lesson is that of variety itself. We have seen, within the confines of what is after all the smallest of the major human religious communities, and one deeply bound to tradition and Scripture, widely divergent types, each of whom has a distinctive approach to the cultivation of inwardness that characterizes all mystics. We further learn that the language of mysticism does not necessarily have to be unitive; the mystic does not have to proclaim, even at the end of the path, "I am God" or "There is nothing but the One." Such formulations as the latter do occur occasionally in Jewish mystical sources, especially in Hasidism, but even there they are very much the exception.* More generally, mystics learn to express themselves within the established limits of those traditions that have nurtured them. Thus the author of the *Zohar,* for example, would himself have considered it entirely improper to speak of a human being rising to unite with the holy Nothingness; to make such a claim in the first person would have been laughable in his eyes. But as he speaks of the coarse matter of the candle feeding the blue flame, the blue flame nurturing the white, and the white flame reaching beyond into the invisible, we may understand that symbolism has provided him a way of understanding the passage of the corporeal into transcendence, without (even mentally) having to tread on theologically dangerous ground.

In our *Merkavah* passage we see another way in which the mystic's inward transformation may be recounted without so much as touching on the question of divine transcendence. Here the vision is one of David and the House of Israel, bestowed by angels who protect the voyager from harm and sustain him amid his fears. But God himself is never even mentioned! Only the Creator's throne slips into this account; the reader presumes that God is seated upon or is above that throne, but our heavenly voyager is content (this is not true of all *Merkavah* texts) to describe the surrounding glories of the heavenly chamber. When he says "Happy is the eye that has seen it," he still refers to the heavenly choirs and the procession of the kings of Israel, making no claim at having seen the king himself.

Such examples should lead us to speculate on the more general question of how it is that mysticism, taking one form or another, will make its appearance in every one of the world's great religious traditions. Judaism would indeed seem, on the face of things, to be somewhat difficult soil in which to root the mystical plant. The transcendent personhood of God being so firmly established, the distinction between God and the human realm so clear (no demigods, no apotheosis), and the commitment to this-worldly activism so total, Jewish mysticism comes as something of a surprise, most of all to those who have a fixed idea of what Judaism is or should be.

* I have treated the appearance of such formulations in Hasidism in a special essay, appearing in *The Other Side of God,* edited by Peter Berger and published by Anchor Books in 1981.

Two major ways have been offered to account for the universality of mysticism in the world's religions. One is collectivist/historical in approach, the other more individual and psychological. Both surely contain elements of truth, and it is probably false (as the Jungians would remind us) to see them as fully separate explanations. The historical view claims that religion goes through a series of developmental stages, and that these involve an increasing abstraction of the deity and positing of distance between human beings and access to religious experience. In its earliest animistic stages, so the account goes, religion provides man with endless access to divinity, in sacred land, trees, sky, and all the rest. As civilization progresses, the deity becomes accessible only in *certain* rocks or trees, in holy sites, and then only in cult objects or in established shrines. As pagan religion gives way to monotheism, the image of the deity becomes more complex and abstract, until philosophical religion finally declares him faceless, possessed of no attributes, and beyond all description. Such a God, however, is not one that ordinary humans can live with, so a counterforce of resurgent myth, in its later stages taking the form of a mystical mythology, goes on as counterpoint to the process of increasing abstraction. In the writings of Gershom Scholem, who is associated with this historical-dialectical approach to the understanding of mysticism, Kabbalah has been described as an example of such a counterforce, emerging in the centuries following the great triumph of medieval Jewish rationalism.

The parallel to this process in the psychological life of the individual will not be hard to trace for anyone with but a smattering of Freud. The infant, surrounded by warmth and secure affection, grows into an increased sense of isolation and abandonment. In religion he seeks a restoration of that primal harmony from which he feels cut off, and it is particularly the testimony of the mystics, with both their openness to feminine/maternal language and their willingness to speak in abstract "oceanic" terms, that the Freudian in this sense would find interesting.

Another aspect of the psychological dimension of explaining mysticism, as yet in its infancy, has to do with the chemistry of consciousness and the place of chemical reaction within the brain in stimulating states of consciousness that seem beyond the ordinary and call forth esoteric and symbolic uses of language in order to approach their seeming "ineffability." Research into this area has of course been stimulated by the claims (dating back to Aldous Huxley's *Doors of Perception*) that states seemingly very similar to those described by the mystics could be induced by the administration of certain "hallucinogenic" drugs. While this avenue of explanation surely needs further study, one must be especially wary here of the dangers of reductionism. Chemistry of the brain may indeed have to do with altered states of mind, as the testimony of yogic practice would also seem to confirm, but the content of no particular mystical text or experience will ever be accounted for by pharmacological explanation alone. Of course reductionism is a danger when it comes to *any* attempt to explain religious phenomena.

In the course of looking at our examples, we should also have learned something more generally applicable about how to read the literature of mysticism. The Kabbalists provide an extreme example of mystics who hesitate to speak directly of mystical experience. This reticence is not primarily brought about, as some would suppose, by fear of persecution were they to speak more openly. It was considered simply improper, showing poor taste and sinful pride, to offer accounts of one's own experiences. (This of course was not yet true for the *Merkavah* period, when first-person narrative was used, albeit through the cloak of pseudepigrapha.) The reader of such sources necessarily must also become a translator, seeking to cull from exegesis of a biblical tale or from some fine point in the interrelationships between the *sefirot* what it is the mystic is saying about his own inner state. Kabbalistic literature in general should be viewed in large part as a projecting of states of soul and stages of consciousness upon the universe, a description of inner states in terms of "upper" worlds. It is the reader's job cautiously to reverse the mirrors, as it were, so that the description of those numerous worlds above, often seemingly so utterly beyond meaning, will allow him to gain some insight into the mystic's own soul as well.

The best example of this need may be seen in a matter that constantly seems to preoccupy writers in the Kabbalistic tradition: that of *rungs* and *levels*. The assertion that a particular moment in the biblical narrative, or a certain word in the daily liturgy, represents such-and-such a level, rung X in world Y, for example, is the very bread and butter of Kabbalistic commentary. Especially the later Kabbalah, that of both Luria and Cordovero, may be read as a constant mapping, remapping, and refinement of the maps of this upper universe. What is the meaning of all these rungs and levels? Surely some of it seems to be nothing more than the Kabbalistic mind having run away with itself, a casuistry of myth not much different from the *pilpul* of legal dialectics as played out by the latter-day Talmudists. But it also may be seen to depict a true and constant need in the Kabbalist's search, a need for definition and moorings in an otherwise compassless sea of contemplation. Though described in terms of mythical cosmology, the repeated statement of rung after rung allows the Kabbalist to know where he has gotten, and also, an ever-important consideration for the inward traveler, what stages he will have to traverse on the return voyage.

Such an approach to the sources is at times difficult to defend; there is no positive scientific test that allows us to know at what point we have ceased looking into the mystic's soul and have begun projecting our own.

Without taking such a risk, however, it will hardly be worth our while to study the mystics. Indeed an appreciation of their writings requires that we develop the critical postures of both historian and psychologist. But the masters of the Mishnah were right when they said that "the matter of the *Merkavah* is not to be taught even to an individual, unless he is both wise and has some understanding of these matters on his own."

Sources

The originals of the four passages translated are to be found respectively in *Merkavah Shelemah* 3b–4a; Sephardic Prayer Book, compared with MS Adler 74 at the Jewish Theological Seminary; *Zohar* I 50b–51a; *Liqqutey MoHaRaN* 65:1, 66:1. Translations are all original, though that of *Yedid Nefesh* is indebted to the prose version of T. Karmi in the recent *Penguin Book of Hebrew Verse*.

Five

Religious Virtuosi and the Religious Community
The Pietistic Mode in Judaism

Ivan G. Marcus

I

It is usually easier to study the religion of the extraordinary few, the elite, than that of the ordinary many.[1] This is because the sources which have been preserved are generally those about and by literate elites, and scholars for their part have tended until recently to be interested mainly in these texts. Occasionally, data do survive from which we can see how a religious elite coexisted within a larger culture of ordinary people. One example from the history of Christianity is examined in *Montaillou*, a study of a fourteenth-century southern French peasant village populated both by pious Christians and by adherents of the dualist heresy of Catharism.[2] Emmanuel Le Roy Ladurie has studied peasants' testimonies preserved in inquisitorial records, and from these documentary accounts of named individuals he imaginatively reconstructed their entire culture, including significant aspects of their religious lives. Especially revealing is his discovery that Christian piety and elitist heresy were in tension not only among members of the same village or the same family but also within the same individuals' minds and hearts, which constantly vacillated between pious and heretical rites and values. If we had only the learned tracts, we might think of the religious systems of Catharism and orthodox Christianity as being mutually exclusive; the actual social-religious contexts turn out to be much more complex and multivalent than the religious texts.

In the history of Judaism, one approximation of the type of evidence found about Montaillou is the documentary part of the thousands of stored Hebrew and Judeo-Arabic papers known as the Cairo Geniza. The Mediterranean is the focus of these documents in which there are scattered impressions of many Jewish communities, rather than unified accounts of individual ones. Nevertheless, the great scholar of the medieval Mediterranean and of the Geniza, S. D. Goitein, has ventured a preliminary sketch of the Judaism of ordinary people as disclosed by a careful, synoptic reading of these sources.[3]

We have no Geniza for European Judaism, but there is at least one case where we have a significantly large number of sources in which followers of Jewish "piety" and those of a new form of Jewish "pietism," as defined below, coexisted. The Jewish Pietists of medieval Germany (Hebrew: *hasidei ashkenaz*) emerged in the middle of the twelfth century, in the Rhineland towns of Speyer, Worms, and Mainz, and their leaders were members of the Qalonimide family, one of the five founding families of German Jewry.[4] Rabbi Samuel, son of Rabbi Qalonimos, known as "the Pietist, the Holy, and the Prophet" (fl. mid-twelfth century); his son, Rabbi Judah, known as "the Pietist" (d. 1217); and the latter's disciple and relative, Rabbi Eleazar, son of Judah, of Worms (d. ca. 1230) produced a body of writings from which we can reconstruct the dynamic patterns of the first religious revival movement in European Judaism. Moreover, the major source for the movement, Judah the Pietist's *Sefer Hasidim* (The Book of the Pietists),[5] gives us a full picture of the interaction in Judaism of Jewish "piety" and "pietism."

After noting the kind of historical source *Sefer Hasidim* is and presenting working definitions of Jewish "piety" and "pietism," I will briefly sketch the new, shared world view which the three Qalonimides developed as a plan for the individual Pietist's religious salvation and then focus on three aspects of Judah's programmatic social, as well as personal-religious, understanding of pietism. These aspects are his attempt to define pietism as a sectarian fellowship of elitist Jews; the various political strategies which this group tried to adopt towards the non-Pietist Jews in Germany, attitudes I refer to as "the politics of pietism"; and, finally, the ways that Judah advises the Pietists to resolve conflicts which arise from the clash between pietism and the piety of Jews who were not Pietists.

Unlike the records from Montaillou or the Geniza, *Sefer Hasidim* is not a documentary source in the usual sense, and this presents a methodological question to the historian who would use it to write the history of German-Jewish pietism. The texture of the book is typological, not specific: the author talks about "a certain Pietist," not about "Rabbi Simeon, the son of Aaron, the Pietist"; about "the wicked," not about Rabbi Simon's cousin, who was "wicked." In almost two thousand numbered paragraphs, Judah combines biblical comments with illustrations about pietistic life in the form of anonymous moral stories, or *exempla*. As a result, the narrative seems to be about Everyman, not about specific people and places.

And yet, despite the anonymity of the protagonists in *Sefer Hasidim*, the stage on which they play is described realistically and corresponds to the picture of everyday life found in contemporary Hebrew and Latin sources.[6] The book talks about princes and prices, occupations and sexual mores, folklore and family relations, political connections with Christians and criticism of Jewish communal leaders, and a host of other social and economic realities documented elsewhere. For this reason, the book is a credible historical source, and the author's reluctance to name names and describe a specific group of individuals seems to be deliberate. Judah describes Pietists and wicked non-Pietists in generic terms and his style gives the book a timeless, traditional quality. *Sefer Hasidim* reads like classical midrashic literature, with its myriads of anonymous *exempla*, and the resulting effect is to disguise the radically innovative quality of the book's world view and social-religious program.[7]

The primary underlying dynamic in the book is between Jewish piety and pietism, and it is necessary to explain how I am using these terms. By Jewish piety I mean the observance of Judaism in any way whatsoever, from its most casual, "popular" forms, to and including the practices and ideologies of any and all extremist elite groups. Piety describes the full gamut of religious life of Jews who identify with the traditional Jewish community. Pietism, however, is a particular kind of extremist expression of Judaism practiced either by individuals or by organized groups. It is that mode of Judaism which claims to know hidden dimensions of the will of God and seeks to transform the Jewish personality and community in accordance with a "hidden revelation" encoded in Scripture. According to these two definitions, Jews who observe Judaism are "pious," but only those who follow the way of pietism are Pietists (Hebrew: *hasidim*).[8] Thus, all Jewish Pietists are pious Jews, but not all pious Jews are Jewish Pietists.

One context within which to understand the pietistic mode in Judaism is to see it as part of a larger process which can be called "the twelfth-century transformation of Judaism." Originating in different communities, apparently without any connection with one another, four modes of Judaism developed in the twelfth century. They were elitist ideologies in that each stipulated what the Torah demands of the Jew who would serve or understand God completely, beyond the demands of

Jewish law (Hebrew: *halakhah*) which are binding on all Jews. Strictly speaking, one of these systems was not new in the twelfth century: the relious philosophical mode had developed in Muslim cultural spheres centuries before, but in the writings of Maimonides (d. 1204), it reached new heights of systematic development and sophistication. Three other contemporary modes were developed independently of the religious philosophical mode and of each other, and each arose in a Jewish community in Christian Europe. One was the innovative theosophical mysticism of Kabbalah, first worked out in Southern France; another, the scholastic study of the Talmud, developed in the academies of northern France and Germany by the Tosafists or Talmud Glossators; and the third, the case at hand, the pietistic mode of the Jewish Pietists of medieval Germany.

Each of these elite rereadings, or, better, creative misreadings, of earlier sacred texts claimed to be the true interpretation of "the complete Torah," that is, of expanded meanings embedded or encoded in Scripture; each thought of itself as the highest expression of Torah and of the will of God communicated in it; each searched for and "found" a rationale for that way in scriptural proof-texts. Moreover, each of these four modes of Judaism, formulated in the twelfth century, became paradigmatic or shaping forces in later Jewish history. For those Jews who embraced one or more of these meta-legal ideologies,[9] these versions of Judaism's sacred symbols enabled them to see the world differently from other Jews. This "re-vision" of Judaism and the meanings assigned to central concepts such as Torah, *ḥokhmah* (true religious knowledge), and *talmud* (legitimate meanings derived from Scripture) influenced various elitist Jews in their treatment of followers of different modes or those Jews who simply tried to be pious observers of earlier Judaism. The history of how these four reformulations of Judaism interacted with one another and with the demands of ordinary Judaism or Jewish piety has yet to be investigated. It is an important way of conceptualizing the history of Jewish culture and community between late antiquity and the emancipation process in the modern period and has implications well beyond the so-called medieval period for understanding how Jewish culture develops.

The more limited intention here is to focus in some detail on the way the pietistic mode pictured in *Sefer Ḥasidim* interacted with the piety of ordinary Jews in medieval Germany. To appreciate the tensions which Judah's social-religious innovation introduced, we should consider briefly the new pietistic ideal shared by the three Qalonimides which addressed the individual Pietist, not the community of non-Pietists.

The Pietist authors agreed about the core meaning of pietism as a personal eschatology, a plan for the individual's otherworldly salvation. Samuel, Judah, and Eleazar shared a vision that the compound, and only partially revealed, divine will demanded more of the Pietist than the norms of Jewish law did. Based on a concern about the personal account-ability for one's motivation as well as external behavior, their ideal of Judaism considered how eagerly one followed the will of God, on the one hand, or how much illicit pleasure one experienced when sinning, on the other. Ascetic, preoccupied with psychological attitudes and motives, the Pietists thought of this world as a continuous trial which God designed to provide the loyal Pietist with opportunities for otherworldly reward. It is difficult to search for the hidden will of God encoded in Scripture; or to be subjected to the influences of one's psychological tempter, the "evil impulse," and undergo temptations of the body or spirit. But if the Pietist succeeds in resisting these temptations and thereby selflessly fulfills the will of God in all of its complexity, the scales of God's reward will tip in his favor.

The Qalonimides' perception of the ideal religious life as a trial sets off German-Jewish pietism from other Jewish views which conceive of the Pietist as a perfected human being. Rather than being represented as an achieved state of moral excellence, German Hasidism is portrayed as an ongoing process towards the achievement of perfection. Instead of being seen as the destination of a journey, German pietism is thought of as a path filled with trials, roadblocks and detours. For the Qalonimides, the Pietist is not simply one who does no evil; rather, the Pietist is a Pietist only insofar as he obeys God's larger will while simultaneously resisting the divine trials posed by the "evil impulse."

II

In *Sefer Ḥasidim,* Judah the Pietist is concerned with social re-sponsibility as well as with the shared ideal of personal religious salvation, and it is he who is the architect of a fellowship of Pietists who have to de-cide how to treat other Jews. Judah's vehicle for the amelioration of Ger-man Jewry is not only a new prescription for the individual Pietist but also a counterelite led, not by non-Pietist communal authorities, but by charismatic religious figures, the Sages (Hebrew: *ḥakhamim*) who serve the Pietists as surrogate communal and rabbinic leaders. The social world presupposed by *Sefer Ḥasidim* is divided into three parts: Christians, Pietist Jews, and non-Pietist Jews. Jews may be rich or poor, scholarly or ignorant, powerful or common. All of these distinctions pale to in-significance in comparison with the one distinction which cuts across the others: is a Jew a Pietist or a non-Pietist? In short, Judah proposes that the German Pietists be a sect.

The idea that a Jewish sectarian group existed in medieval Germany may seem strange. Historians are familiar with Jewish sectarian com-munities in the Greco-Roman period, such as at Qumran, and with the

Qaraites in Islamic and Byzantine Jewish communities.[10] Although the terms "sect" and "sectarian" are used freely in connection with these groups, little attention has been paid to what these terms mean. In particular, no one has tried to understand "Jewish sectarianism" within the conceptual framework of sectarian theory supplied by the sociology of religion. Without directly dealing with the Jewish cases from late antiquity or with the Qaraites, the present inquiry suggests that sectarian theory is applicable to Judah's expression of German-Jewish pietism and that *Sefer Hasidim* has overtones of being a sectarian code.

A number of sociologists of religion have sought to develop and refine the classical theories of sects which were proposed by Weber and Troeltsch.[11] In particular, Peter Berger, Bryan Wilson, and, most recently, Michael Hill have proposed schematic outlines of sectarian characteristics.[12] In view of the fact that sectarian theory has been grounded in data from the history of Protestant Christianity, there is reason for being skeptical of how readily those theories or concepts might apply to data from the history of Judaism. Nevertheless, if one remains open to the differences of the religious traditions, it is useful to compare the results of sectarian theory with the data of Jewish pietism in *Sefer Hasidim*.

In *The Religious Order*, Michael Hill discusses two contrasting ideal types of subgroups within the history of Christianity: "the religious order" and "the sect." For Hill, many of the characteristics of orders and sects overlap. Those shared features include the following: they are "voluntary organizations," not coercive ones such as prisons, and are freely joined by adults; membership requires proof of special merit or commitment; members set themselves apart from nonmembers by adopting special dress and by insisting on various other degrees of separation; they view themselves, to varying degrees, as an elect, possessing special enlightenment; the primary goal is "personal perfection," regardless of any social goals; there is a tendency to oppose excessive compromises with departures from pristine religious values; the commitment required is total—it excludes conflicting loyalties and dominates every aspect of their lives; there is a greater sense of community feeling (*Gemeinschaft*) than in outside religious associations.[13]

In addition to outlining various features which orders and sects have in common, Hill also stresses that the two can be distinguished from one another in view of two crucial, interrelated differences: "While the sect always draws a distinction between itself and both the rest of Christendom and the rest of humanity, the order distinguishes only the heathen."[14] Second, unlike the sect, the order "exists only as part of a Church and has to be sanctioned by that Church. Thus it is based ultimately on an external source of authority. The sect, on the other hand, contains its own authority."[15]

From Hill's point of view, the Franciscans are an order for two reasons: they think of themselves as Christians as well as Franciscans; their source of authority, the pope, is the same as the ultimate authority of the church of which they are a part. In contrast, the Cathari or a host of other "heretical" dissenters can be thought of as sectarian because they claimed to be the true Christians in contrast to all others; and they claimed to possess a higher source of religious authority, independent of the existing ecclesiastical hierarchy.[16]

Despite the existence of a number of differences between Judaism and Christianity, Hill's analysis is helpful in illuminating the world of *Sefer Ḥasidim*. For if we look at the book in light of the categories and distinctions which Hill has raised, we find there traces of a sect rather than of an order. In particular, the author of *Sefer Ḥasidim* views all Jews in his community as consisting of either Pietists or non-Pietists, and the "we" in *Sefer Ḥasidim* includes only the former. Moreover, the non-Pietist Jews are compared to Christians, at least in some respects. Second, the basis of the authority underlying pietism is not only rabbinic learning and lineage but also an esoteric mode of inspired scriptural exegesis by which God discloses to the Pietists the will of the Creator encoded in Scripture. How Judah defines each of these sectarian features requires elaboration.

Throughout the book, Judah employs a variety of apparently interchangeable terms to refer to a group of Jews who are Pietists and another set of synonymous terms to describe the non-Pietists.[17] If one looks at the way these sets of terms are used, it is apparent that Judah has created a cumbersome but technical vocabulary with which to describe not simply "good Jews" and "bad Jews" but two well-defined subgroups within the Jewish communities of the Rhineland.

Judah calls Pietists *hasidim* (Pietists), *zaddiqim* (Righteous), *hagunim* (Proper), *neqiim* (Clean), *yere'im* (God-fearers), *tovim* (Good); and he calls non-Pietists *resha'im* (Wicked), *ra'im* (Evil), *pesulim* (Unfit), *periẓim* (Violent), etc. These terms are used to describe otherwise anonymously introduced people, or *exempla,* and sometimes several appear in the same paragraph or even the same sentence. Moreover, these terms are used as substantives, not adjectives. And while an expression like *tove ha-'ir* (goodmen of the town) can be equivalent to the Latin *boni viri* and refer to the oligarchy of the local Jewish community,[18] the terms enumerated above do not refer to communal leaders. Rather, they denote members of a pietistic fraternity in distinct contrast to all local nonpietistic Jews. That distinction is sectarian.

The sectarian outlook of *Sefer Ḥasidim* is also reflected in the Pietists' claim to have a source of authority which transcends that of rabbinic Judaism. Judah argues that the authority of a learned scholar is insufficient for the Pietist; one must also be learned in pietism as well as in rabbinic law and lore. The latter, without pietism, is worthless:

> If there are Righteous and Wicked in town and both are learned in Torah, even though the Wicked are intellectually more astute [*yoter ḥarifim*], the Righteous should judge a case, not the Wicked.... And if you should object and say that the Wicked is more erudite [*yoter mefulpal*] and will therefore render the correct judgment by virtue of his acumen, realize that the very opposite is the case. He will pervert [justice] and work hard to distort the truth and mislead the just (SHP, 1375; cf. 1816, 1942).

In the advice to the Pietist to value a Pietist judge more than a rabbinically learned one, more is being advocated than group solidarity. Underlying Judah's recommendation is a theory of Pietist authority, and it is his claim that Pietist scholars have a source of religious authority outside of rabbinic channels that constitutes a second expression of the sectarian outlook of *Sefer Ḥasidim*.

In several contexts, we find evidence that the Pietists claim to possess a special knowledge of God's will because "God reveals His esoteric lore [*sodo*] to His servants the prophets" (Amos 3:7) and He reveals it to those that fear the Lord: "The esoteric lore [*sod*] of the Lord is with them that fear Him" (Ps. 25:14). By viewing themselves, the God-fearers, and their own secret lore as a gloss on these biblical verses, the Pietists associate themselves with the prophets. Bearers of a code with which to unlock the will of the Creator, unknown to non-Pietists however great their intellectual acumen in utilizing rabbinic modes of exegesis, they see themselves as being inspired exegetes who can derive their interpretations of God's hidden will directly from Scripture. In this regard, it is noteworthy that one of Samuel the Pietist's epithets was "the prophet" (*ha-navi*),[19] and there are traces of other individuals identified with the Pietists who had the same cognomen.[20] Although no medieval Jew claimed to speak in the name of the deity by directly invoking the classical prophetic formula, "The Lord says this" (*ko 'amar ha-shem*),[21] there is evidence that varieties of semiprophetic claims persisted beyond the time of "Haggai, Zecharia, and Malachi" into late antiquity[22] and even into the Middle Ages.[23]

The two critical criteria of a sect, a sense of separate group consciousness as being the only true members of the larger community, and a claim to a source of religious authority independent of the sources of authority of the larger community, are both present in *Sefer Ḥasidim* and absent in the many writings of Eleazar of Worms. In *Sefer Ḥasidim,* the Pietists are "the good Jews," the non-Pietists are "wicked." Similarly, Judah claims that it is the Pietists, like the prophets, who have possession of God's *sod,* the secret meanings of his will encoded in Scripture. Both aspects of the Pietist fellowship in *Sefer Ḥasidim* are sectarian.

III

Sefer Ḥasidim describes the different ways that the Pietists tried to deal with the non-Pietist "world," and, in so doing, we see the ways pietism and piety collided. They resorted to three basic strategies.[24] If practicable, they preferred either to dominate the Jewish community and thereby impose the will of the Creator on all Jews; or they sought to withdraw from the wicked and form utopian communities apart from the influence of the ungodly. Failing in these alternatives of ruling the world or separating from it, they realized that they would have to live in it but tried to do so on their own terms by insulating themselves as much as possible from the influence of the non-Pietists. It is these three strategies which are being called here the "politics of pietism."

The three attitudes which the Pietists adopted towards non-Pietists can be described as political action. To the degree that they formed groups of religious devotees, led by Sages, the Pietists engaged in political action in the sense described by Peter Worsley:

> Insofar as the believer acts at all, and not only where he tries de-
> liberately to influence others, he is acting politically, not just reli-
> giously. Insofar as he does deliberately seek to influence others, he
> acts "politically," whether he is propagating his religious beliefs as
> theology or challenging the secular authority of the State. No matter
> how spiritual his goals, he will produce political action simply through
> acting, even if as unintended consequences. Political action is thus an
> immanent dimension or aspect of all social action.[25]

The criteria by which the Pietists decided which of the three postures to adopt towards the world were practical: if likely to succeed, they tried to rule over or withdraw from the rest of the Jewish community. If not, they settled for living in, but not of, the non-Pietist majority. Their flexible, practical orientation is reflected in the interpretation which Judah gave to the religious commandment of chastizing the sinner, understood here as the Pietist's obligation to influence non-Pietists to follow the will of the Creator. If the Pietist has the power to influence the non-Pietist and make him stop sinning, he is obligated to criticize him; if not, he is not so obligated.

The practical attitude Judah takes in *Sefer Ḥasidim* towards applying the commandment to rebuke the sinner is consistent with his generally practical orientation towards a number of other situations as well. In deciding whether or not Pietists should come into contact with non-

Pietists or Christians, the practical outcome is all-important. Thus, Pietists are told that they should debate with non-Pietists about the merits of pietism only if they are likely to win the argument. Similarly, Pietists should avoid contacts with Christians unless from a position of relative strength, such as by being creditors. Of course, the Pietists had to treat Christians properly but, again, it is simply dangerous not to do so. Practical considerations also dictate how the Pietist is to educate his son or how a Sage should administer a penance. The child's curriculum will depend on the child's intellectual ability; he should not be forced to study Talmud, for example, if his ability and interest lie more in studying the Bible. Similarly, when a non-Pietist approaches a Sage to confess his sins and receive a penance, the Sage should give him a penance which he is likely to carry out.

Far from being quietistic in their posture towards exercising political power in the Jewish community,[26] the Pietists in *Sefer Ḥasidim* show a considerable interest in trying to achieve and enjoy that power in order to bring about the will of the Creator, when possible. The book reflects the ups and downs of the Pietists both as self-righteous, sometimes devious rulers (according to non-Pietists) and as powerless victims of those they formerly sought to dominate (the Pietists' own self-image).

There were times when the Righteous were in control of the Jewish community (SHP, 1382). Despite temporary setbacks which they encountered, there were places where "most of the communal leaders were Pietists" (*rov roshe ha-qahal ṭovim*) and, as we would expect, "they wanted to enact the will of the Holy one, blessed be He" (*u-vi-reẓonam le-taqqen reẓon ha-QBH*) (SHP, 1343). Although even when they ruled, a wealthy layman (*parnas*) might try to keep them from doing so, there is no doubt that their intention was to impose their Way on the community which they temporarily controlled (SHP, 1344).

Given the power to do so, the Pietist communal leaders used every opportunity to carry out the will of the Creator. For example, if a person was goaded by his relatives to harm a neighbor, the Pietist rulers insisted that the victim be compensated by the instigator if the guilty relative lacked the means to make payment himself (SHP, 1372; cf. 1770). Then there was the case of a criminal who tried to take advantage of a Pietist because Pietists are not supposed to take any kind of oath. The criminal took the Righteous to court by claiming that the latter owed him money, thereby forcing him to take an exculpatory oath that he did not owe the plaintiff anything. In such a case, the Righteous judge is to determine the degree to which the Righteous defendant was responsible for initiating an association with the criminal and to decide the case accordingly. If innocent of any wrongdoing, the Righteous defendant does not have to swear and thereby violate the will of the Creator (SHP, 1382).

When the Righteous are in control and serve as religious judges or other communal leaders, the measures they impose are simultaneously measures of communal as well as religious discipline. Thus, when two are caught fighting on the Sabbath, the Good, if they are in control, are to impose a fine (or penance) on them for desecrating the Sabbath and then the Good are to settle their dispute (SHP, 1770; cf. 1372).

There were times when a Pietist was also a communal servant and this dual status might result in conflicting obligations between one's duty to the larger community and to pietism. When that problem arose, the Pietist was to consult the Sage. Thus, in a certain town, men were suspected of shirking their responsibility to pay their full share of taxes voluntarily, despite the existence of a ban (herem) which required them to do so. A Pietist was therefore appointed tax assessor, to determine how much each should pay and to collect it for the community. But the Pietist tax collector was concerned that if he should enforce the decree, he might inadvertently require some individual to pay more than he actually should. The Sage advised him that it was better for some people to violate the decree of not giving the correct amount rather than for the Pietist to be responsible for making others give more than they should. The latter would, in effect, be robbery (SHP, 1407).

Pietists understood well that wealth is power, and they tried to influence society by using wealth to accomplish their goals. Unlike members in many of the Christian revivalist movements of the twelfth and thirteenth centuries, which sought to revert to an early Christian ideal of apostolic poverty, the Jewish Pietists of Germany considered wealth not an evil but a potential opportunity to serve God. They espoused a theory of noblesse oblige, according to which they associated wealth and power with each other as means for effecting God's higher will on earth. Like power, which is to be used to check the wicked and bad persons in society, wealth is to be employed to sustain the poor, especially, we shall see, the Righteous poor.

The Pietist should do what he can to see to it that the wealthy Pietist, not the poor one, becomes a communal leader, because the former will be better able to implement the will of the Creator and check the ways of the non-Pietists. Thus, if the community should want to appoint a poor Pietist to be its leader, he should yield to a Good person who is wealthy.

To be sure, the times when the Pietists were able to assume control of local communities in Germany were few and far between. There are only a few references in Sefer Hasidim to such a situation; most of the time it represented an aspiration rather than a reality. A second alternative was also attempted for a brief period of time, perhaps simultaneously, at different places. In addition to dominating the non-Pietists by ruling over them, the Pietists also seem to have tried to separate themselves completely from the non-Pietists to avoid being dominated by them. There are signs in *Sefer Hasidim* that the Pietists tried to create a utopian community which failed.

In the best of all possible worlds, if Pietists could not rule over non-Pietists, they would try to live in their own towns free from non-Pietist influence; marry only within the holy circle of fellow Pietists; and live out their lives in total dedication to searching out and fulfilling the infinitude of religious obligations demanded by the will of the Creator. Given the vulnerability of even large Jewish communities in the Rhineland and the persistent antagonism which the non-Pietists expressed towards fellow Jews, it is not surprising that the Pietists had to compromise almost from the very beginning of their brief experiment of living in splendid isolation. The ideal of creating a separate commune is mentioned in the context of its failure:

> In certain places, Pietists who had Pietist leaders assembled by themselves. One of the elders said: What good is it if we intermarry with non-Pietists and our children end up following non-Pietist ways? Let us enact [a communal decree] that unless a majority of Sages agree that a person is Proper [*hagun*] that no one [of us] marry his daughter to someone from out of town even if he moves here, for he might ruin the rest of us. The same [applies] to a woman from out of town. Only if the Sages say that she is Proper may she settle here. This is the way it was for a while. But soon afterwards, the following generation did not want to follow that enactment. Although the Sages did not want to rescind it, they were pressured [to do so] until they finally agreed. That generation married their children to outsiders who then settled down with them and ruined the town on account of their sins, lying, and non-Pietist ways (SHP, 1301; cf. 1300, 57, 233).

IV

The two ideal political situations of Pietists ruling over non-Pietists or over themselves failed. Instead, the most frequently mentioned case in *Sefer Hasidim* is of non-Pietists ruling the Jewish communities in which Pietists live as members of a sectarian fellowship, under the guidance of the Sages, persisting in their Pietist way but living among non-Pietists. As some scholars have correctly noted, the Pietist is usually described as a victim of ridicule and mockery, if not of outright persecution by fellow Jews. This tension was partly the result of the self-righteous and cocksure attitudes which the Pietists assumed towards non-Pietists, who were frequently perfectly conscientious and punctilious religious Jews. One wonders, however, if another source of the hostility which the Pietists experienced was not the result of the fact that they once enjoyed the power to impose their will on the non-Pietists. When the Pietists were out of power, it was only natural for the non-Pietists to get even, and with a vengeance.

Whatever the complex causes which led up to the situation of this tense coexistence, it is clear that *Sefer Ḥasidim* portrays Jewish society as made up of circles of Pietists who are living among non-Pietists, even while they try to insulate themselves from the influence of the Wicked. The Pietists made a virtue out of necessity. For by finding that they could not rule over or withdraw from the non-Pietists, they rationalized their subjection as a trial which God designed in order for them to earn merit in the next world.

The alternative to domination or withdrawal was avoidance of unnecessary contact with the wicked. *Sefer Ḥasidim* offers advice to the Pietist about how he should conduct his life while living in, but not as a part of, the non-Pietist Jewish community. Choices had to be made throughout the Pietist's life in answer to the question: How can I insulate myself and fellow Pietists from the influence of the Wicked? We will look at how these conflicts were supposed to be resolved in the areas of child-rearing, marriage, and burial, and then explore in more detail the interactions anticipated during times of public worship and in connection with philanthropy. In all of these areas, as well as in many others, Judaism imposes on all Jews an elaborate set of norms and religious obligations. The Pietists superimposed upon the requirements of Jewish *piety* an additional set of demands which they understood to be derived from the larger Will of the Creator, that is, from *pietism*. But by expanding and transforming piety into pietism, Judah the Pietist stimulated religious and social tensions between Pietists and non-Pietist Jews who continued to follow Judaism as they knew it.

The tension between piety and pietism arises when a potential or real conflict develops between the Pietists' obligations *qua Ḥasid* and the demands of piety of the larger religious community. From the clashing perspectives held by the Pietists and non-Pietists flow a series of questions as to priorities. How must the Pietist treat non-Pietists, including members of his own family, when he regards all non-Pietists as the Wicked, who are to be equated with Gentiles? Does a Pietist Jew have the obligation to honor his father and mother even if they are non-Pietists or if they want him to marry a non-Pietist? Does the Pietist insist on proper, that is, pietistic rituals in the synagogue and even risk wars of words or does he draw back from the brink of social conflict and find other ways of serving the complete will of God as he understands it? Does the Pietist have to give charity to his needy family first, if they are non-Pietists, or pass them over in favor of needy Pietists who are not related to him? In short, when pietism and piety clash, what is the Pietist to do?

The tension was an unexpected but real outcome of the "politics of pietism," and this disruptive force probably was responsible for the disappearance of the Pietist fellowship within not much more than Judah's own generation and its neutralization into Eleazar's personalist, nonsocial mode.

Separation: In, But Not Of

Rabbinic Judaism records a teaching ascribed to the first-century Sage, Hillel, that a Jew should not separate himself from the community,[27] but Pietists held to different considerations. In view of the strength which the Wicked commanded, it was necessary to build strong social safeguards or risk being influenced by the ungodly. In general, Pietists were taught not to live near non-Pietists, nor to celebrate religious meals together. Social contact was dangerous and to be avoided, and Pietists were to try to convince non-Pietists not to settle in town. Even to take in a non-Pietist lodger was to be avoided (SHP, 116, 305, 229, 60, 1504, 1880, 181, 1899, etc.).

Childhood, marriage, and death were times for special concern about keeping the proper company, and "proper" meant with Pietists. When the time came for a son to go away to school, it was better for him to remain among Pietists in a small village than to risk being influenced by non-Pietists in the larger town: "For it is difficult for someone who wants to be a Pietist to see someone his own age in town pursuing a different way of life. If he does not also follow, he will be embarrassed, and he would be better off living in a different town" (SHP, 1484 [end]). As careful as Pietists were to insulate their young children from non-Pietist teachers and companions, they were even more persistent in trying to find Pietist marriage partners for their daughters and sons. Although the experiment of living in Pietist communes that practiced endogamy failed, efforts were made to avoid "intermarriage" between Pietist and non-Pietist when both groups lived together. The values of the Pietist way of life are reflected in the priorities they assigned to finding an appropriate marriage partner. According to Sefer Ḥasidim, it is preferable to marry a convert to Judaism who is a Pietist rather than a native Jew who is not (SHP, 1097). One should not marry a woman from a non-Pietist family because of her money or beauty (SHP, 1094, 1100, 1132, 1826, 1900, 1901), and daughters of Pietists should not marry non-Pietists (SHP, 1879). Only if one is choosing between two Pietist women may one marry the one whose pietism is inferior but who is wealthier. This is advised in order for the Pietist to avoid destitution and the temptation to sin (SHP, 1126). But if no moderately Pietist woman of means is at hand, a Pietist should take public charity rather than marry the daughter of a non-Pietist (SHP, 891, 1879–

1881, 1883). In extreme cases, when there are no suitable women, one is to leave town rather than marry into a non-Pietist family at home (SHP, 1880).

The issue of whom to marry created tensions between parents and children, and *Sefer Ḥasidim* indicates that the Pietist's obligation to marry only another Pietist takes precedence over the commandment to honor one's father and mother.

> There are local women who are Good and their brothers are Good and there also are Bad women whose brothers are Bad. The latter want to pay a boy's parents to arrange for their son to marry one of their daughters, but the Good do not intend to pay the boy's parents anything. If the parents order their [Good] son to marry the daughter of the [Bad] people who are paying them, but the son only wants to marry one of the Good, he should not obey them, even if his parents get aggravated over his refusal. [He should do so] because they treat him improperly [*lo ke-hogen,* i.e., contrary to pietism] (SHP, 953; cf. 1902).

The author argues further against such marriages by adding a warning: marrying the daughter of wealthy non-Pietists because of their money, instead of a Pietist's daughter, will not be beneficial. Not only will the couple's children turn out as badly as the wife's brothers, but even their wealth will not last. When such a Pietist's own sons reach marrying age, he will not be able to marry them to members of his own family who are Pietists [*le-hithaten be-ṭovim*] (SHP, 1900, 1901, 1903, 1880–3).

Marriage should revolve around the fellowship needs of the Pietists, and the Sage plays an important role in counseling Pietists about how to marry when choices must be made from among the godly. The initiative of finding a marriage partner can come from the woman as well as the man and either can approach the Sage for advice. Suppose a young woman tells the Sage that she wants to marry a handsome young widower who has no children, is from a Pietist family, and is himself a scholar and a Pietist. But the Sage, here as a matchmaker, also knows of another widower who is not so handsome but who has children. If the woman's father wants to marry his daughter to the second widower, the Sage is to ignore the father's desire so as not to violate the verses: "you shall not place a stumbling block before the blind"; "Do not degrade your daughter, making her a harlot" (Lev. 19: 14, 29) (SHP, 1112). Given the fact that the daughter's choice is for a Pietist, her wishes should be honored. Otherwise, the woman will not honor the marriage and the Sage will be contributing to the woman's downfall.

The matter is much simpler for the Sage if one woman asks the Sage to arrange a marriage with a young man who is handsome but not a Pietist, and a second woman wants a man who is a Pietist. If there are two young men, one of whom is handsome and a Pietist and the other a Pietist but not handsome, the Sage should give the handsome Pietist to the woman who asked only for the Pietist: "give her better than she herself requested" (SHP, 1113).

As with childhood and marriage, so with death and burial—the Pietists were to avoid contamination by non-Pietists. Thus, *Sefer Hasidim* makes it clear that a Pietist is not to be buried next to non-Pietists:

> It once happened that a Pietist scholar [*talmid hakham zaddiq*] was buried next to a non-Pietist [*mi she-'eno hagun*]. The Pietist [*ha-zaddiq*] appeared in a dream to the townspeople saying: You have caused me harm because you buried me next to an outhouse. The stench is foul and the smoke bothers me. They placed stone partitions between the grave of the Pietist [*ha-zaddiq*] and the non-Pietist [*ha-rasha*ʿ] and he no longer appeared to them in a dream (SHP, 266; cf. 265, 267).

In addition to devising specific ways of insulating themselves as much as possible from non-Pietists, the Pietists persisted in applying their programmatic interpretations of Judaism in sectarian ways. They restricted a number of religious obligations to apply only to fellow Pietists, instead of to all fellow Jews, and this sectarian focus resulted in social tensions with neighbors and even with family. In particular, they demanded that Pietists pray and give charity in such a way that only Pietists and pietism define the applicability of these obligations. Only Pietists' prayers could reach God. Hence, ever practical, the Pietists reasoned that they alone should serve as cantors. True to their principles that pietism is Judaism, they held that only needy Pietists should be supported by the commandment to give charity. Their stipulations about how Pietist Judaism should be lived led to hostility from other Jews who were offended by the Pietists' exclusiveness.

The clash between the values of pietism and non-Pietist Judaism led to other kinds of conflict as well. For in trying to follow the will of the Creator while living among non-Pietists, the Pietist always faced choices between values of their fellow Pietists and those Jews whom they regarded, in some respects, as no better than Christians. Symbolic of their sectarian zeal is the following indication of their priorities: "It is preferable to provide essential clothing for the wife of a Fellow [*haver*] than to save the life of a non-Pietist. This holds so long as the wife is as pious as the husband, acts piously towards God, her husband, and other Pietists" (SHP, 1676).

Public Worship

One area which led to a great number of tense confrontations between Pietists and non-Pietists was that of prayer and other rituals associated with public worship. Whenever possible, Judah required that Pietists be in charge of religious services and other rituals because non-Pietists would not be effective petitioners for the community. Always practical in their thinking, they argued that it would be of no purpose to pray to God if God was not listening.

But one knew a Pietist by his appearance even before he entered the synagogue. The Pietists apparently attached ritual fringes (ẓiẓit) to the four corners of an outer garment, thereby making it into a four-cornered prayer shawl (talit) which they wore, not only during the morning prayers, but "all day" (SHP, 1036, 1666, 1584; cf. 976 [?], 439, 1589). In a responsa collection of Rabbi Meir of Rothenburg (d. 1298), we find the following in the name of R. Samson b.R. Abraham:

> And I have heard that talitot made like c[h]aperons are like the talitot of Ḥaside Ashkenaz. It has four corners and when it is removed one folds it and then wraps oneself in it. There are those who say, however, that a garment is not a [proper] talit unless it is like ours, that is, made [not to wear] but [solely] to be wrapped in and covered with.[23]

From this indirect evidence, the Pietists of Germany may have appeared to wear prayer shawls all day because they made a cape or poncho into a shawl by tying ritual fringes on each of its four corners. But since the prayer shawl worn in the synagogue requires that one recite the blessing "Who commanded us to *wrap ourselves* in fringes," they removed the cape, folded it, and wrapped themselves in it when about to pray in the synagogue in the morning.

More reliable is the following report taken from Judah the Pietist's Commentary to the Pentateuch: "Rabbi J[udah] the Pietist rendered the following decision [pesaq] to those people who wear a talit all day: When entering the synagogue, they should put on an additional talit which they should wrap around themselves and then recite the blessing a second time [over that talit]."[29] Whether or not the cape was removed and temporarily made into a conventional prayer shawl or a second one was worn on top of the fringed cape, the sources agree that some German-Jewish Pietists did wear ritual fringes on an outer garment. This practice evidently accounts for references in *Sefer Ḥasidim* that the Pietists wore a prayer shawl all day, and it was this peculiar type which did not go unnoticed by non-Pietists.

Such display could easily rub outsiders the wrong way, and not surprisingly this practice attracted the hostility of non-Pietists from time to time. For example, there was the non-Pietist who was politically well-connected, religiously observant, and "ethical," but who terrorized Pietists by taking a Pietist's prayer shawl and giving it to a "fool" to wear in order to embarrass the Pietist publicly (SHP, 1344).

But the area in synagogue life which drove non-Pietists to distraction was the Pietists' peculiar way of reciting the prayers. *Ḥaside Ashkenaz* were known for their penchant of counting the letters of the prayers in order to ruminate on esoteric meanings associated with the number of letters and the numerical equivalents of the Hebrew letters. To be able to do this, they insisted that the prayers should be recited *be-meshekh,* in a drawn out or deliberate style (SHP, 479, 839), and this practice was not conducive to speedy non-Pietist worship. Given their own needs, it would have been helpful if they had prayed in their own synagogues, and they recommended this whenever possible: "If there are two synagogues in town, one of which is closer than the other and the Pietist synagogue is farther away, it is better to go to the one farther away where they pray correctly" (SHP, 481).

Not to pray "correctly" meant to risk participating in prayer with the Wicked, whom God would not hear; not to pray "correctly" meant rushing through the prayers without the time to pray *be-meshekh.* And yet, in the small Jewish communities of the Rhineland, there would probably be only one place for conducting public worship. Of necessity, Pietists would have to pray with non-Pietists and somehow coexist:

> If there is only one synagogue in town and it is known that the Jews there are not [Pietists; lit., stand to pray in a boorish manner], and that it is impossible to pray [there] with concentration [*be-khavanah*], he should first pray at home with concentration and then go to the synagogue for the Sanctification prayer [*qedushah*] [which requires a *minyan*] (SHP, 481).[30]

Sefer Ḥasidim provides the Pietist with various techniques for praying with "deliberate concentration," even when sitting next to an unsympathetic non-Pietist worshiper. For example, the Pietist should close his eyes at various prescribed times, such as before each time a section of the Torah is read publicly, during the daily penitential prayers (*taḥanun*), and when reciting the prayers which mention the morning or evening. Immediately afterwards, one should open one's eyes and look up towards Heaven (SHP, 1597, 1575, 1582, 455, 1586)[31] despite the talmudic dictum that one's eyes should look down and one's heart should be directed up.[32]

Such practices appeared excessive to a non-Pietist and earned the Pietist more than a little contempt and ridicule. Advice is also given for the Pietist to develop ways of achieving concentration while minimizing opportunities for others to ridicule him. Ribbing was not all a Pietist might get for his efforts to concentrate during prayer. That same well-connected non-Pietist who terrorized Pietists would also hurry the recitation of the service, thereby preventing the Pietists (*ha-ẓaddiqim*) from observing the commandments, and he would chase out of the synagogue anyone he pleased, thus aiding "sinners" and insulting Pietists (*yir'e ha-shem*) (SHP, 1344).

Nor were the Pietists' preferences for exclusive control in conducting the service likely to win them any friends from non-Pietist Jews. One can imagine the lack of sympathy of those otherwise religious, but not-Pietist, Jews towards the Pietists, who believed that they, and they alone, merited serving as cantors to conduct the public worship; sounding the ram's horn on Rosh Hashanah or Yom Kippur; rolling up the Torah scroll before returning it to the Ark (SHP, 1591, 1590, 972 [239, lines 9 ff.]). Again, the reason offered is practical: "when Pietists [*zaddiqim*] pray, prayer is heard" (SHP, 1628).

For the same reason, the Pietists did not want to count non-Pietists in the *minyan* (SHP, 1573) and proscribed sitting next to one or even in a non-Pietist's empty seat because non-Pietists drive away the Divine Presence (*shekhinah*) on account of their improper thoughts (SHP, 403). Pietists also should avoid anything which a non-Pietist has made. Thus, they may not pray from a prayer book copied by a non-Pietist scribe, and Pietists cannot use it even as recycled scrap paper but must burn it (SHP, 405; cf. 1621). Liturgical poems which non-Pietists composed, we recall, are not to be recited even if they are superior to poems written by Pietists (SHP, 470, 1619–21).

Yet, there were limits. For when Pietists confronted other Jews with such behavior in the same small synagogues, there was bound to be an explosion. For the sake of community harmony, Judah drew back from the full implications of his position when Pietist exclusiveness was likely to result in open dissension (*mahloqet*). Thus, if non-Pietists did serve as a cantor or sound the ram's horn or read the Book of Esther on Purim, the Pietist is told to repeat these rituals after the non-Pietists leave the synagogue or at least recite the words of the prayer in private if doing them again in public will result in dissension (SHP, 444; cf. 502). Similar restraint is reflected in the advice that a Pietist who wants to be seated in the synagogue near the Ark, a place of honor, should not argue about the seat if it is already occupied but should take a different seat (SHP, 407; cf. 495). The reason is practical: "For since the Bad [*ha-raʿim*] outnumber the Pietists [*ha-hasidim*]" (SHP, 1085; cf. 1591, 1599), they should let others do these things. Avoiding dissension takes precedence over pietism. The motivation of working to save the community would be undermined if the Pietists ended up destroying it.

Philanthropy

Giving charity (*zedaqqah*) is still another religious obligation which Judah interpreted and applied in a sectarian fashion despite the risk of creating tensions with non-Pietist acquaintances and even family. By indicating how a Pietist should give, *Sefer Hasidim* reveals the author's exclusivistic scale of values.

When it comes to deciding which individuals should receive charity, the Pietist must try to give to other Pietists while at the same time balancing his religious obligation to his family. The ideal recipient in *Sefer Ḥasidim* is not one's family but a needy Pietist (*ẓaddiq ve-ẓarikh*) (SHP, 857, 917). If one's relatives are Pietists and in need, there is no conflict between giving to one's relatives and to fellow Pietists: Pietist relatives have priority over Pietists who are not related to the donor (SHP, 888, 918).

But when one must choose between poor relatives who are non-Pietists and those who study Torah for pietistic reasons, the Pietist is to ignore the relative. Even if they say that they will study properly in the future, they are not to be considered, because their motives for saying so are suspect: perhaps they are making the pledge to study in order to get the charity (SHP, 919). Similarly, a father cannot favor one of several children in his will just because he loved that child more than the others but only if that child was more pious (SHP, 1703; cf. 893).

On the other hand, one is obligated to support one's own Pietist relatives even if funds from other sources become available:

A Sage was told: So-and-so died and told me to dispense so much money to poor Pietists [*le-ʿaniyyim ṭovim*] according to your advice. To whom should I allocate it? Do you think that I can give it [to my relatives] . . . who are Pietists [*ṭovim*]? The Sage answered: If you are used to giving your money to your relatives anyway, and you now want to ease your own burden by using some of the money which he gave you to dispense for charitable purposes and you are wealthy [enough to help your family with your own money], realize that [using that money for your relatives] would be sin because you would be robbing the poor. But if you do not reduce the usual amount of your gift to your own relatives, we can allocate [to your relatives the money your friend entrusted to you]; [if you do reduce your own family contribution], we cannot allocate it [for them] (SHP, 1683).

When relatives are not involved, one is to give charity to Pietists in need (SHP, 1680, 1689). One recipient may give a contribution to someone else, but only to another Pietist in need; money can be given to a needy Pietist either directly or indirectly but only by means of another Pietist or a Sage (SHP, 1700, 1679, 1683, 1684). Moreover, giving money to a non-Pietist is a sin; not giving charity to a non-Pietist is itself an act of Pietism (SHP, 840; 917, 1705). One should go to great lengths, even leaving town, to avoid supporting non-Pietists, including one's own father (SHP, 1679, 1705). Unless a non-Pietist threatened to murder someone if a Pietist does not give him charity, a Pietist must not yield to threats to commit a sin. Even if the non-Pietist should threaten to apostatize, the

Pietist is to resist helping him: "Let the non-Pietist go to Hell" (SHP, 857).

Conclusion

The tension between piety and pietism underlies Judah's *Sefer Hasidim* and resulted from his attempt to create a new socioreligious expression of Jewish spirituality. In so doing, he not only provoked those Jews who were pious but not Pietists, he also made it increasingly more difficult for Pietists to resist the social pressures from non-Pietist Jews. The unstable social situation produced by Judah's effort to establish pietism as a religious fellowship could not last, and the tension was resolved in two ways. On the one hand, Jews in Germany simply did not follow a regimen which required a sharp break with much of Jewish piety; on the other hand, Eleazar of Worms salvaged the Qalonimides' shared plan for personal salvation by ignoring the socioreligious categories which Judah had emphasized.

By focusing in his writings exclusively on pietism as a personalist eschatology for the individual, Eleazar broke down the social distinction between Pietist and Jew. In marked contrast to the sectarian orientation of *Sefer Hasidim*, Eleazar's writings do not refer to Sages or to groups of Pietists. His audience is the individual Pietist or Jew—the distinction is no longer clear—and his expression of pietism is personal, not social, sectarian, or political. Moreover, the process by which Eleazar transformed pietism into piety is important. By putting his summaries of pietism and ascetic atonement into a book of Jewish law, the central expression of Jewish piety, Eleazar "normalized" the shared personalist formulation of German-Jewish pietism. Instead of being included in a book like *Sefer Hasidim*, which Judah wrote for the benefit of the extraordinary few, Eleazar's law code, *Sefer ha-Roqeah* (The Book of the Perfumer) put the shared, nonsocial pietistic vision into the hands and hearts of the ordinary many. In so doing, Eleazar made it possible for any Jew to be a Pietist simply by being a pious Jew.

Judah the Pietist and Eleazar of Worms represent two stages in the history of one case of Jewish pietism. Judah was a socioreligious innovator and, as such, represents an effort to challenge the existing communal and rabbinic order of the medieval Jewish community. Eleazar, in contrast, provides a mechanism of adaptation by which religious symbols are introduced into the religious life of the community when the social challenge to it is eliminated. This dynamic pattern of radical socioreligious revival, modulated by a conservative, personalist-legal adjustment, has implications for the study of other cases of Jewish pietism, such as later Hasidism in its various permutations. Our single case study of the interaction between pietism and piety in Judaism suggests how the study of elite forms of Judaism and the Judaism of ordinary people can illuminate the mutual relationships between these two expressions of religious life. Pietism and piety are not the same thing in Judaism, and this distinction will, one hopes, stimulate further thinking into the dynamics of socioreligious contexts and religious texts.

Notes

1. A different version of this paper appeared with complete annotation as "The Politics and Ethics of Pietism in Judaism: The *Ḥasidim* of Medieval Germany," *Journal of Religious Ethics* 8 (1980): 227–58, and is part of my larger study, *Piety and Society: The Jewish Pietists of Medieval Germany* (Leiden: E. J. Brill, 1981).

2. Emmanuel Le Roy Ladurie, *Montaillou: The Promised Land of Error* (New York: Vintage Books, 1979).

3. S. D. Goitein, "Religion in Everyday Life as Reflected in the Documents of the Cairo Geniza," in *Religion in a Religious Age,* ed. S. D. Goitein (Cambridge, Mass.: Association for Jewish Studies, 1974), pp. 3–17.

4. On the founding families of early German Jewry (Hebrew: *ashkenaz*), see Avraham Grossman, *Ḥakhmei Ashkenaz ha-Rishonim* (Jerusalem: Magnes Press, 1981), esp. chap. 10.

5. Citations are by paragraph number from the Parma manuscript recension of Jehuda Wistinetzki, edited with an introduction by Jacob Freimann, *Sefer Ḥasidim* (Frankfurt am Main: Wahrmann, 1924). Quotations from and references to this recension will be cited in the body of the chapter as SHP (*Sefer Ḥasidim,* Parma), followed by the paragraph number.

6. Cf. Caesarius of Heisterbach, *Dialogus miraculorum,* ed. Joseph Strange, 2 vols. (1851; reprinted, Ridgewood, N.J.: Gregg, 1966).

7. See Tamar Alexander, "Sipporet ve-Hagut be-*Sefer Ḥasidim*" (Ph.D. diss., University of California, Los Angeles, 1977), pp. 10, 26–27.

8. The history of the major developments of Jewish pietism (*hasidut*) has yet to be written. It is not identical, by any means, with either the history of Jewish mysticism (*qabbalah*) or the history of Jewish piety (*musar*). Cf. Gershom Scholem, "Three Types of Jewish Piety," *Eranos Jahrbuch* 38 (1969): 331–48, who makes other distinctions and uses the term "piety" in a different way. The conceptualization of German-Jewish pietism as depending on a new vision of the hidden, secret will of God was first formulated in my "Penitential Theory and Practice among the Pious of Germany: 1150–1250" (Ph.D. diss., Jewish Theological Seminary of America, 1974), pp. 10–12, 98–99, and, especially, 121–31. It was developed further in *Piety and Society* (see above, n. 1) after consideration of Haym Soloveitchik, "Three Themes in the *Sefer Ḥasidim,*" *AJS Review* 1 (1976): 311–57, who stresses the "will of the Creator."

9. Cf. Isadore Twersky, "Religion and Law," in S. D. Goitein, ed., *Religion in a Religious Age,* pp. 69–74.

10. See Geza Vermes, *The Dead Sea Scrolls: Qumran in Perspective* (Cleveland: Collins & World, 1978), and Zvi Ankori, *Karaites in Byzantium* (1959; reprinted, New York: AMS Press, 1968).

11. See H. H. Gerth and C. Wright Mills, eds., *From Max Weber: Essays in Sociology* (New York: Oxford University Press, 1946), chap. 12; cf. Michael Hill, *A Sociology of Religion* (New York: Basic Books, 1973), chaps. 3 and 4; Ernst Troeltsch, *The Social Teaching of the Christian Churches* (London: George Allen and Unwin, 1931), pp. 328–49.

12. Especially suggestive are Peter Berger, "The Sociological Study of Sectarianism,"

Social Research 21 (1954): 478–81; Bryan R. Wilson, *Patterns of Sectarianism* (London: Heinemann, 1967), introduction and chap. 1; Michael Hill, *The Religious Order* (London: Heinemann, 1973), chaps. 1–4.

13. Hill, *Religious Order,* pp. 61–84.

14. Ibid., p. 71.

15. Ibid., p. 70.

16. See Jeffrey Burton Russell, *Dissent and Reform in the Early Middle Ages* (Berkeley: University of California Press, 1965), pp. 8, 75–81, 188–229.

17. Terms such as *zaddiq* (Righteous), *hasid* (Pietist), *tovim* (Good), etc., are used interchangeably in *Sefer Hasidim.* The exception is the special usage of *zaddiq* as one of two righteous people whose existence makes the cosmos exist. See SHP, 1517 and Eleazar of Worms, *Hokhmat ha-Nefesh* (Knowledge of the Soul), (Safed, 1913), pp. 10c–10d.

18. See, for example, SHP, 21, 201, 395, 402, 1300; Yizhaq Baer, "Ha-Megamah ha-Datit-ha-Hevratit shel Sefer Hasidim," *Zion* 35 (1937): 42; Salo Baron, *The Jewish Community,* 3 vols. (Philadelphia: The Jewish Publication Society, 1942), 2:55.

19. See Eleazar of Worms, *Moreh Hatta'im* (Guidebook for Sinners), in *Kol Bo* (Naples, 1490), p. 89a.

20. Gershom Scholem, *Major Trends in Jewish Mysticism* (New York: Schocken, 1941), p. 84.

21. Cf. Ezekiel 22:28.

22. See B. Sanhedrin 11a; Ephraim E. Urbach, "Matai Paseqah ha-Nevu'ah?" *Tarbiz* 17 (1955): 1–11.

23. See A. J. Heschel, "'Al Ruah ha-Qodesh bi-me ha-Benayim," *Alexander Marx Jubilee Volume* (New York: The Jewish Theological Seminary of America, 1950), passim, and Gershom Scholem, *Ursprung und Anfänge der Kabbala* (Berlin: Walter de Gruyter, 1962), pp. 210–11, 218, and the literature cited, especially at p. 211, n. 70.

24. On these three basic ways a sect can interact with the "world," see John Milton Yinger, *Religion, Society and the Individual* (New York, 1957), pp. 144, 146, and Berger, "The Sociological Study," p. 478.

25. Peter Worsley, *The Trumpet Shall Sound* (New York: Schocken, 1968), pp. xxxvi–xxxvii.

26. Cf. Gerson D. Cohen, "Messianic Postures of Ashkenazim and Sephardim," in *Studies of the Leo Baeck Institute,* ed. Max Kreutzberger (New York: F. Ungar, 1967), pp. 143 ff.

27. M. Avot 2:4.

28. R. Meir b. Barukh of Rothenburg, *Responsa* (Prague, 1608), no. 287.

29. Yizhaq Lange, ed., *Perushe ha-Torah le-R. Yehudah he-Hasid* (Jerusalem, 1975), p. 176 *ad* num. 15:36.

30. A *minyan* is a quorum of ten adult males (over age thirteen) required for certain parts of each of the public services.

31. For these features of the Jewish liturgy, see Abraham Millgram, *Jewish Worship* (Philadelphia: The Jewish Publication Society, 1971), pp. 178–86, 461–63, 98–101.

32. B. Yevamot 105b.

Six

Religion and the Religious Intellectuals

The Case of Judaism in Medieval Times

David R. Blumenthal

Introduction

Jacques Le Goff, in his *Les intellectuels au moyen âge* (Editions de Seuil, 1960), maintained that the true intellectual did not appear until the advent of the cities (10, 67) and that he was primarily a professional (p. 16): "L'intellectuel du XIIe siècle est un professionnel, avec ses materiaux, les anciens, avec ses techniques, dont le principale est l'imitation des anciens." Furthermore, the intellectual was molded by the general *mentalité* of the urban worker-producer (68): "Les écoles sont des ateliers d'où s'exportent les idées, comme des marchandises. Sur le chantier urbain, le professeur côtoie dans un même élan producteur, l'artisan et le marchand."

Jean Leclercq, in his *The Love of Learning and the Desire for God* (Fordham University Press, 1961), developed a different model. Pointing to the difference between the schools for clerics (that is, for practicing clergy) and the schools for monks, he reasoned that the two social settings caused two types of theology to evolve (pp. 3–4):

> In general, the monks did not acquire their religious formation in a school, under a scholastic, by means of the *quaestio*, but individually,

* I wish to acknowledge with deep thanks the critical reading of this manuscript by my colleague and friend Will Beardslee.

under the guidance of an abbot, a spiritual father, through the reading
of the Bible and the Fathers, within the liturgical framwork of the monastic life. Hence, there arose a type of Christian culture with marked
characteristics: a disinterested culture which was "contemplative" in
bent. Very different from this are the schools for clerics, situated in
cities, near cathedrals, they are attended by clerics who had already
received a Liberal Arts formation in rural, parochial or monastic
schools and are intended to prepare them for pastoral activity, for
"the active life." It is in these schools for clerics that "scholastic
theology" is born, the theology of the schools, that which is taught in
the schools. . . . Does this imply that the monks have no theology?
They do have one, but it is not scholastic, it is the theology of the
monasteries, "monastic theology." The men of the twelfth century
were clearly aware of this distinction. . . . Let us note carefully that the
monastic and the scholastic milieus are not in constant opposition;
they form a contrast but are also interrelated and they owe much
to each other.

The social situation of intellectuals in Islam was somewhat different.
After the death of Mohammed, there ensued a religious and political
struggle for control of the Islamic movement. The eventual triumph of the
Abbasids led to several crucial decisions that affected the intellectual life
of Islam (and the political and social life, too). First, the new rulers
brought religious authorities from Medina to Baghdad and installed them
as consultants in all matters. Second, the new rulers established schools
for the study of grammar, for the study of Islamic law, and for the translation of the works of Greek civilization. (For this, see L. Gardet and M.-M.
Anawati, *Introduction à la théologie musulmane* [Vrin, 1970], pp. 39–46.)
The effect of these decisions was to create a class of intellectuals who
were working for the state and who were housed in state-supported
schools (the *madrasas*). The Islamic intellectual was then, in large measure, a part of the established orders. (This would be one of the charges
made by Sufis and reformers in subsequent eras.)

The position of the Jewish intellectuals resembled none of these situations. There were, to be sure, some men who were heads of yeshivot
(academies) in communities that could support such institutions. There
were Jewish community functionaries and some were paid. But they were
teachers of children, itinerant preachers, cantors, beadles, ritual
slaughterers, and judges. There were educated laymen, men who continued studying, sometimes achieving certain titles. These were busi-
nessmen and, if they served from time to time as judges, they might be
compensated. They were not, however, necessarily intellectuals. And
there were rabbi-scholars whose function it was to render decisions in
Jewish law (particularly in the laws of marriage and divorce) and to
preach. The local rabbi-scholar was often not paid at all or compensated

only in a minimal way. He too, however, was not necessarily an intellectual. The intellectual, the man who wrote books or essays, was not employed as such. Even the head of a yeshiva was employed to train rabbis, judges, etc., and not just to study or learn. Furthermore, philosophy and theology "seem not to have formed part of the regular syllabus of the establishments for Jewish higher studies" (S. D. Goitein, *A Mediterranean Society* [University of California Press, 1971], 2:210).

Who, then, was the Jewish intellectual and under what conditions did he work? First, the Jewish intellectual was an isolated individual. He was not a professional, supported by the state, the church, or a religious order. He was not, except in the rarest of circumstances (as the head of a well-attended yeshiva), surrounded by students, libraries, and colleagues. On the contrary, the Jewish intellectual worked on his own; his contact with colleagues was through books and letters. This is not surprising when one remembers that there simply were not many Jews in the world in medieval times and, furthermore, they were not concentrated enough to sustain full-blown universities and *madrasas*. Second, the Jewish intellectual was largely an autodidact. He was a rabbi or doctor who continued to read books on logic, science, poetry, law, grammar, theology, or mysticism.

These two facts had important effects on medieval Jewish intellectualism. First, medieval Jewish intellectualism was largely a matter of the exchange of written material. A question would come up in theology, philology, polemics, mysticism, literature, law, or science. Someone would put his thoughts into writing. The writing would be read. New questions would be generated and old ones answered. New thoughts would be written down. And so on. Second, often in the attempt to grapple with these new ideas, someone would create a new literary form in which to communicate and he would write a whole book on the subject. This, in turn, created the possibility and precedent for other such whole books to be written. For instance, systematic theology became a concern in the mind of Saadia Gaon (tenth century, Baghdad). He formulated his thoughts in one book and so created "the book on theology." His book stimulated others. Eventually, a genre of books on theology developed. Similarly, genres of books on philology, polemics, mysticism, literature, law, and science developed. The ideas generated the books which generated other books which, in effect, created whole genres of literature on varied subjects. The particular questions raised and the answers proposed varied in time; but the genres remained. And they remained because books were the medium of discourse for Jewish intellectuals in the Middle Ages. These genres became the marketplace for ideas. They were the sociological reality of medieval Jewish intellectuality. And, interestingly, almost all these works are signed, a procedure not common in late antiquity.

Our first task, therefore, must be to determine what the genres were of medieval Jewish intellectualism. What were the topics that stimulated the creation of books and the exchange of ideas?

Returning to the Christian and Islamic models, we must ask about motivation. Le Goff has set forth the claim that the medieval Christian intellectual ensconced in his university was motivated by *la passion iconoclaste* (p. 42). This set him over against his sponsors and accounts for the slow and often violent struggle of the university against the church and later against the state. It also accounts for the periodic traditionalist revivals and inquisitions. Leclercq has maintained that the medieval Christian intellectual ensconced in his monastery was motivated by his spiritual experience. "The corrective for literature is the experience of God, the devotion to heaven. . . . He [i.e., the cultivated monk] is a scholar, he is versed in letters but he is not merely a man of science nor a man of letters nor an intellectual, he is a spiritual man" (pp. 316–17). In the area of Islam, Franz Rosenthal, in his *Knowledge Triumphant* (E. J. Brill, 1970), has traced meticulously the "charismatic role of knowledge" (p. 243) in all areas of Islamic culture and religion. In that world, it was taught (pp. 297–98):

> The twin fundamental qualities a professor must possess are dignity and piety. He must observe decorum in the way he dresses and the like and, indeed, in everything he does. But he must also be properly modest. Above all, he must always remain willing to learn even from those younger and of a lower status than himself, as confirmed by the fact that "a number of the ancient Muslims used to acquire knowledge they themselves did not have from their students." It is the professor's duty to write and to publish. In his teaching, he must follow a suitable gradated method of instruction. He must try to overcome the bashfulness of students, test their progress from time to time, and, in general, show concern and consideration for them and for their welfare. Students must basically possess the same qualities of earnestness and piety as professors . . . "the rank of knowledge is the rank of the heritage of the prophets" and "the scholars are the heirs of the prophets."

The intellectual, then, in the Islamic milieu was the messenger, the representative of the tradition and its teachings.

What, however, was the motivation of the medieval Jewish intellectual? That is, given the isolated social setting and various literary genres as the marketplace and medium of communication, why did medieval Jewish intellectuals respond to certain issues? What, if anything, united the work they did, given the prodigious range of topics they treated and methods they employed? Was there a *mentalité de l'intellectuel juif?* Was it a function of social class? of political debate? of the impact of ideas passing from one generation to another? Or, was it some factor completely external to the mind? Was it mental restlessness? Writing a book takes energy and those who expend it must have some motivation. This will be our second task: to probe motivation.

It will be the theses of this essay: (1) that, from time to time, new literary genres appeared in medieval Jewish culture; (2) that these new genres were generated by, and in turn generated, new structures of thinking, new questions, and new sets of problems; (3) that the role of the medieval Jewish intellectual was to respond to the challenge of the new structures of thought embodied in the new literary genres; and, (4) that this response was motivated by a sense of intellectual integrity and by a perceived need to defend the faith.

The Genre of "Theology"

One new genre of religious literature in medieval Judaism was the book on theology. Such books had three characteristics: they were signed, they dealt topically with certain issues crucial to religion, and they did this in a systematic way. Saadia Gaon's *Book of Beliefs and Opinions,* Moses Maimonides' *Guide of the Perplexed,* Judah Halevi's *Kuzari,* and Joseph Albo's *Ikkarim* are among the best known. But there are hundreds of lesser-known works—some of them elegant in conception and execution, some of them unoriginal and dull. All of these books share the fact that they were the work of one author; they were not anonymous compilations. The topics generally dealt with included: creation and the current scientific view of the universe, God's existence, his attributes and man's language, man's free will, the role of Torah in society, the nature of prophecy and revelation, the problem of evil, the problem of divine retribution, the nature of wisdom, God's oneness, the eschatological dimension of religious belief, miracles, the image of God in man, etc. All of these books shared a preoccupation with these topics. Finally, each of these books attempted an ordering of the discussion of these ideas, beginning with the most basic and proceeding to the most subtle. The authors differed in their ordering, according to the prevailing school of thought and their own judgment, but each attempted some ordering.

The moment in time and the conditions which produced the first book of theology are not relevant (although in the case of theology there is some knowledge on that subject). The important realization is that, once having been written, the first book on theology (sometimes erroneously called "philosophy") set a precedent. It could be, and was, imitated. It called forth further production within its genre. The first book in theology also raised certain questions which required answers. As time and intellectual background changed, so did the answers. But the questions demanded responses. After the first book in theology, Judaism was never the same, and the intellectual was always the one who rose to the challenge and responded to the ebb and flow of questions in that genre. Sometimes, theological material was treated in an exegetical setting, or in a poetic form, or even in a legal context. But the questions and answers that formed the substance of theological inquiry received their fullest treatment in the separate treatises that constituted the genre of theological literature.

One example. Judaism of the biblical period and of late antiquity seems not to have bothered much with the problem of the language we use to describe God. He had revealed himself and man related to him in piety and ritual, in law and belief. Nothing more in the way of systematic thinking was necessary. But, at a certain point in time, someone raised the question "Just what is God? What is his nature? What language can one use in truly describing him, in describing his true being?" This question posed the problem of predication and became known as the problem of God's attributes. The solutions had to come from two systems of thought: from the Bible itself, for that book was regarded as God's revelation (no one in the Middle Ages doubted that authority); and from the general theory of predication, whichever was current. All the theories of predication in the Middle Ages, however, implied an ontology; that is, a hierarchical arrangement of all the beings in reality that culminated in God, who, because he was at the summit, was the most perfect of them. Given this arrangement, there were two answers to the question "What is God's nature? What can we say about him as he truly is?" The first answer presupposed that God, because he is at the top of the great chain of being, must contain certain perfections. These are his basic qualities, his "attributes of essence" or "essential attributes." This theory was easily supported by Scripture and rabbinic tradition. All other predicates were secondary, or "accidental" (in the technical sense of the word, meaning the opposite of "essential"). The second answer presupposed that God must not be on the scale of being at all, for "being" itself was created. God, therefore, cannot be described at all (not even by such words as "existing," "one," "good," etc., each of which logically implies a class of beings in which God can be only the highest). Medieval Jewish theology alternated between these two answers, each presented in a more or less elegant manner according to the intellectual power of the author. Both were attempts to deal systematically with a topic, the question and the systematization being peculiar to the genre of literature called "theology."

Why did the intellectuals of the Middle Ages elect to respond to the questions posed? Even if we grant the givenness of the genre, the motivation for responding to it is not clear. Here, the authors themselves help us.

Saadia Gaon in his *Book of Beliefs and Opinions* (trans. S. Rosenblatt [Yale University Press, 1948]) stated very clearly (pp. 6–7):

> What has prompted me to speak explicitly about this matter is my observation of the state of many people in regard to their beliefs and convictions. . . . When, now, I considered these fundamentals and the evil resulting therefrom, my heart was grieved for my species, the species of rational beings, and my soul was stirred on account of our people, the children of Israel. For I saw in this age of mine many believers whose belief was not pure and whose convictions were not sound, whilst many of the deniers of the faith boasted of their corruption and looked down upon the devotees of the truth although they were themselves in error. I saw, furthermore, men who were sunk, as it were, in seas of doubt and overwhelmed by waves of confusion and there was no diver to bring them up from the depths nor a swimmer who might take hold of their hands and carry them ashore. But inasmuch as my Lord had granted me some knowledge by which I might come to their assistance and had endowed me with some ability that I could put at their disposal for their benefit, I thought that it was my duty to help them therewith and my obligation to direct them to the truth.

Similarly Moses Maimonides in his *Guide of the Perplexed* (trans. S. Pines [University of Chicago Press, 1963]) also stated clearly (pp. 3–4):

> Then I saw that you demanded of me additional knowledge and asked me to make clear to you certain things pertaining to divine matters, to inform you of the intentions of the Mutakallimun [earlier Islamic philosophers] in this respect . . . you were perplexed, as stupefaction had come over you; your noble soul demanded of you to "find out acceptable words" [Eccl. 12:10] . . . to compose this Treatise, which I have composed for you and for those like you, however few they are.

Further on in the Introduction, Maimonides made it clear that this type of book was intended to "teach a demonstrated truth" even if it be to a single virtuous man while displeasing ten thousand ignoramuses, "for I claim to liberate that virtuous one from that into which he has sunk, and I shall guide him in his perplexity until he becomes perfect and he finds rest" (pp. 16–17).

The evidence is clear. The intellectual who chose the genre of theological literature chose it because he perceived intellectual confusion around him. This confusion, he felt, was not justified intellectually and it also led (or could lead) to a weakening of religious faith. Therefore, the intellectual had to respond with a work of his own, growing out of his own comprehension of Scripture and systematic thinking. As Joseph Albo put it in his *Book of Principles* (Hebrew, reprint of the Warsaw edition, pp. 14–15, my translation).

Knowing the principles and understanding the beginnings upon which
the ways of the foundations of all religions are based is easy from one
point of view and hard from another. It is easy because all the known
men in the world today are members of religions, and it cannot be
imagined that one of them be such, or align himself with a religion,
without knowing the principles of that religion or [at least] that he have
some imaginative understanding of them such that he believe in
them—just as a doctor cannot be called such if he have no knowledge
of the beginning principles of medicine, or an engineer who has no
knowledge of the beginning principles of engineering.

This sensitivity to intellectual confusion and this response of topical
thinking, arranged systematically, in an independent book were, to be
sure, not limited to medieval Jewish culture. Theology became central to
Christian and to Islamic civilization, too, and, I think, for the same reasons.

The Genre of "Philology"

Another new genre of religious literature in medieval Judaism was the
book that dealt with words and their usages: the dictionary and the grammar. Such books had two characteristics: they were signed and they
attempted to systematize both the form of Hebrew words and the usages
thereof. Saadia Gaon's *Egron,* Menahem Saruq's *Mahberet,* Ibn Janah's
Book of Roots, and Abraham Ibn Ezra's *Yesod Diqduq, Sefer Sahot,* and
Safah Berurah are among the best known. But there are dozens of
lesser-known treatises on the subject. In addition, this kind of material
was very frequently not included in a separate book but incorporated in a
commentary to a sacred text, or it constituted a section of a larger work in
an area such as theology. Thus, for instance, much of the first part of
Maimonides' *Guide of the Perplexed* is devoted to matters of word usage:
explication of terms and explanation of the proper types of predication.

Just as the first book of theology set a precedent, so did the first book
of philology. Having raised certain types of questions about the morphology and meaning of words, this first work evoked a continuing response
by intellectuals as they considered and reconsidered the received answers
in the light of new knowledge and of further reflection.

One example. In Treatise II, Chapter 10, of his *Book of Beliefs and
Opinions* (pp. 116–22), Saadia Gaon listed thirteen anthropomorphic expressions used by Scripture in connection with the heavens and the earth.
He noted that they were clearly metaphoric. He then listed a similar set of
anthropomorphic expressions used by Scripture in connection with God
and concluded that these expressions, too, must be taken as figures of
speech. For dogmatic reasons, Saadia did not take this insight to its ulti-

mate conclusion. Maimonides, several centuries later, however, pushed
the concept further, denying all anthropomorphism and all anthropopa-
thism to God. Subsequent thinkers took Maimonides' position even further. Indeed, much of the history of medieval (and modern) Jewish thought
revolved around questions pertaining to the exact form and meaning of
words.

If we are to understand why medieval intellectuals devoted so much
time and energy to philological problems, we must know that, while these
questions were philological in origin, they had remarkable theological
consequences. What, for instance, does "Let us make man in our image
according to our form" mean if it has no anthropopathic content? And,
what does "And God spoke unto Moses saying" mean if it does not mean
what it says? What does "beginning" mean? and "created"? Whole doctrines hung on the meaning of certain words. The intellectual, then, had as
his first task to clarify the meaning of words. As Maimonides put it in his
Guide of the Perplexed (pp. 5–6):

> The first purpose of the Treatise is to explain the meanings of cer-
> tain terms occurring in books of prophecy.... For the purpose of
> this Treatise and of all those like it is the science of the Torah in its
> true sense ... he [the observant educated person] would remain in a
> state of perplexity and confusion as to whether he should follow his
> intellect, renounce what he knew concerning the terms in question,
> and consequently consider that he had renounced the foundations of
> the Torah. Or [whether] he should hold fast to his understanding of
> these terms and not let himself be drawn on together with his in-
> tellect.... This Treatise also has a second purpose: namely, the ex-
> planation of very obscure parables occurring in the books of the
> prophets.... But if we explain these parables to him ... he will take
> the right road and be delivered from this perplexity.

Attention to the proper form and usage of words was, thus, motivated by
a sense of intellectual integrity and a need to interpret and defend the
faith. This was facilitated by the existence of an entire genre of philological literature, in independent book form and in exegetical or essay form,
which raised philological questions and proposed various answers. But
the whole was motivated by a concern for God, for his book, and for his
people's belief in him.

The Genre of "Polemics"

Another new genre of religious literature in medieval Judaism was the
book intended to counter the claims of another religious tradition or of
some rival (and "incorrect") stream within Judaism. Again, while
polemic literature was embedded in commentaries, in theological works,

in legal codes, and even in poetry, it is primarily with the development of the independent essay, the book, that polemics became a genre unto itself. Joseph Kimhi's *The Book of the Covenant,* Isaac Troki's *Faith Strengthened,* Nahmanides' *Vikuah,* and parallel books within the sphere of Islam are among the best known of the "disputations"—the interfaith polemical literature. The extended polemic against the Karaites, the so-called Maimonidean controversy over rationalism, and the ongoing denunciation of false messiahs form the core of what is known as the "controversies"—the intrafaith polemical literature.

Here, too, the conditions and date of the first disputation and the first controversy are not relevant. The important realization is that, once having been engaged, the process of discussion and the limits of argument were firmly established. In fact, the literature is cumulative, arguments recur in later books, are refined, and are passed on to still later authors. Once disputation and controversy had come into Jewish life, Judaism could never again be the same and, again, it was the intellectual who bore the burden of learning the literature, of devising new arguments, and ultimately of entering into the political battle.

Here, too, the stakes were very high: The true meaning of the sacred texts was up for discussion. The true path to God and Torah was at issue. Often, the coherence of the Jewish community—religiously and socially—was a major concern. In the interfaith disputations, the very existence and safety of the community was frequently at stake. And so was God's honor, and Israel's. The intellectual had no choice but to respond. It was his sacred duty.

In this area of disputation, Judah Halevi began his *Kuzari* (trans. H. Hirschfeld [Pardes Publishing, 1946]) as follows: "I was asked to state what arguments I could bring to bear against the attacks of philosophers and followers of other religions, and also against [Jewish] sectarians who attacked the rest of Israel" (p. 31). Halevi then proceeded to write one of the most widely read books in medieval Jewish civilization, a set-piece debate between a Jew and his cultural opponents. Thus, too, Joseph Albo justified writing his *Book of Principles* partly as an answer to the question "Shall the religion of God be one or many?" (pp. 16–17).

Similarly, in the matter of intra-Jewish controversy, the intellectuals felt compelled to speak out. The Karaite schism produced strong reactions among Rabbinites such as Saadia, Maimonides, and others in their theological, legal, and other works. Some felt impelled to defend philosophy. Thus, Isaac Albalag, in his *Sefer Tiqqun ha-De'ot* (ed. G. Vajda [Israel Academy of Sciences and Humanities, 1973]) justified his work in these words (p. 2):

> And, because most of the talmudists and many of the ignorant people who profess Judaism think that the philosophers are destroying the

foundations of the Torah and are uprooting the principles of the faith, especially these four [previously enumerated] beliefs up to the point that they reject the books [of the philosophers] and accuse them of things that are not true, my heart has moved me to translate this book.

Others felt impelled to attack philosophy and defend traditional rabbinic theology. Nahmanides in his *Torat Ha-Adam* (ed. C. Chavel [Mosad Harav Kook, 1964]) stated (p. 14):

My son, if sinners seduce you, do not acquiesce. For you will find many essays of the Greek philosophers and of those who have become wise through their wisdom, who strengthen the hearts and reinforce thoughts. [But] they rejoice without reason, they extend comfort for vain labor, they deny the future, and they despair of the past. Their memory will be as dust. Abomination is chosen because of them and each is a heretic. Socrates, one of their wise men, said to the common people. . . .

Jacob ben Sheshet in his *Sefer Meshiv Devarim Nekhohim* (ed. G. Vajda [Israel Academy of Sciences and Humanities, 1968]) put it strongly (pp. 66–68):

And He commanded man to work and to preserve his Garden of Eden, to guard it as the apple of his eye. Do not try to be too smart and do not yearn for much knowledge and intelligence lest you become a ruin and traveler's dust; cursed be he who deceives. From every tree of the Garden you shall eat but from the tree of knowledge of good and evil; my advice is: "Do not disturb it. How beautiful it is; how good; do not destroy it because it contains a blessing. . . . " How long has the hope of the wise men endured! They are as many, now, as the grains of sand from the sea. So much so that the intelligent ones of the age say, "There is no more righteous man who is saved. The land has been given into the hand of wicked. Faith has been cut off and lost. There is neither judgment nor Judge." . . . This has started them toward breaking down fences and accusing God, for they have learned the wisdom of the people of Greece and the men of India. They think, with them, that all the abominations of God which they did for their gods must not be moved from them, [nor] their books of wisdom; that they will mix with the nations and learn their ways. They think to build a city of wisdom . . . but Torah is almost lost from their children. There are no pious; faith has evaporated; and the time has come that the Sages, peace be upon them, predicted: "The Torah is destined to be forgotten from Israel. . . . " From this I learned to strengthen myself as best I can, not from much talking. And so I have girded my loins and bared my face. The time has come to act for God.

Similarly, in the matter of false messiahs, Maimonides, in his *Epistle to Yemen* (ed. and trans. A. Halkin [Jewish Theological Seminary, 1952]) mixed anti-Christian and anti-Muslim polemic with the teaching of truth-Torah and with exhortation to adhere to rabbinic Judaism. On the subject of the false messiah who had put forth his claims, Maimonides wrote (p. xvi):

> You mention that a certain man in one of the cities of Yemen pretends that he is the Messiah. As I live, I am not surprised at him or at his followers, for I have no doubt that he is mad, and a sick person should not be rebuked or reproved for an illness brought on by no fault of his own. Neither am I surprised at his votaries, for they were persuaded by him because of their sorry plight, their ignorance of the importance and high rank of the Messiah, and their mistaken comparison of the Messiah with the son of the Mahdi [the belief in] whose rise they are witnessing. But I am astonished that you, a scholar who has studied carefully the doctrines of the rabbis, are inclined to repose faith in him. Do you not know, my brother, that the Messiah is a very eminent prophet, more illustrious than all the prophets after Moses? Do you not know that a false pretender to prophecy is liable to capital punishment, for having arrogated to himself unwarranted distinction, just as the person who prophesies in the name of idols is put to death, as we read in Scripture "But the prophet that shall speak a word presumptuously in My name, which I have not commanded him to speak, or that shall speak in the name of other gods, that same prophet shall die" (Deuteronomy 18:20)? What better evidence is there of his mendacity than his very pretensions to be the Messiah?

Part of the task of the medieval intellectual, then, was to respond to the intra- and extracommunal pressure to debate the nature of truth, to define true salvation, and to defend the honor of God, Torah, and Israel. The genre of polemical literature provided the framework and the main content. But it was up to the individual intellectual to take up the task.

This sensitivity to the conflict of definitions of salvation was not limited to medieval Jewish culture. Polemics became a major way of life in both Christianity and Islam—internally and externally—and intellectuals in those traditions, too, were charged with such responsibilities. Some undertook them with glee; others probably reluctantly. But "the time to act for God" came to all.

The Genre of "Mysticism"

The Jewish mystical tradition was, as Scholem has noted (*Major Trends in Jewish Mysticism* [Schocken, 1941]), extremely reticent in the matter of personal accounts of mystical experience. Nonetheless, as Jean Leclercq has put it (*Love of Learning*): "There is no spiritual literature without spiritual experience: it is the experience which gives rise to literature, not the reverse" (p. 322). Jewish mystics might be reticent and oblique, but they had to give an inkling of what it was that impelled them to write. This led to a new genre of literature: the book that dealt with mystical experience directly, or indirectly as part of an essay on mystical theology and symbolism. Such books had two characteristics: they were usually signed and they attempted an exposition of various types of Jewish mystical experience set into an exposition of Jewish mystical theology. The works of Abraham Abulafia, Moses de Leon, Joseph Gikatilia, Ezra of Gerona, and in a certain sense Moses Maimonides are among the best known. But there are hundreds of lesser-known treatises (not to speak of the eighteenth-century Hasidic books) on the subject.

As we have seen previously, the moment and the generative conditions of the first book of Jewish mysticism are not relevant. As time and intellectual background changed, so did the intellectual and experiential elements of this genre. (I have tried to illustrate this in my two-volume work, *Understanding Jewish Mysticism* [Ktav Publishing, 1978, 1982].) But, once questions about the nature of intense Jewish religious experience and the accompanying intellectual framework had been raised, Jewish intellectuals of mystical bent were committed to an ongoing conversation with the past, God, and themselves.

One example is the question of the definition of *devekut* ("communion with," "clinging," or "adherence" to God). Scholem has traced this in *The Messianic Idea and Other Essays* (Schocken, 1971). Another example is the question of "Know Thyself." This has been traced very carefully by Altmann in his *Studies in Religious Philosophy and Mysticism* (Routledge and Kegan Paul, 1969). Another is the overlap of philosophical and mystical systems of thought. This has been illustrated with exceptional clarity in the work of Joseph ibn Waqqar in Vajda's *Recherches sur la philosophie et la kabbale dans la pensée juive de moyen âge* (Mouton, 1962). Many more such topical studies exist.

To understand what is truly at stake, however, we must again turn to the authors themselves. Scholem has cited an anonymous fragment from a disciple of the Abulafian tradition. The author began as follows (*Major Trends*, pp. 147–55, passim):

> I, so and so, one of the lowliest, have probed my heart for ways of grace to bring about spiritual expansion and I have found three ways of progress to spiritualization: the vulgar, the philosophic, and the kabbalistic way. The vulgar way is that which, so I learned, is practiced by Moslem ascetics. They employ all manner of devices to shut out from their souls all "natural forms" . . . they summon the Name of Allah . . . the very letters Allah and their diverse powers work upon them. They are carried off into a trance without realizing how . . .
>
> The second way is the philosophic, and the student will experience extreme difficulty in attempting to drive it from his soul because of the great sweetness it holds for the human reason. . . . At best, he can

perhaps enjoy a [contemplative] spinning out of his thought and to this
he will abandon himself, retiring into seclusion. . . .

The answer lies, as I am going to demonstrate with the help of
Shaddai, in the third way of spiritualizing. And I, the humble so and
so, am going to tell you what I experienced in this matter.

The author went on to relate his experiences and then resumed his narrative:

And behold I was still speaking and oil like the oil on the anoint-
ment anointed me from head to foot and very great joy seized me
which for its spirituality and the sweetness of its rapture I cannot describe.

All this happened to your servant in his beginnings. And I do not,
God forbid, relate this account from boastfulness in order to be
thought great in the eyes of the mob, for I know full well that greatness
with the mob is deficiency and inferiority with those searching for the
true rank which differs from it in genus and in species as light from
darkness.

Now, if some of our own philosophers, sons of our people who feel
themselves attracted toward the naturalistic way of knowledge and
whose intellectual power in regard to the mysteries of the Torah is
very weak, read this, they will laugh at me and say: See how he tries to
attract our reason with windy talk and tales, with fanciful imaginations
which have muddled his mind and which he takes at their face value
because of his weak mental hold on natural science. Should however
Kabbalists see this, such as have some grasp of this subject or even
better such as have had things divulged to them in experiences of their
own, they will rejoice and my words will win their favor. But their difficulty will be that I have disclosed all of this in detail. Nevertheless,
God is my witness that my intention is *in majorem dei gloriam* and I
would wish that every single one of our holy nation were even more
excellent herein and purer than I. Perhaps it would then be possible to
reveal things of which I do not as yet know. . . . As for me, I cannot
bear not to give generously to others what God has bestowed upon me.
But since for this science there is no naturalistic evidence, its premises
being as spiritual as are its inferences, I was forced to tell this story of
the experience that befell me. Indeed, there is no proof in this science
except experience itself. . . . That is why I say, to the man who con-
tests this path, that I can give him an experimental proof, namely, my
own evidence of the spiritual results of my own experience in the science of letters according to the book of *Yetsirah.*

It was, then, spiritual experience that generated and justified the work and
the genre.

Another prominent Jewish mystical-thinker, Moses de Leon, the author of the classic book in the Jewish mystical tradition, *The Zohar,* began

one of the books he signed as follows (*Sefer Or Zarua*, ed. B. Altmann, *Kovetz al Yad*, n.s. 9 [Jerusalem, 1980], pp. 245–49):

The author has said: When I was standing on my watch to study and to go through the house of my glory [some work he was studying may be meant], as I was standing, waiting, I lifted up my eyes and behold a man stood opposite me. And behold the hand of God touched me, my spirit awoke within me, and the spirit of the Lord God was upon me. He answered me, saying: "Son of Man, stand on your feet that I may speak with you. Have I not directed you in searching the plan, in studying and going through wisdom, in explaining matters that are in the search for secrets—by vision and not by riddles? These matters have been chosen by the ancients, yet the gate has been closed and they have hidden their words in the recesses, for the pursuers have gone out after them, pressing upon their chosen ones. Jerusalem has hills around it. Therefore, they were careful to hide their wisdom . . . no person who has a blemish shall draw near. But the man of wise heart may go up as he wishes, according to his intelligence, to have visions of the grace of God and to visit His sanctuary. A light is sown and a radiance of the bright ones. The aura in which God is."

Now, when I heard these words, I drew strength, the words which were with me I took [unto myself], and my soul was enclosed in the plan. I swore that I would not give sleep to my eyes or rest to my lids, nor would I let my heart or my thoughts be at ease until I found a place for God. So I studied the plan deeply and found the secret of the ways of wisdom: that He, may He be blessed, and the secret of His true being cannot be grasped by the mind, even by souls which have visions . . . though we can comprehend a part of His true being from the secret of the ways of Torah, all of which go from darkness to light. The Jews had light. And, from it, we can understand the secret of His hidden concealment and we can climb the steps of the ladder. For all who wish to comprehend Him must go up, step by step. . . .

See now that my eyes have become bright for I have tasted a little of the honey. House of Jacob, let us go in the light of God.

(It is impossible without an extensive explicative apparatus to catch in translation the enormously learned and skillful weaving of quotations into the text and the beauty of the rhymed prose. See Altmann, however, for the references.)

There are similar types of quotations from Ezra of Gerona, Joseph Gikatilia, and others in whom experience is used to justify writing a work. I wish to add only a few words from Maimonides, who is not usually thought of as a mystic, to illustrate that this genre was not limited to those whom moderns explicitly identify as mystics. In chapter 51 of Part III of his *Guide for the Perplexed*, Maimonides brought his major work to a climax and wrote about the highest type of piety one could expect of man (p. 618):

This chapter that we bring now does not include additional matter over and above what is comprised in the other chapters of this Treatise. It is only a kind of conclusion, at the same time explaining the worship as practiced by one who has apprehended the true realities peculiar only to Him after he has obtained an apprehension of what He is; and it also guides him toward achieving this worship, which is the end of man, and makes known to him how providence watches over him in this habitation until he is brought over to the *bundle of life*.

Maimonides, then, went on to various topics in order to differentiate between the love of God (Hebrew, *'ahava;* Arabic, *mahaba*) that is identical with having knowledge of him and the passion for God (Hebrew, *hesheq;* Arabic, *'ishq*) that is a love so strong it is totally preoccupied with him. Maimonides, then, offered the following (p. 627):

The philosophers have already explained that the bodily faculties impede in youth the attainment of most of the moral virtues, and all the more that of pure thought, which is achieved through the perfection of the intelligibles that lead to passion for Him, may He be exalted. For it is impossible that it should be achieved while the bodily humors are in effervescence. Yet in the measure in which the faculties of the body are weakened and the fire of the desires is quenched, the intellect is strengthened, its lights achieve a wider extension, its apprehension is purified, and it rejoices in what it apprehends. The result is that when a perfect man is stricken with years and approaches death, this apprehension increases very powerfully, joy over this apprehension and a passion for the object of apprehension becomes stronger, until the soul is separated from the body, at that moment, in this state of pleasure.

A brief explanation of the "death by a kiss" as exactly this kind of spiritual death followed, and then Maimonides concluded this chapter (p. 628):

After having reached this condition of enduring permanence, that intellect remains in one and the same state, the impediment that sometimes veiled it having been removed. And it will remain permanently in that state of intense pleasure, which does not belong to the genus of bodily pleasures, as we have explained in our compilations and as others have explained before us. Bring your soul to understand this chapter, and direct your efforts to the multiplying of those moments in which you are with God or endeavoring to approach Him, and, to decreasing those times in which you are with other than He and in which you make no efforts to approach Him. This guidance is sufficient in view of the purpose of this Treatise.

The evidence is clear. Part of the task of the medieval Jewish intellectual was to respond to the reality of his own religious experience: to put it into writing, to teach it to others, to study other such texts, and to evolve the intellectual structure that generated and supported the experience. Here, too, what was at stake was not simply a kind of intellectual mystical geometry. What was at stake was the experiential and intellectual core of Jewish religion, as perceived by this type of Jewish intellectual. The reality of one's religious experience was a testimony to the reality of God, and the honest intellectual was compelled to testify, to reflect and study, and then to testify again.

This sensitivity to experiential religious reality and to the need to put it into writing was not limited to medieval Jewish culture. Again, for the same reasons that mystical writing became important in Judaism, it became important and more developed in Christianity and Islam.

The Genre of "Literature"

Another new genre that made its appearance in medieval Judaism was the book of poetry, the collection of short stories, and the book on rhetoric. Such books had as their common characteristic a literary aspiration, an attempt to create something of cultural elegance through the artful use of language. The poetry of Solomon Ibn Gabirol, of Judah Halevi, of Moses Ibn Ezra, of Samuel the Nagid, and of Abraham Ibn Ezra are among the best-known examples of this genre. So are the stories of Judah al-Harizi's *Tahkemoni,* or the *Travels* of Benjamin of Tudela, or Joseph Ibn Zabara's *Book of Delight,* or the *Maasehbuch,* or the various histories and chronicles. But there are hundreds of lesser-known examples, and who knows how may people tried their hand at these cultural arts and failed to survive the test of time? In fact, within the cultural sphere of Islam, every person of some substance learned to write, to compose, and to do some calligraphy; that is, every person of standing learned to be a cultured gentleman. The Arabic language even had a word for this: *adab,* the art of being cultured.

The educational goals of one trained in this genre were as follows (quoted from al-Mutanabbi by Bahya ibn Paquda, cited in Bezalel Safran, "Bahya ibn Paquda's Attitude toward the Courtier Class," *Studies in Medieval Jewish History and Literature,* ed. I. Twersky [Harvard University Press, 1979], p. 156):

> Do not preoccupy your mind with any studies except those through which you can ingratiate yourself into the favor of your contemporaries and through which you can become acceptable to the great ones of your generation—the vizir, the chief of the royal police, the royal finance officer and political dignitaries. [These are studies of] the unusual features of language, the laws of prosody, the principles of grammar and poetry. [Know the] choice anecdotes, exotic parables

and strange tales. Frequent the sessions of eloquent men, learn to communicate with all sorts of people. Master the science of the stars, on the basis of which the appropriate course of action for the public and for individuals can be determined.

When the evil passion will discern your desire to pursue wisdom it will say to you: Does it not suffice for you [to study] that which suffices for the great ones of your generation and your elders, that is, the [condensed] knowledge of the Torah? Are you not aware that study has neither an end nor a limit? Set therefore as your goal knowledge merely of the roots of religion and basic principles of Torah. Focus your attention on that with which you can adorn yourself in the eyes of people—poetry and its meter, knowledge of the unusual features of language, strange tales, traditional parables. Leave aside matters of law and the discussion of scholars regarding them. Do not turn to the mastery of the principles of logical demonstration, principles of dialectics, or the various syllogisms; [turn away from] the various kinds of proofs, the way to relate the cause to its effect, [or the allegorical method through which to relate] the exoteric to the esoteric meaning—[turn away from these studies] because of their profundity and subtlety of meaning. Lean on the masters of religious tradition even concerning those matters which you can verify independently.

Similarly, the social ethics of this courtier class were such that members were taught to do whatever was necessary to bring honor to oneself among the great and to enhance one's reputation. One must avoid bad grammar and diction. One must strive for elegant style. One must study only insofar as it is necessary for witty conversation. One must cultivate the art of writing poetry, especially the flowery kind one uses with a patron. Even philanthropy came under the utilitarian perspective: "Charity may diminish your fortune but it will increase your glory," taught Samuel the Nagid. And, in considering the purpose and goal of life, he wrote (Safran, pp. 166, 171):

> Can one restrain himself whose soul is pure,
>   and who, like the moon, aspires to rise? . . .
> Until he and his accomplishments are renowned,
>   and he surpasses his reputation like the sea . . .
> I will roam until I ascend and reach the peak,
>   which will as a result be known forever. . . .

> Do not spend the entirety of your days in His service,
> Rather make time for God, and periods of time for yourselves,
> Give Him half the day, and the other half [set] for your own activities,
> And during your nights, give no respite to wine [drinking]. . . .

> When you are awake, let your right hand stretch to a
>   winecup which is like a candle in the darkness,

And refrain from making a day of respite from the glass,
　　at night too let your sleep be little
For your lifetime is short, and in the grave there will
　　be plenty of slumber.

To be sure, there were other intellectuals, of a more rabbinic and pietistic
bent, who expended a great deal of energy criticizing the product of the
literary intellectuals. The most wide read book in the Jewish Middle Ages
was probably Bahya ibn Paquda's *Duties of the Heart*. This book, vari-
ously claimed by philosophers, mystics, and ethicists, was really a book
on piety of a mildly ascetic and definitely rabbinic type. In it Bahya
criticized strongly the courtier attitudes and goals. (Safran has argued the
case, although one wonders if Bahya's attack was not broader than Safran
has stated.) The true goal of the Jewish man was piety, trust, contemplation, and a certain reserve vis-à-vis the allurements of society. It is true
that Bahya, Halevi, Ibn Gabirol, and even Saadia wrote poems in the
literary cultural style of the age. But their redeeming virtue was (until
modernity) their piety. The art therein was secondary, appreciated only
by those who had been so trained.

The absorption of the *adab* style of culture, its incorporation even into
the liturgy, and the fight that ensued over its legitimacy (Maimonides
objected even to liturgical poetry) was really a fight over the nature of
human and Jewish identity. Could one be truly "Jewish" and still be
cultured? Those who answered affirmatively—and some of them were
community leaders, liturgists, and creators of secular culture in Hebrew,
a language not quite fit to the task—were intellectuals motivated by a deep
aesthetic sense, as well as by that joie de vivre that comes from participating actively in the life of the surrounding society. Social life and beauty
were part of the joy of Creation and, hence, participation in them was
seen to be within Jewishness even though rabbinically not central to it.
Those who answered negatively—the minority of intellectuals who
formed the sober rabbinic leadership—were intellectuals motivated by a
deep sense of the seriousness of revelation and law. God had spoken, and
life could not be a frivolous pursuit of the joy of Creation. It was to be a
sober pursuit of the demands placed upon man by God. Historiographic
hindsight may tempt us to justify the one and denounce the other but, in
the Middle Ages, there was simply variety, represented by the contesting
sides.

This sensitivity to cultural milieu and aesthetic conventions was not
limited to Jewish intellectuals. The *adab* way of life and the ideal of
chivalry developed in Islam and Christianity respectively. In both civilizations secular culture absorbed a great deal of the energy of the intellectuals and generated a great deal of concern among intellectuals of the more
conservative religious bent.

The Genre of "Law"

Another new genre of religious literature in medieval Judaism was the book that dealt with Jewish, that is, rabbinic, law. There were three main literary forms for this genre: the commentary or supercommentary on the Talmud or on other legal texts; the responsum (a formal legal response to a formal legal inquiry); and the code of law. It must also be understood that this material was cumulative and, hence, that the corpus was (and is) always growing. The commentaries on the Talmud of the north European Tosafists, the responsa of Maimonides, and the codes of Maimonides and Joseph Karo are among the best known examples of the three literary forms of this genre. But there are untold numbers of commentaries and supercommentaries, thousands of responsa, and many other codes or handbooks of lesser scope which are well known to scholars in the field.

The first code of law evoked a strong response, leading to commentative modification and even complete revision. As rabbinic Judaism gained momentum and as time allowed accretion, Jewish law grew. As always, it fell to the intellectual to occupy himself with the intricacies of the law: interpreting, devising new conceptual tools, meeting the challenge of new situations, and harmonizing inconsistencies. It particularly fell to the legal intellectual to reach out and grasp the greater sense of the law, always with the sense of responsibility engendered by revelation.

An example. In the twelfth century, Maimonides organized and wrote the first code of Jewish law, the *Mishneh Torah*. There appear to be three, possibly four, reasons why he broke with the previous noncodificatory forms of Jewish legal literature. (The first three are reported in I. Twersky's careful analysis in his *Introduction to the Code of Maimonides* [Yale University Press, 1980], pp. 61–81. The fourth is my own suggestion.) First, Maimonides shared the historiographic view of many medieval Jewish intellectuals that the entire revealed tradition was deteriorating because of time and the oppressive effects of the exile. Thus he wrote (Twersky, p. 62):

> In our days severe vicissitudes prevail, and all feel the pressure of hard times. The wisdom of our wise men has disappeared; the understanding of our prudent men is hidden (cf. Isa. 29:14). Hence the commentaries of the Geonim and their compilations of laws and responses, which they took care to make clear, have in our times become hard to understand, so that only a few individuals properly comprehend them. Needless to add, such is the case in regard to the Talmud itself—the Babylonian as well as the Palestinian—the Sifra, the Sifre, and the Tosefta, all of which works require for their comprehension a broad mind, a wise soul, and considerable study.... On these grounds, I, Moses the son of Maimon the Sefardi, bestirred myself... [to compose a work from which] the entire Oral Law might become systematically known to all.

Second, Maimonides felt deeply that other people, as well as he, needed a simple, direct guide to action. People, even scholars, had need of a book in which they could look up the law without having to have recourse to the complicated, and not always unambiguous, legal literature of the day. Thus he wrote (Twersky, pp. 40–41, 42, 44):

> My sole intention in composing this text was to clear the paths and re-move the obstacles from before the students of the law, so that they should not become discouraged or distressed (literally: their minds be-come faint) by the overabundance of debate and argumentation, and consequently err in adjudicating the law correctly. May the Lord, blessed be His name, aid you as well as us to study His law and to at-tain knowledge of His oneness. Let us not err, and let the following verse be fulfilled in our lifetime: I will put my law in their inward parts, and in their heart will I write it (Jer. 31:33). . . .
>
> Know that I did not compose this work in order to become great (in renown) in Israel because of it; or in order that I might acquire fame in the world; and consequently [it is not to be expected] that I should be grieved at any opposition to the purpose for which I composed it. But in the first instance I composed it—and my Witness is in heaven (Job 16:19)—for my own sake, in order to free myself from the burden of investigating and searching for the *halakot* which are needed con-stantly, and then for use in my old age (as my memory weakens), and for the sake of the Lord, may He be blessed. For I was most zealous for the Lord God of Israel when I saw before me a nation that does not have a comprehensive book (of laws) in the true sense nor true and accurate (theological) opinions. Therefore I have done what I did, only for the sake of heaven. . . .
>
> The fact is that when we ventured forth in a pioneering effort to compose a work concerning the laws of the Torah and the elucidation of its rules, we intended thereby to fulfill the will of God, blessed be He, not to seek recompense or honor from men, but to smooth the path, interpret, and, as we thought necessary, help those who could not understand the words of the Torah scholars, of blessed memory, who preceded us, to understand them. It seems to us that we facili-tated (literally, brought close or made reasonable) and simplified abstruse [apparently nonritual] and profound subjects; we collected and compiled subjects which were scattered and dispersed; and we knew, at any rate, that we were achieving something valuable. For if the case was as we thought it to be, then by simplifying, facilitating, and compiling, in a manner that none of our predecessors had ever done, we have already achieved something by benefiting people and have earned divine recompense. But if it proves otherwise, and we have not succeeded in clarifying or simplifying the subject to any greater extent than our predecessors did in their works, then we have at least earned God's reward; as the Talmudic saying has it, "God de-sires the heart [i.e., the intention of the act]. . . . "

Third, Maimonides, working in the intellectual setting of theology and in the social setting of intra- and extracommunal religious polemics, felt compelled to establish correct belief as a matter of law. Theology and spirituality were not to be separated from law (as is the case of modern society) but were part of a whole revealed and prescribed view of the nature of religious obligation (Twersky, pp. 44–45):

> And when we ventured to undertake this project (the *Mishneh Torah*), we saw that it would be wrong to aim at our goal—to interpret and facilitate details of the laws—and at the same time to neglect its foundations (*yesodot*), i.e., that I should not explain them or guide (the reader) to their truth. . . . We saw that it would be necessary for us to explain the foundations (principles) of religion in our Talmudic works in a descriptive-apodictic fashion rather than in a demonstrative one, because a demonstrative approach to these religious principles requires an intellectual facility and familiarity with many sciences which the Talmudists do not possess, as we have explained in the *Moreh Nebukim*, and we preferred that the fundamental truths at least be accepted as articles of tradition by all people. Consequently, we mentioned at the beginning of our *Commentary on the Mishnah* principles which should be believed concerning (various matters) [e.g., prophecy]. In *Perek Helek* [chapter 10 of Sanhedrin] we explained principles. . . . We did the same also in our great work entitled *Mishneh Torah*, whose true worth will be recognized only by those men of religion and wisdom who acknowledge the truth and are predisposed to study intelligently, who can understand how the work was composed, and who can recognize both the extent and how we arranged them in order. We have also stated therein all the religious and juridical principles, and we have intended thereby that those who are called disciples of the wise (*talmide hakamim,* scholars), or Geonim, or whatever you wish to call them, should build their branches [i.e., details of the laws] on juridical roots; that their Torah knowledge should be properly grounded; that all this should be built on religious principles; and that they should not cast the knowledge of God behind them, but should direct their utmost efforts and zeal to that which bring them perfection and enable them to draw nearer to their Creator, not to the things that the masses deem to be perfection.

This aspiration to teach correct belief even led Maimonides to devise a code so comprehensive that it dealt with the building plan of the Temple and the sacrificial system (for the time when that would be restored) and with the rules applicable to the messianic king. Fourth, I think the precedent of Islamic codes of law must have seemed salutary to Maimonides. In Islam, as in Judaism, not only civil and criminal law were codified but also ritual and theology.

Maimonides called his great code the *Mishneh Torah,* "the second Torah" or "the second-in-authority to the Torah." It was never accepted as such. All were awed. All studied it. No one ventured into rabbinic law without it. But many remained skeptical. They were skeptical of its apodictic form. They were skeptical of some of its conclusions. Mostly, they were skeptical of its arrogation of authority. No one put it better than his contemporary, Rabbi Abraham ibn Daud of Posquières (in I. Twersky, *The Rabad of Posquières* [Harvard University Press, 1962], p. 131):

> He intended to improve but did not improve, for he forsook the way of all authors who preceded him. They always adduced proof for their statements and cited the proper authority for each statement; this was very useful, for sometimes the judge would be inclined to forbid or permit something and his proof was based on some other authority. Had he known that there was a greater authority who interpreted the law differently, he might have retracted. Now, therefore, I do not know why I should reverse my tradition or my corroborative views because of the compendium of this author. If the one who differs with me is greater than I—fine; and, if I am greater than he, why should I annul my opinion in deference to his? Moreover, there are matters concerning which the Geonim disagree and this author has selected the opinion of one and incorporated it in his compendium. Why should I rely upon his choice when it is not acceptable to me and I do not know whether the contending authority is competent to differ or not? It can only be that "an overbearing spirit is in him."

The great debate of the intellectuals of legal bent of mind began with Rabad but did not end there. It went on, provoked bitter controversies, and, to some extent, still goes on. Even the wide-ranging scope set by Maimonides' towering intellect for a code of Jewish law was rejected, and later codes and manuals confined themselves to more functional matters and a more functional structure (cf. Twersky, *Code,* pp. 515–37).

What was really at stake in the terribly complex, passionately fought issue of the forms of the genre of Jewish law? It was God. He had revealed his law to men. The law was his, not man's. He had entrusted only its interpretation, application, and enforcement to man—to the intellectual. The intellectual, therefore, always had to act in such a way that his decision reflected the best that his mind, heart, and instinct could produce. It was really God's reputation, as well as the intellectual's, that was at stake, at all times.

Medieval Islamic and Christian fellow intellectuals understood this, for the *shari'a* and canon law were shared concepts. In an orderly world, with revealed traditions and established interpretive authorities, the Jewish intellectual of a legal bent of mind was not alone.

The Genre of "Science"

Another new genre of literature, not exactly religious but with wide-ranging influence on religious intellectuals, was the book that dealt with medicine, mathematics, biology, physics, astronomy, alchemy, and astrology (the latter two were sciences in the Middle Ages). Characteristically, these books were signed. They were also usually, but not always, written by men who had reputations in other fields as well. Thus, Maimonides was known for his medical works as well as for his legal and philosophical works. Ibn Ezra, the exegete and linguist, developed extensive astronomical tables and wrote a book on astrology. Gersonides, the exegete and philosopher, wrote extensively on arithmetic, geometry, trigonometry, and astronomy. He is credited with inventing the Jacob staff, a device to measure the angular separation between celestial bodies, that was of great importance as a navigational tool in the century that first saw circumnavigation of the globe. In addition, treatises on the Jewish calendar appeared, commentaries on the early *Sefer Yetsirah* ("Book of Creation") were written, chronologies (histories) were developed, and countless chapters were set into larger works that dealt with the same issues. Thus, Maimonides devoted a sizable section of Part II of his *Guide* to the faults of the Ptolemaic account of the heavenly motions. In fact, no medieval Jewish intellectual of any cast could avoid the realm of science. A centuries-long dialogue developed among Jewish intellectuals on matters of science itself and on the relationship of scientific knowledge to religious knowledge.

The case of astrology is probably the most curious one. Medieval Jewish intellectuals accepted the idea that the world was created and therefore orderly. They further accepted the idea that God imparted this orderliness through the heavenly bodies. Finally, they acknowledged the common idea that all change was a function of motion, that all motion came from the momentum imparted by a body, and hence that all motion-change was traceable to the motion of the heavenly bodies. Astrology, therefore, was an eminently reasonable science. Only the doctrines of free will and repentence stood in the way. A great deal of scientific-religious dialogue by medieval Jewish intellectuals took place in the effort to resolve this problem. Abraham bar Hiyya, for example, wrote several books on mathematics, geography, intercalation, and astronomy. He also believed in astrology. At one point, he clashed with a distinguished contemporary, Judah ben Barzillay of Barcelona, himself a commentator on the "Book of Creation." Abraham bar Hiyya wanted to move the date of a wedding because he had determined that the astrological signs were not favorable. Rabbi Judah, rejecting astrology as pagan custom, refused to have it moved. For the record, it seems that most Jewish intellectuals—rationalists, kabbalists, legalists, etc.—approved of, or at least allowed, astrology, Maimonides being the most prestigious and aggressive denier.

Again, what was at stake was a theological commitment, an intellectual assent to a proposition about the nature of God's world. It was not just a scientific difference of opinion discussed in the halls of the academy. It was a matter of faith and morals. It was a matter of the truth within a system of thought that reached out and encompassed all of life, not just a segment thereof. Life was given. Life was whole. And the intellectual had to try to reconcile the apparent diversity of life with its givenness and its wholeness.

Galileo, al-Biruni, and many others understood this, and sensitivity to science and its relation to the broader definition of life in a created world were preoccupations of intellectuals in all medieval traditions.

Conclusion

In the Introduction to this chapter it was noted that the medieval Jewish intellectual, unlike his Christian and Islamic counterparts was, first, an isolated individual and, second, an autodidact. He did not have the benefit of large universities or *madrasas* with significant numbers of students, books, and colleagues. Nor did he usually enjoy substantial state or church financial support. Because of this, books became his medium, various genres of religious literature became his marketplace.

These genres, it was further noted, comprised books on various topics. The first book in each genre was revolutionary because it created a new literary form for expressing and discussing new ideas—the whole book, systematically arranged (as opposed to the more traditional commentary). Subsequent books were responses, building upon the precedent of the first. The content and substance changed; but the form, the genre, remained. Sometimes these genres overlapped, with one book containing several topics or forms. (On this, see M. Buss, "Principles for Morphological Criticism: With Special Reference to Letter Form," in *Orientation by Disorientation,* ed. R. A. Spencer [Pickwick Press, 1980], pp. 71 ff.). Nonetheless, the genres of medieval Jewish intellectualism are identifiable: theology, philology, polemics, mysticism, literature, law, and science. Throughout, form and content influenced one another.

In the Introduction it was also noted that the Christian intellectual was seen as motivated by intellectual iconoclasm (Le Goff) or by monastic piety (Leclercq) while the Islamic intellectual was seen as motivated by a sense of the all-pervasiveness of knowledge and by a perception of the intellectual as the prophet or messenger of the tradition and its teachings (Rosenthal).

The motivation of the Jewish intellectual, we have seen, resembled more closely the Islamic model, even in Christian Europe, than it did either of the Christian models. The Jewish intellectual was not iconoclastic and, except for the mystic-intellectual, he was not pietistic (in the monastic sense.) He did have a very broad definition of knowledge, of what he felt was within the purview of that which one could, and ought, to know. He was challenged by that knowledge. And, he was motivated to seek accommodation between knowledge and culture on the one hand, and Scripture and tradition on the other. In this sense, the Jewish intellectual was a person possessed of intellectual curiosity and integrity, but he was also committed to God and to his Torah and, hence, to a Jewish theology and a Jewish way of life. There could be no theology, philology, polemics, mysticism, literature, law, or science without God and his Torah being in the center. The faith had to be defended and the intellectual was the one to do it. The *mentalité de l'intellectuel juif*— whether he was in the Islamic sphere of influence or in the European sphere; whether he was a rationalist or a mystic, a philologist or a polemicist, a legal scholar or a student of science or literature—was based on mind. This is succinctly exposed in the fact that, while Maimonides denied absolutely that God could be described in positive terms, he insisted on positing knowledge as man's way to God and as the conduit of his Providence toward man. Furthermore, Maimonides chose to codify this doctrine in his "Book of Knowledge," the first book in his *Mishneh Torah*.

In retrospect, the medieval Jewish intellectual—isolated, self-taught, acting through the medium of his genres to maintain his intellectual integrity and to defend his God and his faith—achieved, quite unintentionally, a goal which modern intellectuals would, later, find most laudable. He permitted new ideas and new experiences to penetrate the tradition and to contribute to the living religious reality that is indicated by the word "tradition." The issues and problems in theology, the precise meaning of words in philology, the sharpening of ideological lines in polemics, the various types of spiritual experience in mysticism, the aesthetic and cultural challenge of literature, the regulation of the law code, and the new knowledge of the sciences—all were able to penetrate and interact with rabbinic Judaism through the medieval Jewish intellectual who read, reflected, and wrote on these topics. I do not think that medieval Jewish intellectuals consciously intended to participate in "the evolution of Jewish tradition." On the contrary, my own conclusion is that they saw themselves as conducting a rear-guard action to defend the faith. But history, or Providence, enabled them to have a different role. And who knows what medieval (and even modern) Jewish life would have been if the medieval Jewish intellectual had not felt himself challenged to do the work that was to be his.

Part Three

Interpretation
Judaism Today and Tomorrow

Introduction

The analysis of Judaism brings us down to our own day. It is not possible to do justice to so complex and subtle a creation of humankind as religion when we deal with what is yet alive and changing, important and therefore subject to ongoing controversy. How shall we (merely) analyze and describe that about which people care deeply? Analysis demands the capacity to entertain many possibilities. If we are alive and deeply care, we see only a few. Description demands detachment, reflective selection of suggestive facts. By definition we cannot release our bond to faith yet with us, and we with it. Hence the present task, to confront Judaism today and tomorrow, is somewhat different from the one carried out in the first and second parts of this book. To deal with the here and now I have defined the labor in ways at once descriptive and analytical. A clear statement of the types of classical response to contemporary life within the present-day world is demanded and forthcoming at the start. At the same time a principal labor of contemporary religion is to shape a usable and credible past. Hence how Judaism has served, and now serves, as a mode of organizing history, of turning this-and-that into destiny and national calling—that seems a fine example of one approach to the interpretive study of the present. Two striking exercises in historical interpretation are offered. Neither makes any pretense at description, just as, in all matters contemporary, an approach claiming to believe and advocate nothing and merely to describe is pretense. An exercise in the description and analysis of Judaism as a timeless cultural system is accomplished by an anthropologist who quite properly makes no pretense at indifference to the society he proposes to study and interpret. A look at how today the past is organized, on the one side, and a picture of how today a religion lives in an ongoing, eternal present, as if it has no past—these complement the picture of acutely contemporary life within a world view and way of living created by a vital, and evidently lasting, religion.

Let me point to what, at the end of the twentieth century, constitutes the principal trait of Judaism. It is the unraveling of a long-standing compromise, the upsetting of what had for ages remained at rest in exactly balanced scales. To explain, let me start with a question of the most fundamental character: What made the modern period *modern?* The break with those long centuries in which Judaism was defined by the rabbis of the Talmud was marked by the fact that classical Judaism, for many, became implausible in the face of a contemporary context. Jews, emerging from the perspective of rabbinic world views, found that the promise of modernity was closed off by those world views. The longtime reticence about a Messiah and the messianic age did not credibly explain that wonderful age people in the nineteenth century thought had dawned—an age of liberalism in the acceptance of difference in general, an age in which Jews in particular might find themselves citizens like all others, subject to a common law and enjoying common rights. One important component in the shift of Judaism in the modern period, therefore, is the demise of long-established skepticism in the face of claims of Messiahs and new dawns and new ages. Through much of the nineteenth century and even down to World War II, that skepticism proved to be incredible and implausible, so powerful was the optimism of the age. That remarkable optimism, together with a renewed interest in history, therefore politics, is one-half of the curious syzygy of modernity—a gravitational system made up of opposite forces, each pulling at the Jews from its side of the planet, Israel.

The other half was equally persuaded that history, therefore politics, matters. But it placed its own, negative valuation upon both. From the last third of the nineteenth century onward, many Jews gave up the optimism of the day. They began to understand that the golden promises of the Enlightenment and the emancipation would never be kept, indeed, were false to begin with. There was no place in Western civilization for the Jews. They therefore had to build their own state as a refuge from the storms that were coming upon them—and that did break. These Jews rejected not only the high hopes of Enlightenment and Reform. They also abandoned fundamental teleological optimism, rationalism, yielding patience, and quietism, with which classical Judaism had viewed the world. They did not believe that the world was so orderly and reliable as Judaism had supposed. They regarded Judaism as a misleading and politically unwise view of the Jewish people and their worldly context. So what was needed was not prayer, study of Torah, and a life of compassion and good deeds. What the hour demanded was renewed action, a reentry into politics, and the repoliticization of the Jewish people. But while the Reform Jews entered the politics of the nations, the Zionist did not. Zionism was the movement that redefined the Jewish people into a nation. Zionism revived the ancient political status of the Jews.

So far as Zionism saw the world as essentially irrational and unreliable, unable to proceed in the orderly, calm, reasonable fashion in which Judaism assumed the world would always conduct its affairs, Zionism marked an end to Judaism as it had been known. The fact that, in time to come, Zionism would take up the old messianic language and symbolism of Judaism and make over ancient vessels into utensils bearing stunningly new meaning is not to be ignored. But at its beginning, Zionism marked a break from Judaism. It was not because of Zionism's messianic fervor, but because of its rejection of the quiet confidence, rationalism, and optimism of rabbinic Judaism.

These two things—the promise of emancipation and the advent of racist and political anti-Semitism to which Zionism responded—fall far outside the world view of rabbinic Judaism. Citizenship in the nations or a Jewish state—these choices could not be satisfactorily interpreted and explained within the established system. The result has been the breakdown of the Judaic system for many Jews. The system of Judaism was not overturned. For these people, it simply became implausible. It lost the trait of self-evidence.

So, in all, Judaism was and is a system of balance between cosmic, teleological optimism and short-term skepticism—a system of moderation and restraint, of rationalism and moderated feeling. Just as it came into being at the end of the first century in response to the collapse of unrestrained messianism, feelings unleashed and hopes unbounded by doubt, all in ashes in the Jerusalem Temple, so it came to an end, where and when it did come to an end, in a renewed clash with those very emotions and aspirations which, in the beginning, it had overcome. These were passionate hope and unrestrained, total despair. A system of optimistic skepticism and skeptical optimism, creating a world grasped with open arms, loved with a breaking heart, could never survive those reaches toward the extremes, those violations of the rules and frontiers of moderate and balanced being, that characterize modern times. Jews as equal, free citizens of the nations, Jews as smoke up the chimneys—these extremes defied Judaism.

When the balance was upset, it hardly mattered whether it was shifted toward one extreme—optimism become messianism—or toward the other—skepticism turned into utter despair, even nihilism. The extremes would meet, in due course, in the remarkable messianization of Zionism in the last third of the twentieth century. But at that point, it would appear, even avatars and exponents of rabbinic Judaism would take up the messianic fervor of the moment. That unanticipated phenomenon—the messianism of rabbinic Judaism in the persons of its (self-described) "most authentic" exponents—would mark a moment in the history of Judaism so completely contemporary and so utterly unanticipated as to permit no comment whatsoever.

Yet as students of religion, we may at least take note of the unpredictable character of religion. If, as I argue, Judaism today constitutes re-messianization of a Judaism formerly distinctly skeptical of messianic claims, then there can be no more certainties, only surprises. The one thing not to be predicted even as recently as 1967 was that Orthodoxy would invoke messianic language and symbolism in behalf of the State of Israel. Nor could anyone have imagined that a claim to return to the promises of the patriarchs through settlement in the territories of Judea and Samaria would impress the sober and cautious intellects of that enduring world view. Yet in the 1970s and early 1980s that is precisely what took place. In the face of the advent of what any reasonable student of Judaism would have declared impossible, what is there to be said? Only that religions have a way of surprising students of religion.

If there is one lesson to be learned from the case of Judaism, it is to avoid excessive contemporaneity in the study of religions. For what is valid as analysis and description today—Judaism as a syzygy in which messianism is kept in place by an opposed gravitational field of skepticism, in which hope for an enchanted unimaginable future generates energy and support for a disciplined and controlled, predictable present—turns out in a span of years or even months to be all wrong. And yet, in yet a little while, what is all wrong may turn out to be right again. So it goes. That is why studying religions is interesting and may prove illuminating. Everything is always changing. Yet despite time and change there is what can be subjected to analysis, description, and interpretation.

J. N.

Seven

Religion and the Chaos of Modernity

The Case of Contemporary Judaism

Charles Liebman

Modernity, or modern consciousness, is defined by the necessity to choose (Apter, 1965:10; Berger, 1979).[1] Men and women, and in increasing measure even children, are confronted by alternatives in matters which previous generations accepted as given. Rapid technological change and the severe economic dislocation attendant upon such change, accumulation of wealth or the consciousness of abject poverty, increased education, conceptions of political freedom and equality, and the breakdown of extended family relations, especially when all of these things occur more or less simultaneously, chip away at the taken-for-grantedness that characterizes the world view of traditional societies. Modernity forces the individual to confront his own identity; to ask himself, consciously or unconsciously, who he is, to what groups or communities he really belongs, and what the models are that he must choose in responding to the world about him.

Modernity came to Jews of western and central Europe in the late eighteenth and early nineteenth centuries although its roots are in an earlier period (Katz, 1973). Its echoes evoked responses from Jews of eastern Europe by the middle of the nineteenth century. Jews today choose models of Jewish life many of which originated in that period.

The two major choices which modernity forced

and continues to force upon Jews are the meaning of being Jewish, that is, the nature of Jewish identity, and the choice about how committed one will be to Judaism, that is, how much of one's life space will be occupied by being Jewish. Jews have to decide if they are to express their identity as a national group, as a religious group, as a cultural group, as an ethnic group, or as some combination of these. And Jews have to decide, assuming they decide to remain Jewish, how much time, effort, and energy, how much of their sense of self is to be dedicated to being Jewish (Liebman, 1973).

The two types of choices are not unrelated, although they are certainly not identical. How one defines one's Jewish identity has implications for how much of one's self is to be involved in that identity. But the implications may differ by the time or place of choosing, or by the person who does the choosing. It doesn't necessarily follow that any one definition of Jewish identity necessarily implies a greater or lesser commitment.

It is misleading to think that the choices were or are entirely matters of subjective preference or taste. There were cultural, social, economic, and political restraints then, as now, which channeled responses. Furthermore, people, then as now, were not always pleased by the fact that they had to choose. Choice necessitates obligations and responsibilities which are always onerous. The result is that some people look to leaders to make their choice, and the leaders, whether they are rabbis, communal leaders, patriarchs or matriarchs, often present their decisions as though choices were limited or nonexistent.

To identify the major choices that were made in the nineteenth century is really to label the major movements and tendencies in Jewish life in the modern era. Assimilation, Jewish Enlightenment, Reform Judaism, Zionism, Jewish Socialism, and Orthodox Judaism are all types of Jewish responses to modernity. I want to look more carefully at one such major response, Orthodox Judaism.

Orthodoxy is the self-conscious effort by Jews to meet the challenge which modernity poses to the tradition while retaining the binding authority of *halakhah* (Jewish law and way of life) as it was traditionally understood and interpreted. Looking backward, one can easily observe that modernity posed problems to the traditional Jewish world view and to Jewish identity. Assimilationism stands at one end of the continuum of responses to modernity. It unequivocally welcomed the new era and assumed that its price (or benefit) was the disappearance of Judaism. Orthodoxy represented the other end of the continuum. Superficially, at least, it made the fewest concessions to modernity and demanded the greatest degree of Jewish commitment from its adherents. Orthodoxy is of special interest not only because it stands at one end of our theoretical continuum of responses but because, despite the limits to its flexibility (no deviation from the halakhah), it exhibits both a variety of types of responses and, in some cases, a remarkable capacity to reconcile religion and modernity.

Before we undertake a closer look at Orthodoxy, two points must be clarified. First, there is a strong conservative bias built into religion. And Orthodoxy, unlike Zionism, for example, defines Judaism as a religion in the broadest sense of the term. Religion claims some kind of absolute truth. One cannot deny all of that truth and still claim religious adherence. So, almost by definition, the religious elite not only exercise extreme caution in reformulating doctrines of the past but tend to deny that they are changing anything by their reformulation. Intrareligious controversy is not phrased in terms of "what ought to be" but in terms of "what has been." Those who take religion's claims seriously (it is a mark of a religion's worldly success that not all its adherents or even its leaders do take its claims seriously), are committed to a certain past which obligates them with respect to what they ought to be doing in the present and the future. Hence, controversy within the same religion inevitably is phrased in terms of the meaning of the past. Once a group proclaims that the past is no longer binding, the possibility for intrareligious discourse is seriously jeopardized if not futile. This is why, for example, Reform and Orthodox Jews have so little to say to one another at a religious level although they may share, along with other Jews, important and compelling ethnic, cultural, and political concerns.

Second, the Jewish religion, like any other religion, consists of the practices, customs, and behavior of nominal adherents whose religious folkways generally deviate, sometimes more so and sometimes less so, from the formulations of the elite. I am going to discuss four responses of Orthodox Judaism to modernity. These responses are divided between those that received theoretical articulation but had no followers in practice and those that represent responses in practice, by groups of Orthodox Jews, that were never legitimated in theory. The four responses are to be understood as my formulation. They are mental constructs. I will try to show how, in reality, the thinking of major Orthodox leaders and the behavior of groups of Orthodox Jews conformed to these constructs and how, over time, these responses to modernity continued to evolve. However, since we are dealing with ideas and behavior classified in accordance with mental constructs, it should not surprise us if, in practice, we do not have many cases of pure types. Most Orthodox Jews fall between two or even three types of responses.

Neotraditionalism

The first response, neotraditionalism, rejects modernity. In contrast to modernity, which promotes perceptions of alternate identities, neotraditionalism seeks to create a society where identity is taken for granted and traditional perceptions of reality are presented without alternatives. Carried to its logical extreme, it must construct an alternate society which will insulate its adherents from the spirit of modernity—most especially from choice and the assertion of individualism.

Neotraditionalism is not the same as traditionalism.[2] The traditional Jewish world view emerged as part of the environment in which Jews found themselves. Basing itself on the sacred texts of the tradition (the Bible and the Talmud), the religious elite evolved a code of law and the people developed norms of behavior and conceptions of reality which explained the Jewish condition.[3] But the mark of the traditional elite was its unconscious permissiveness and openness to plural interpretations and new meanings precisely because it was not challenged by radically different interpretations or alternatives. When such challenges did arise, for example, the challenge of Karaitism (Baron, 1957; Nemoy, 1952), traditional leaders exhibited many characteristics associated with neotraditionalism.

Neotraditionalism, conscious of the threats to the integrity of its interpretation of the tradition, is characterized by elitism (clear demarcation of leadership groups—i.e., the rabbi-sage), authoritarianism and hierarchy (the rabbi-sage's authority is final and independent of the wishes of the community which he leads; there is, in turn, a hierarchy of rabbinical leaders), strictness in the interpretation of religious law (laxity in any form is intolerable because it may represent not only a weakness in character but the choice of some deviant interpretation of Judaism), and uniformity in the interpretation of the tradition. Paradoxically, the neotraditional elite themselves may reinterpret the tradition by censuring rabbinical texts, filtering out ideas which are suspect of bearing the seeds of deviation, and denying discordance and difference within the tradition. While neotraditionalism seeks to insulate its adherents from the modern world in general through the creation of independent schools, communications media, neighborhoods, and, where possible, independent economic institutions, it is most threatened by other Jews.

There are differences of opinion among neotraditionalists about the proper attitude to be adopted toward nonreligious Jews. The differences are limited on the one hand by religious injunctions which assert that a Jew, even though he sins, remains a Jew and that all Jews are responsible for each other's behavior. On the other hand, association with nonreligious Jews poses various problems including the violation of a host of injunctions against association with evildoers. Neotraditionalist groups and leaders have adopted various strategies for dealing with nonreligious Jews; but all the strategies are characterized by the sense that a vast spiritual and behavioral gap separates the religious and the nonreligious Jews.

Rabbi Moses Sofer (1762–1839), more than any single individual, fashioned the ideology of neotraditionalism, coining the slogan "all that is new is forbidden by the Torah," a play on words of a rabbinic injunction. Nevertheless, unlike many later rabbinical leaders, including those who counted themselves among his disciples, he did not oppose all secular education in principle (Katz, 1967:141). He went so far as to assert that a knowledge of some secular subjects is helpful in resolving certain questions of Jewish law. But what characterizes the neotraditionalists today is that, even when they do not oppose secular education, they legitimate it in instrumental, primarily economic terms.

It is difficult to estimate the number of neotraditionalists, in part because there are no accurate demographic data on Jews in general, much less data on different types of Jews, and, in part, because as I noted, there are so few pure types of Orthodox Jews (or Jews with any kind of pure ideology). However, neotraditionalists, precisely because of the supreme importance which they ascribe to proper conduct and ideology, are institutionally isolated, and one can specify their dominant institutional affiliations. They include the followers of most Hasidic rabbis,[4] the hareydi (pious) community of Jerusalem and of Bnei Brak, those identified with the world of yeshivot (academies for advanced Talmudic study), and most of the adherents of Agudat Israel.[5] There is a great deal of institutional overlapping. I would estimate their number as about 4 percent of the Jews of the United States and Israel with a higher proportion in Israel than in the United States.

Neotraditionalists today juxtapose their own world view, which they are convinced is the only authentic one, and those aspects of the modern world which they reject: anarchy, relativism, bodily license, meaninglessness. The neotraditionalist tendency, other things being equal, is continually to broaden the scope of halakhah. Halakhah is interpreted by rabbinic masters (experts in Talmudic study) whose authority is absolute. Logic and rationality are highly esteemed but only within the context of the authority of the legal code and traditional rabbinical interpretation. The neotraditionalist aspires to a life directed toward holiness and purity. By definition, observance of God's law and study of his revealed Scripture brings one closer to God, the source of holiness and purity. This requires great self-control. Temptations, especially in the realm of sexual behavior, always exist. Under modern conditions, the temptations reflected in the mass communication media, in the manner in which women dress and conduct themselves, in the social and physical contacts between the sexes which modern Western society takes for granted, lead to impure thought if not impure action. Strict separation of the sexes and avoidance of the mass media are helpful in the constant struggle to overcome these temptations. Since the modern world is characterized by ever greater sexual license, ordinances governing separation and avoidance must be ever more rigidly adhered to. (There are in addition reasons for avoiding contact with secular culture in general and the mass media in particular. They challenge religious tenets at a variety of levels. At best they waste time that could be devoted to study of sacred texts.) The virtuous life is one lived in accordance with Jewish law and devoted, as far as possible, to study of sacred texts. This is the ultimate life of meaning. It is not only a religious obligation but becomes, in time, the fulfillment of one's self and the realization of one's purpose. Hence, the Orthodox Jew is truly blessed and rewarded. Whatever else he may think of the non-Orthodox Jew, the neotraditionalist also pities him.

Modernity has led the more extreme and consistent of the neotraditionalists to create structures and institutions to prevent its penetration. This often requires the duplication or imitation of technically advanced instrumentalities which are shorn of their overt antireligious effects (Friedman, 1975). (For example, buses transporting neotraditionalists to work in which seating is segregated by sex and sexually offensive advertisements are eliminated.) The effort to harness modern science to religious needs, both politically (Mintz, 1979) and technologically, may seem naive to contemporary social scientists who argue that political mobilization and technological advances bear the seeds of modern consciousness. Nevertheless, Jewish neotraditionalism has shown a remarkable vitality. This vitality is reflected, in part, in the differences among neotraditionalists themselves. Despite all that unites them and the gulf that separates them from the remainder of the Jewish world, there are sharp differences in outlook and perception, not to mention politics and behavior, among neotraditionalists. The other side of the same coin is the built-in instability in the neotraditional response. Unable to insulate themselves entirely from the modern world (Schneller, 1980), the temptations to concession always exist. These, in turn, evoke a posture of greater rigidity on the part of other elements and lead to continual tensions, threats of schism, and sectarianism.

Adaptationism

A second Orthodox response, at the opposite pole from neotraditionalism, is most appropriately labeled adaptationism. The adaptationist response to modernity is to affirm that the basic values of the modern world are not only compatible with Judaism but partake of its essence. Freedom, individual autonomy, equality of man, rationalism, science, rule of law, etc. are all found to be inherent in the Jewish tradition. Secular study is affirmed as a positive religious value—an instrument whereby man might learn more of God's creation. Not least important, adaptationism includes an effort to reinterpret the tradition including those aspects of the law which seem to stand in opposition to modern values.

Adaptationism characterizes some early leaders associated with what is today known as Conservative Judaism (Davis, 1963; Siegel, 1978). Until recently, when more radical and self-conscious reinterpretations of Jewish law and conscious deviations from its norms have become pronounced, the label "adaptationism" suited leadership groups within the Conservative movement in particular. In fact, until the last few years, that which distinguished Orthodox adaptationists from some leadership groups within the Conservative movement was institutional, familial, and social ties no less than the degree of adaptation.

Orthodox adaptationists were ready to affirm the spirit and values of modernity but were far more cautious in the realm of religious behavior. Some, however, countenanced dancing, "mixed" swimming, married women uncovering their hair, and some degree of leniency in Sabbath observance law. There are Israeli religious authorities (Chief Rabbi Goren is an example) whose rulings tend to be adaptationist, without any ideological self-consciousness or philosophical underpinning. Emanuel Rackman, whose work is best known in the United States though he now resides in Israel, is the leading theoretical exponent of Orthodox adaptationism. He writes that:

> The only authentic Halakhic approach must be that which approximates the philosophy of the teleological jurist. The teleological jurist asks: what are the ends of the law which God or nature ordained and how can we be guided by these ideal ends in developing the law? (Rackman, 1961:14).

The results, Rackman says, must not only meet the challenge of revelation but of history and of Jewish life in the present. By way of example he notes that:

> If rabbis have no sympathy whatever with the demands of modern women for equal status in the Jewish law of marriage and divorce, they will find texts adequate to support their intransigence. If, however, they feel that the present situation is simply intolerable and an insult to God and God's law, they will be vociferous and militant in making use of the halakhic authorities and the texts available to propose revisions in the *halakhah*. They are no less "Orthodox" than their colleagues, and indeed, they may even be more halakhically "authentic" (Rackman, 1976:143).

There are limits to the extent to which adaptationists can affirm every aspect of modernity; they do not adapt Judaism to everything that is in current vogue; nor is everything which is in current vogue a necessary concomitant of modernity. There is an apologetic as well as an adaptive side to Orthodox reform. As in other religions (Smith, 1970:3) family law and relations between the sexes evoke the most conservative sentiments. (Though, even here, adaptationists are far more accommodating than neotraditionalists.) Nor is there any record of those associated with an adaptationist response directly confronting the problem of modern consciousness, the choices and alternatives which break down the taken-for-grantedness of Jewish identity. Instead, there is an implicit assumption that, given a really free choice, intelligent, well-meaning, and honest Jews will choose a Jewish-Orthodox identity. But, in fact, the Orthodox adaptationists have acquiesced in and even promoted an educational system structured to inculcate the values of Orthodoxy, paying lip service to the style of modernity.

Adaptationism's strength is also its weakness. It appeals to Jews who want to be or who are in fact "modern"; that is, Jews whose occupations, education, interests, and proclivities orient them toward the values of modernity. Adaptationism is, therefore, the most comfortable and convenient Orthodox response to modernity for many Jews, and this in itself raises problems about its religious authenticity. In addition, the adaptationists suffer from the classical dilemma of all liberal religion. The affirmation of modernity, the acceptance of its assumptions about the nature of reality, undermines religious faith and the belief in the efficacy of religious practice. Once religion legitimates the assumptions of modernity, it negates its own presuppositions. Of course, many modern Jews seek to retain their allegiance and identity with the Jewish people, Jewish customs, and Jewish tradition while living in the "modern" world. But, in such cases, adaptationism is not their only alternative. Non-Orthodox interpretations of Judaism which reinterpret Jewish law in more radical fashion or deny its binding authority or substitute Jewish culture or Jewish social concern or Zionism for religion are more palatable options than adaptationism.

On the other hand, the adaptationist response, other things being equal, appears compromising and lacking authenticity to many modern Orthodox Jews. We must remember that Orthodoxy defines proper Jewish life as adherence to Jewish law. Hence, the more precisely one adheres to such laws, the better Jew one becomes. While the adaptationists argue that their interpretation of Jewish law is no less valid than that of the strict constructionists, their case is weak. First of all, no recognized Talmudic authorities are identified with their approach. Hence adaptationists must not only engage in a fight over the interpretation of the Judaic tradition in which the logic of their position might or might not be persuasive but in an argument over the nature of rabbinic authority in which, as in any religious argument, the conservative side has a clear advantage. Second, it is difficult for them to escape the charge that their "reforms" are motivated by their attraction to the modern secular world rather than by their commitment to what is authentically Jewish. Third, the adaptationists are at a competitive disadvantage with other Orthodox interpretations. The former recognize the legitimacy of the latter's interpretation of Jewish law but demand legitimacy for their interpretation as well. In other words, they pose a pluralist model of interpretation. Other Orthodox leaders, on the other hand, deny the legitimacy of the adaptationists' conceptions. This provides them with a distinct psychological advantage.

In countries such as the United States where other religious interpretations of Judaism are found, the Orthodox adaptationists had to be self-conscious about distinguishing themselves from, for example, Conservative Judaism. As long as the adaptationists continued to identify institutionally with Orthodoxy, they had to look over their shoulders at what others were saying about them. But in Israel, particularly in the early years of statehood, when non-Orthodox religious interpretations of Judaism were almost unknown and the Orthodox establishment was weak and divided, there was room for a more radical development of adaptationism. Furthermore, the need for an adaptationist response was also more evident because the creation of a Jewish state raised questions without precedent in the tradition. A few, led by Israel's first minister of religion, Judah Leib Maimon (1875–1962), favored a reconstituted Sanhedrin, a tribunal of legal authorities which was the ultimate legislative authority for Jewish law in the period of the Second Temple. A Sanhedrin would presumably have the authority to legitimate the kind of change in Jewish law which many Orthodox Jews felt was necessary to adapt that law to the needs of a modern political society. Yet Maimon, despite his personal influence and the power of his office, never attracted enough support for his proposal to permit its implementation. The most radical proposal of reform in Jewish law, offered by Yeshayahu Leibowitz, would transfer the right to legitimate change from rabbinic authorities to the community of Jews committed to Jewish law, a community

> acting in accordance with its understanding of Torah and with the honest intent to preserve it. In other words, the changes are made from the need and necessity to maintain the Torah and not for the convenience of people or the gratification of their personal desires (Leibowitz, 1975:53).

Leibowitz, for example, suggested the need to reform the laws of Sabbath observance to permit work by those engaged in providing services which any state must provide. Such work, he argued, would be the fulfillment of a religious obligation. He criticized those who believed they could extend religious law to include the whole of Israeli society without acknowledging that this required the introduction of changes in the law itself. Leibowitz's proposals evoked little positive response within Israeli Orthodoxy.

The founders of the religious kibbutzim (collective settlements) were also adaptationists in their orientation (Fishman, 1975:184–248). Indeed, they called the ideology of religious labor Zionism "the holy revolt." But in the final analysis they shied away from the boldest step—seeking to legitimate their interpretation of Judaism in the absence of rabbinical authority. A number of explanations have been offered for their reticence. Not least important, I suspect, was their fear that once one questions the authority of recognized religious leaders it is easy to fall into an atmosphere of laxity and permissiveness out of indifference and laziness rather than principle. In order for adaptationism to survive as an authentic religious response, in order that it not degenerate into an excuse for religious laxity, it requires an enormous degree of religious enthusiasm and self-discipline because, by definition, it lacks the fixed and rigid framework of religious authority. But religious enthusiasts tend to be attracted to more rigorous and demanding forms of religious expression than that which adaptationism cultivates.

Nevertheless, adaptationism, for all its signs of weakness in the United States (Liebman, 1979) remains an attractive option for many Jews. Some of the largest Orthodox synagogues and some of the most prominent Orthodox rabbis are best characterized by an adaptationist approach, though they might be reluctant to admit it. In Israel, where the self-conscious adaptationist approach has also been declining in recent years (Liebman, 1982), a group of Orthodox intellectuals, joined by members of religious kibbutzim have organized a group called Neemaney Torah V'avodah (Faithful to Torah and Labor—"Torah and Labor" was the slogan of the religious labor Zionist movement) to counter the tendency away from adaptationism and toward what they call religious extremism.

Compartmentalization

A third response is labeled compartmentalization. Traditional Judaism constituted a total way of life. Whereas it recognized distinctions between sacred and secular, holy and profane, it aspired to encompass under the rubric of its norms all activity in which a Jew engaged. Nothing is foreign, irrelevant, or immaterial to Judaism. No Orthodox leader has ever argued that it is legitimate to distinguish between aspects of life or conduct which are Jewishly relevant and aspects of life which have nothing to do with Judaism. No Orthodox leader, in other words, favored compartmentalizing life, thereby neutralizing, from a Jewish point of view, certain aspects of conduct. Compartmentalization, however, was the response of many Western European Jews to modernization and was associated, however improperly, with the slogan *Torah im derekh eretz,* which was interpreted to mean "Torah and the ways of the world," and with the intellectual and organizational efforts of Samson Raphael Hirsch (1808–88) (Breuer, 1953). Hirsch and his followers constructed a community in Germany in the late nineteenth century generally referred to as neo-Orthodoxy (Schwab, 1950). As Ismar Schorsch (1972:10) observes:

> While the Old Orthodoxy attempted to salvage as much of judicial au-
> tonomy and separatism of the medieval Jewish community as was pos-
> sible under an unwelcome emancipation, the Neo-Orthodoxy ad-
> vanced by Samson Raphael Hirsch enthusiastically embraced the
> multiple opportunities it would provide. Like the spokesmen for re-
> form, Hirsch dropped all demands for judicial autonomy and con-
> tinuance of Jewish civil law. He insisted upon the wholly religious
> character of Judaism, reduced the significance of the periods of Jewish
> national independence, and divested the messianic concept of political
> overtones. . . . Hirsch too emphasized the ethical content and univer-
> sal mission of Judaism.

Having surrendered large areas of life heretofore defined as Jewishly relevant, the neo-Orthodox sought vigorously to defend, unchanged, those areas of life which they retained under Jewish norms. In so doing they drew sharp ideological and institutional lines between themselves and the non-Orthodox who would abrogate the law. On the other hand, unlike the neo-traditionalists, the compartmentalizers saw no need to reduce their interchange with the general non-Jewish culture. Rather, it was modern society's definition of religion which neo-Orthodoxy accepted as normative. Areas which remained under the dictates of halakhah were those which nineteenth-century German society viewed as falling within the prerogatives of religion. Superficially, at least, there was no basic incompatibility between contemporary culture and religion, no points of conflict, but a division of areas of authority and responsibility.[6]

Elsewhere, I argued that compartmentalization is also the unself-conscious strategy adopted by most American Orthodox Jews (Liebman, 1979). This is true in Israel as well. The behavior of most Orthodox Jews is characterized by de facto compartmentalization—multiple identities through which they relate to different aspects of life. Compartmentaliza-tion is especially suited to the Diaspora, where the dominant culture model encourages the distinction between one's religious identity and one's orientation to economic, political, and even many social and cul-tural aspects of life. In Israel it is a more difficult model to legitimate since it seems puerile to define the culture, society, and political institutions of a

Jewish state as matters of Jewish irrelevance.

Despite all its ideological and theoretical limitations, compartmentalization offers an attractive model for responding positively to many aspects of modernity while retaining ostensible commitment to the Jewish
tradition. It is not surprising that many Orthodox Jews continue to legitimate this approach by attributing it, however incorrectly, to one of the
great leaders of Western Orthodoxy. Nor does compartmentalization
evoke the kinds of psychological difficulties one might anticipate. Daniel
Breslauer (1978:32), following Robert Wuthnow, notes that since modern
man divides his world into social realities and inner realities he may
accept a social consciousness which "sees the world as a series of pressures and stimuli which condition human actions" and he "may also
reserve a space of reality free of such determinism."

Expansionism

The final Orthodox response to modernity is most appropriately
labeled expansionism. Compartmentalization is an Orthodox folk response without ideological legitimation. Expansionism, as I understand it,
has an elaborate legitimation and many enthusiastic adherents in theory
but none in practice. This also merits attention.

Expansionism affirms modernity by reinterpreting it through the prism
of the Jewish tradition. Like adaptationism and unlike compartmentalization, the expansionist response is monistic. It aspires, in theory, to bring
all aspects of life under the rubric of its interpretation of Judaism. It is
necessarily associated with Jewish nationalism since a necessary condition to its realization is control of all aspects of political and social life.

There are a number of theoretical expositions of expansionism but the
formulation of greatest contemporary significance is that of Rav Kook
(Rabbi Abraham Isaac Hacohen Kook, 1865–1935) (Yaron, 1974; Bergman, 1963:121–41), first chief rabbi of the modern settlement in Palestine. Whether Rav Kook comprehended modernity and modern consciousness in its entirety is a moot point. One of the foremost contemporary Jewish thinkers, Eliezer Schweid, argues that Rav Kook never really
understood the idealistic secular Zionist settlers for whom he had so much
sympathy and whom he was so anxious to influence (Schweid, 1980). Rav
Kook's writing is a blend of legalism, metaphysics, and poetry. Much of it
is difficult to understand, parts almost defy comprehension. But those
who have studied his work attest to the affinity between his thought and
many attitudes which characterize modern consciousness. Aviezer
Ravitsky, in a paper delivered in Jerusalem in February 1981 on "Rav
Kook and the Modern Condition," demonstrates this by citing a number
of different statements scattered through Rav Kook's work—for example,

the emphasis that man must be attentive to his inner feeling which, Rav Kook says, is often the voice of God or insistence on the importance of love of self. Rav Kook saw the purpose of Judaism as the sanctification of all of life. The characteristic features of expansionism which supported such a world view and made its realization feasible, in addition to its commitment to Jewish nationalism, were a redefinition of secular-religious distinctions and a belief that divine redemption was immanent.

Expansionism is necessarily nationalistic since Jews must live a natural life in all its physical manifestations in order to invest all of life with the divine spirit. But, after all, the early Zionists were overwhelmingly secularist, often antireligious. Rav Kook answered this objection by redefining secularism. He not only blurred distinctions between the holy and the profane but between ostensibly religious and ostensibly secular Jews. This view broke through the traditional Orthodox perception of religious Jews as a beleaguered minority surrounded by hostile Jewish secularists with whom they might at best, and even at their peril, cooperate at an instrumental level.

Whereas most religious thinkers accepted secularism as a fact of life, however unpleasant, Rav Kook defined secularism as a superficial manifestation lacking inner content, meaning, and a firm foundation in existence. But, like every aspect of reality, it contains sparks of holiness which stem from a divine source and are hidden throughout all creation. Everyone is obliged to attempt to uncover the sparks of light and holiness concealed behind the manifestations of secularism and to expand the influence of holiness to all areas of life.

All human beings are partners in this effort but the primary responsibility rests upon the Jewish nation since the expression of holiness and good stems from and is influenced by the unique qualities of *knesset yisrael,* the hypostasis of Jewish spirituality which is particularly attached to and associated with the divinity. In accordance with Rav Kook's philosophy of "all-encompassing unity," everything that is good and positive from a moral or aesthetic point of view stems from Judaism and Torah, even when no association is apparent.

As a consequence, religious Jews dare not segregate themselves from modernity and contemporary society; nor are any manifestations religiously neutral, as the compartmentalizers believe. On the contrary, it is important to identify the positive aspects of modernity and secularism by revealing the associations between these elements and their sacred sources.

Rav Kook saw manifestations of holiness in sports which strengthen the body, in physical labor, in education, in science and languages, and in the fields of culture, art, aesthetics, and manners (Kook, 1950:67–69, 77, 78, 80). But he attached greatest significance to the nation. The individual is perfected only by his total incorporation into the life of the nation. On the other hand, complete national life is not possible unless the nation possesses its own territory and establishes a system of social and political institutions which will provide full expression to the national spirit.

The renewal of independent statehood, he believed, would permit the sanctification of all aspects of life by directing them in accordance with the Torah. According to Rav Kook, many of the commandments of the Torah are intended to sanctify life within an independent statist framework, and their fulfillment is only possible within that context; hence the value and sanctity of a Jewish state which will represent the spirit of Judaism. Writing prior to the creation of Israel, he said:

> That the state is not the greatest happiness for man can be said about a normal state whose merit does not exceed that of a society of mutual responsibility.... But this is not true of a state upon whose existence the noblest ideas are inscribed.... Such a state is truly the greatest happiness and such a state is our state of Israel... whose only wish is that God shall be one and His name one which is truly the greatest happiness (Kook, 1950:160).

Expansionism is a philosophy of religious optimism and confidence. Its assumptions about the benign nature of secularists and secularism and the capacity of authentic Judaism to overcome all opposition by the inner force of its truth and its light do not stand up to the test of contemporary Jewish experience. Rav Kook's basic conceptions were formulated before World War I and he never knew the Holocaust or the decline of the idealistic socialist-humanist tradition in modern Israel. No less important, expansionism requires an openness to nonreligious ways of life and thought which is contrary to the structure of Orthodox life. The great achievement of Orthodox Jewry in this generation has been its establishment of child-rearing networks (schools, peer groups, extended-family associations and neighborhoods) which have socialized its own youth to its norms and values. This has been achieved through segregation of Orthodox from non-Orthodox and from filtering out modern values. Rav Kook's expansionism, sociologically speaking, runs contrary to Orthodoxy's prescription for its own survival. Nevertheless, Rav Kook, as a role model and as a prophetic thinker, occupies a central place in the pantheon of Orthodoxy's modern religious figures. The apparent paradox is not difficult to understand. Rav Kook and his philosophy symbolize the belief that strict Orthodoxy and modernity, properly understood, are not incompatible. On the contrary, modernity, properly understood, is really one aspect of authentic Judaism. Second, Orthodox and secular Jews can and ought to live as one community. It is important for many Orthodox Jews to retain these beliefs. This, in itself, is a powerful testimony to the continuing force of modernity.

In its most recent evolution, the major movement of Rav Kook's followers center around his son Rav Zvi Yehudah Kook. Politically, the son's followers are among the most extreme nationalists. They insist on Israel's right (religious obligation) to retain and settle all the lands captured in the June 1967 Six Day War. In the realm of religious ceremonial and ritual the followers of Rav Zvi Yehudah Kook are hardly distinguishable from the neotraditionalists.

Expansionists never developed a school curriculum consistent with their ideology, a curriculum which taught secular studies in the light of the Jewish spirit. Rav Kook's own efforts in this direction failed (Yaron, 1974:199–202). As expansionism has elaborated itself, institutionally and politically, it has become far less sympathetic to modern values. The followers of Rav Kook opposed the introduction of secular studies into schools which they founded (Bar-Lev, 1977:121–22). When parents who wanted their children to receive a high school degree forced the adoption of secular studies, the expansionists acquiesced but resisted their integration into the religious study program and continued to oppose the introduction of humanist study (Bar-Lev, 1977:155–156). Neotraditional modes and categories of behavior have exercised an important influence on expansionism. On the other hand, the expansionists have retained certain basic values of modernity which distinguish them from the neotraditionalists. They do not prohibit reading of newspapers, viewing television, or attending concerts, theater, etc., although there are efforts to channel leisure time to sacred study. In other words, they are far less prone than the neotraditionalists to insulate themselves from cultural and social influences of modern society, despite increasing signs of impatience with Western civilization. Their attitude toward the non-Jewish and non-Israeli world has become increasingly disdainful. Details of proper dress have become increasingly important and appropriate relations between the sexes less and less a matter of subjective feeling and more and more codified in halakhic standards of conduct. But women are assigned important roles in political activity, are encouraged to study sacred texts, and, as far as one can tell, are treated as social equals. Finally, and most important, the expansionists continue to cooperate with nonreligiously observant Jews willing to join with them in their nationalist efforts. While it is true that this cooperation is purely tactical for some, it is a matter of principle for others. These expansionists refuse to recognize the conception of secular nationalism, arguing that Jewish nationalists are by definition fulfilling the most important religious commandments and hence are more suitable partners than the antinationalist neotraditionalists.

Given the fact that more moderate, permissive, humanistic variants of Orthodoxy have developed among other followers of Rav Kook, one cannot argue that expansionism inevitably leads in one direction or another. But, it is not, I think, surprising that the son's understanding of expansionism is dominant. Given the assumption that not only does Judaism encompass all aspects of life but is instructed to engage itself with all aspects of the world, the reality of the engagement dictates either some compromise with the secular world (adaptationism) or a struggle. The struggle itself is so futile that it invites redefinitions of reality, through mystical formulations, faith in imminent supernatural redemption on the one hand and socialization to the values of struggle on the other. In the process of socialization, in the struggle for its goals, Rav Kook's conception of Orthodoxy has probably become institutionalized in forms he would have hardly recognized. This makes his followers no less dedicated or sincere in their commitments or their conviction that they are indeed his true disciples. It does suggest that there is a dynamic to the expansionist response which makes it difficult to predict its future direction.

Summary

To the outsider, Orthodox Judaism appears monolithic. Orthodox leaders themselves occasionally project such an image. The image does not even suit neotraditionalism, the most reactionary and authoritarian of Orthodoxy's four responses to modernity. Obviously there is a great deal that unites Orthodox Jews. In the area of ritual ceremonial and faith it is quite true that all Orthodox Jews have more in common with one another than with non-Orthodox Jews. But most Jews, even in Israel, do not live their lives solely in the framework of ritual, ceremonial, and faith, and it is in this respect that differences among Orthodox Jews become very pronounced.

The second striking feature of Orthodoxy characterizes all living religion. If it is to live, and this is surely one of its mandates, it must respond to its environment. As it responds, it evolves and changes even when it legitimates change by denying its reality. Third, the development of Orthodoxy suggests that the nature of the response is only determined in part by the environment and the structure of the religion. Subjective forces, individual proclivities, and even chance all play their part.

Notes

1. The central ideas of this essay were initially developed in Liebman (1982), and parts of that paper are reproduced here in revised form.

2. There is an artificiality in use of the term "Jewish tradition" or "traditionalism," with its implication of a uniform way of life, socioreligious structure, and mode of confronting problems. Jews differed greatly over time and place. The term "tradition" is also a mental construct for dealing with that which preceded the modern period. But, when viewed from a contemporary perspective, and only from that perspective, despite the simplifications and generalizations involved in the term and despite the many exceptions which a more careful analysis would have to indicate, the use of the term is not without justification.

3. For an excellent illustration of the development and adaptation of the tradition see Katz (1961).

4. The *hassidim* are religiously observant Jews who are subdivided into a number of groups according to their adherence to one *rebbe* or another to whom they attribute charismatic qualities.

5. For some essays by and studies of neotraditional groups of different types see: Friedman (1975, 1977); Shaffir (1974); Schneller (1980); Marmorstein (1969); Rosenheim (1968); and Wasserman (1942).

6. On the educational program of the neo-Orthodox and the implications of compartmentalization, see Breuer (1979).

References

Apter, David. 1965. *The Politics of Modernization*. Chicago: University of Chicago Press.

Bar-Lev, Mordechai. 1977. "The Graduates of the Yeshiva High School in Eretz-Yisrael between Tradition and Innovation" (Hebrew). Ramat-Gan: Ph.D. Thesis, Bar-Ilan University.

Baron, Salo W. 1957. *A Social and Religious History of the Jews*. Vol. 5, *High Middle Ages: Religious Controls and Dissensions*. New York: Columbia University Press.

Berger, Peter. 1979. *The Heretical Imperative*. Garden City, N.Y.: Anchor Press.

Bergman, Samuel Hugo. 1963. *Faith and Reason: An Introduction to Modern Jewish Thought*. New York: Schocken, paperback.

Breslauer, S. Daniel. 1978. *The Ecumenical Perspective and the Modernization of Jewish Religion*. Brown Judaica Studies. Missoula, Mont.: Scholars Press.

Breuer, Isaac. 1953. "Samson Raphael Hirsch." In Leo Jung, ed., *Jewish Leaders*. New York: Bloch Publishing Co.: 163–77.

Breuer, Mordechai. 1979. "Ideal and Reality in Orthodox Education in 19th Century Germany" (Hebrew). Annual of Bar-Ilan University, vols. 16–17. Ramat-Gan: Bar-Ilan University.

Davis, Moshe. 1963. *The Emergence of Conservative Judaism*. Philadelphia: The Jewish Publication Society.

Fishman, Aryei. 1975. "The Religious Kibbutz" (Hebrew). Jerusalem: Ph.D. diss., Hebrew University.

Friedman, Menachem. 1975. "Religious Zealotry in Israeli Society. On Ethnic and Religious Diversity in Israel." Ramat-Gan: Bar-Ilan University, 91–112.

———. 1977. "Society and Religion: The Non-Zionist Orthodox in Eretz Israel, 1918–1936" (Hebrew). Jerusalem: Yad Izhak Ben-Zvi.

Katz, Jacob. 1961. *Exclusiveness and Tolerance: Studies in Jewish-Gentile Relations in Medieval and Modern Times*. New York: Oxford University Press.

———. 1973. *Out of the Ghetto: The Social Background of Jewish Emancipation, 1770–1870*. Cambridge, Mass.: Harvard University Press.

———. 1967. "Contributions towards a Biography of R. Moses Sofer" (Hebrew). In E. E. Urbach et al., eds., *Studies in Mysticism and Religion Presented to Gershom G. Scholem on His Seventieth Birthday*. Jerusalem: Magnes Press: 115–48.

Kook, Avraham Isaac. 1950. *Orot* (Hebrew). Jerusalem: Mossad Harav Kook.

Leibowitz, Yeshayahu. 1975. *Judaism, Jewish People and the State of Israel* (Hebrew). Jerusalem: Schocken.

Liebman, Charles. 1973. "American Jewry: Identity and Affiliation." In David Sidorsky, ed., *The Future of the Jewish Community in America*. New York: Basic Books: 127–52.

———. 1979. "Orthodox Judaism Today." *Midstream* 25 (August–September): 19–26.

———. 1982. "The Growth of Neo-Traditionalism among Orthodox Jews in Israel"

(Hebrew). *Megamot* 27 (May 1982):233–50.

Marmorstein, Emile. 1969. *Heaven at Bay*. London: Oxford University Press.

Mintz, Jerome R. 1979. "Ethnic Activism: The Hassidic Example." *Judaism* 28 (Fall): 449–64.

Nemoy, Leon, ed. 1952. *Karaite Anthology*. New Haven: Yale University Press.

Rackman, Emanuel. 1961. "Sabbaths and Festivals in the Modern Age." *Studies in Torah Judaism*. New York: Yeshiva University.

———. 1976. "Halakhah: Orthodox Approaches." *Encyclopaedia Britannica, 1976 Yearbook*.

Rosenheim, Yaakov. 1968. *Yaakov Rosenheim Memorial Anthology: A Concise History of Agudath Israel*. New York: Orthodox Library.

Schorsch, Ismar. 1972. *Jewish Reactions to German Anti-Semitism, 1870–1914*. New York: Columbia University Press.

Schneller, Raphael. 1980. "Continuity and Change in Ultra-Orthodox Education." *Jewish Journal of Sociology* 22 (June): 35–46.

Schwab, Hermann. 1950. *The History of Orthodox Jewry in Germany*. London: The Mitre Press.

Schweid, Eliezer. 1980. "Two Neo-Orthodox Responses to Modernity: Rabbi Samson Raphael Hirsch and Rabbi Abraham Isaac Hacohen Kook" (Hebrew). Paper presented to the Summer Seminar of the Kotlar Institute for Judaism and Contemporary Thought. Kibbutz Lavi.

Shaffir, William. 1974. *Life in a Religious Community: The Lubavitcher Chassidim in Montreal*. Toronto: Holt, Rinehart, Winston.

Siegel, Seymour, ed. 1978. *Conservative Judaism and Jewish Law*. New York: Ktav.

Smith, Donald E. 1970. *Religion and Political Development*. Boston: Little, Brown.

Wasserman, Elhanan. 1942. "The Footsteps of the Messiah" (Hebrew). Bnei Brak: Histadrut Z'erei Agudat Israel.

Yaron, Zvi. 1974. *The Philosophy of Rabbi Kook* (Hebrew). Jerusalem: The Department of Torah Education and Culture in the Diaspora of the World Zionist Organization.

Eight

Religion and History

Power, History, and the Covenant at Sinai

Richard L. Rubenstein

How shall we understand Judaism, with its God of history, as a system of interpreting history? History itself can be understood as the record of the ways in which men have employed power that have been deemed worthy of memory. Every reflection on history is therefore a consideration of the nature and the use of power. Nor is the understanding of power irrelevant to the understanding of religion, especially a religion of history, for one of the most important questions in both religion and politics is this: what is the ultimate source of power and how are men and women to relate to that power? Power itself has been defined as "the possibility within a social relationship of imposing one's will, even against opposition."[1] In view of the fact that the state can be understood to be a "human community that successfully claims the monopoly of the legitimate use of force within a given territory," the ultimate source of power must be either the state, which is the human agency with the greatest power, or a suprahuman agency. The suprahuman agency, if such there be, would have to be a god.[2]

The idea that there could be a power greater than and unrelated to that of the state would be most likely to arise in the aftermath of a natural or social catastrophe, in which the state's claim to ultimacy proved dysfunctional to a substantial number of its subjects. In recent times, the failure of the secular government of the Shah in Iran to cope with the social dislocations of rapid modernization and sudden affluence led to the theocratic regime of the Ayatollah Khomeini. In the Near East, the inability of the rulers of the Canaanite city-states to cope with the economic and social needs of their subjects had the effect of facilitating the entry of the Israelites into Canaan and the adhesion of large numbers of the indigenous population to the new community.[3] The religious transformation initiated by ancient Israel was the first in which a human community was organized on the basis of the idea that the ultimate source of power in human affairs is an absolutely unique Divine Being whose potency is greater than and distinct from that of any of the gods of the nations as well as of any divine-human ruler. Once initiated, that idea has had an enduring, vexing, and problematic history. It has continued to be a source of hope, liberation, and vexation down to our own day.

It is, however, important to remember that the religio-political system opposed by ancient Israel has not lacked intelligent and informed defenders to the present day. I refer to the institution of divine kingship. That institution probably has been the most effective means of governing without the use of overt force known to mankind. Perhaps the oldest method of exercising power over human beings involved the threat of force. However, naked fear is an unstable incentive. A state that governs solely by the threat of force must always guard against the possibility of revolt. Moreover, the resources necessary to govern a hostile population are far greater than for a loyal population. Such loyalty is likely to be strongest when members of the community are convinced that the ruler's authority has divine sanction or, better still, when the ruler is regarded as being the living incarnation of a divine being. At its best, divine kingship can assure members of the political community that, whether they be of high or low estate, they can have a secure place in the order of things. The system can offer them the further assurance that the governed can normally expect equitable treatment from their rulers, although, as we shall see, that is not always the case. That assurance was implicit in the Egyptian belief that Pharaoh ruled by *maat* or divinely certified justice.

Nevertheless, the institution of divine kingship has also been a source of misery and even degradation for large numbers of the men and women who have been bound to it. This was certainly the case in the ancient Near East. At the time of Israel's entry into Canaan, the sacralized city-kingdoms of the land were largely governed by foreigners or their descendants who had imposed their dominion on the indigenous population by means of the superiority of their weaponry.[4] One of the king's most important social functions was to serve as the authority responsible for the redistribution of the total wealth of the community. The agricultural surplus of the countryside provided the food for the city. The labor of the agrarian villagers, often exacted with little or no concern for their well-being, was forcibly placed at the disposal of the king and his retainers. Redistribution was frequently little more than naked exploitation exacerbated by the fact that it was practiced by arrogant and alien rulers.[5] The abuses to which the institution of monarchy was prone in the ancient Near East are often depicted in Scripture. In one well-known passage, the prophet Samuel is depicted as warning the people against asking for a king:

> This is the sort of king who will govern you. . . . He will take your sons and make them serve in his chariots and with his cavalry, and will make them run before his chariot. . . . Some . . . will plough his fields and reap his harvest; others again will make weapons of war and equipment for mounted troops. He will take your daughters for perfumers, cooks, and confectioners, and will seize the best of your cornfields, vineyards, and olive-yards, and give them to his lackeys. He will take a tenth of your grain and your vintage to give to his eunuchs and lackeys. Your slaves, both men and women, and the best of your cattle and your asses he will seize and put to his own use. He will take a tenth of your flocks and you yourselves will become slaves. (1 Sam. 8:11–17).

Clearly, the claims of the individual, even when just and reasonable, were subordinated to those of the state in the sacred kingdoms of the ancient Near East.

The fundamental political purpose of the institution of sacral kingship is to legitimate the unconditional character of the state's right to govern every sphere of human activity. Theoretically, in a sacralized kingship there can be neither private property nor what is today called "human rights." Strictly speaking, in such a system the ruler can do no wrong. As a divine being or, at least, a divinely sanctioned being, all of his actions are self-legitimating. Whatever privileges the ruler or his agents bestow on the governed derive solely from his cosmically grounded authority.

Obviously, sacral kingdoms are not the only states whose rulers regard their actions as self-legitimating. It can be argued that any form of sovereignty that recognizes no transcendent divine authority is self-legitimating. Moreover, there are undoubtedly many rulers who pay lip-service to the idea of a transcendent divine authority, or even to the "will of the people," but who nevertheless regard sovereignty as self-legitimating. Unfortunately, whether the state be sacral or secular, when it is regarded as the ultimate authority, those men and women who, for any reason, find themselves stateless cease to be human beings in some crucial ways. At the very least, such persons enjoy the protection of no institution that can give them any assurance that they will be treated as human beings. When Aristotle argued that "outside of the polis man is either a beast or an angel," he reflected a common conception that the limits of humanity were coterminous with the limits of one's group.[6]

The Nazi extermination of the Jews is but a contemporary example of one of mankind's most enduring codes of behavior. Knowing that the Jews of Europe belonged to no human community capable of assuring them of any security whatsoever, the Nazis saw no reason to limit the destructiveness they inflicted upon the Jews as well as upon all those whom they regarded as unassimilable to their community and, hence, as they clearly stated, devoid of human status.[7] Nor have the Nazis been alone in their belief in the self-legitimating authority of the state and the total denial of human treatment to those who were perceived to be unassimilable to the body politic. The age-old strategies of enslavement, expulsion, and extermination of the unassimilable stranger have been widely practiced throughout the modern world.

In some important respects there is a similarity between modern doctrines of race as the basis for political unity and the ancient doctrine of the divinity of the king. Both doctrines seek to establish the basis of political and social community in a metaphor of biological kinship. Racism proclaims the unity of common biological origin; the doctrine of divine kingship treats society as an extended family under the leadership of a divine-human parent-figure. However, racism's myth of common origin is often implicit in sacral kingship's view of society.

As we have noted, such societies can work well over long periods of time. Such a system works best where, as in Japan, the emperor is neither a conquering foreigner nor the descendant of conquering foreigners but the leading member of the first family. We have also noted that such societies can work intolerable hardships on outsiders and those at the bottom of the social hierarchy. When conditions become intolerable in any society, the victims may finally be tempted to change their situation through force. Such revolts usually fail. However, Scripture does preserve the memory of a revolt against a sacred kingdom that not only succeeded but became the basis of a decisive transformation in the religious and political life of humanity. I refer, of course, to the Exodus from Egypt.

As is well known, the Egyptian state depended upon a system of corvée labor for many of its most important projects such as the building of the pyramids and temples. As a living god, Pharaoh was regarded as the sole proprietor of all goods and services within the nation. In redistributing the nation's wealth, Pharaoh's agents were thought of as redistributing that which in any event belonged to him. One Egyptian tomb inscription reads: "What is the king of Upper and Lower Egypt? He is a god by whose dealings one lives, the father and mother of all men, alone by himself without equal."[8] As Henri Frankfort has observed, the Egyptians were without any concept of personal freedom. Nevertheless, they did not regard any service they rendered to Pharaoh, whether in the form of goods or labor, as a form of slavery.[9] However, this was not true of those non-Egyptians who had been condemned to corvée labor because they were prisoners of war, hostages, or had experienced a radical degradation in status, such as occurred to the "Hebrews" after the Semitic Hyksos domination of Egypt had been overthrown in the thirteenth century C. E.[10] We have terse evidence of this degradation of status in Scripture: "And there arose a new King who knew not Joseph" (Ex. 1:11). Scripture also records that the Egyptian state dealt with the degraded persons in a manner that has been perennially characteristic of sacred or totalitarian societies when confronted with unwanted persons or groups. They were either enslaved or exterminated. The "Hebrews" were condemned to slavery, and, when their numbers increased beyond the labor requirements of the slavemasters, all male Hebrew infants were ordered put to death at birth (Ex. 1:16). Apparently, extermination was a method of eliminating a surplus population in ancient as well as modern times.

As the story is told in Scripture, it would appear at first glance that the "Hebrews" enslaved by the Egyptians shared a common religious and ethnic background. This is, of course, the way they are normally regarded within the Judeo-Christian tradition. In reality, Scripture offers hints that the group that escaped with Moses did not share a common inheritance. Referring to the band of Moses' followers in the wilderness, Scripture tells us: "Now there was a mixed company of strangers who had joined the Israelites" (Num. 11:4). For several centuries before the Exodus, people from Palestine and Syria had entered Egypt, some as prisoners of war, some who were forced to take up residence by the Egyptians after engaging in activities hostile to Egypt in their home communities, others who were merchants. Not all were slaves, but the situation of all resident aliens tended to deteriorate as time went on. It is thought today that each group within the resident aliens retained something of their own identity, particularly insofar as their religious traditions involved some elements of ancestor worship.[11] As we know, Scripture identifies the resident aliens as "Hebrews," but that name probably designated a number of peoples who shared a common condition and social location in Egypt but were of diverse origins.[12] In some respects, the situation of the "Hebrews" was like that of members of a modern multi-ethnic metropolis, in which diverse groups share common problems in the present but remain distinct from each other because of differences in origin, religion, and culture.

When the time came for the escape from Egypt, the "Hebrews" shared a common yearning for liberation and a common hatred of their overlords, but little else. This was enough to unify them so that they could escape. However, as soon as they were beyond the immediate reach of the Egyptians, a compelling basis for unity beyond shared hatred and a desire to escape had to be found, if the band of fugitives and outcasts was to survive the natural and human hazards of the wilderness. Fortunately, the escape provided a further shared experience, the Exodus itself.

An important function of any new religion that originates in a radical break with past tradition is to facilitate the founding of a community for those who share no community.[13] There could be only one basis for communal unity in the ancient Near East where the distinction between group membership and religious identity was unknown. The diverse peoples could only become a single people if they were united by a common God. Moreover, the God had to be a new God whose power was greater than that of the Egyptian God-king. It would have been difficult for any of the peoples among the escapees to assert that its particular ancestral god ought to be the God of the entire band without arousing the mistrust and hostility of the others. *The "Hebrews" shared a common historical experience rather than kinship.* Ancestral gods were an impediment to unity. Only a God who was the author of their shared experience could have unified them. Of course, *after* the new God had unified them, it was natural for the assorted peoples to read back elements of continuity between the new God and their ancestral gods. That process is visible in Scripture.[14]

We know that under Moses the new God and the new unity were found. It also appears that within a relatively short time, the united escapees experienced an extraordinary increase in numbers and energy and that the enlarged group was able to gain control of much of the territory of Palestine and Jordan. The details of the conquest are unimportant for our purposes. What is important is that we understand something of the nature of the new God and his utterly novel relationship to his people.

From the very beginning the followers of this God were convinced that he shared his power with no other being, human or divine. All human power was thought to be subordinate and accountable to his power. Moreover, the new God was thought to exercise his power in a manner that was both rational and ethical. It was rational in that there was nothing gratuitous, arbitrary, or purposeless in its exercise; it was ethical in the sense that it was fundamentally concerned with the well-being of persons rather than with the maintenance of political, social, or even religious institutions. His power was also thought to be ethical and rational in the sense that he gave his followers the assurance that there was a predictable and dependable relationship between their conduct and the way he exercised his power over them.

The structure by means of which the new God offered the followers of Moses a secure relationship resembled a form of treaty that had been used in the ancient Near East in international relations, especially among the Hittites, in order to define the relationship between a suzerain and his vassals. It had, however, never been employed before by a God to define his relationship to a people whom he had adopted as his own. The treaty form was that of a *covenant*.[15] The character of the relationship between the new God and his people was *covenantal*. Unless this fundamental fact is understood, there can be no comprehension of the conception of God to which normative Judaism has been committed from its inception to the present day. Although one cannot speak of Judaism until long after the Exodus, one can with justice assert that the covenant at Sinai was decisive for the Jewish conception of God, the relationship between God and man, and the relationship between man and man.

Modern biblical scholarship has given us a fairly accurate picture of the origins of the covenant form.[16] There were two types of covenant, one between equals, which need not detain us, and the other, the suzerainty type, which was a pact imposed by a powerful lord upon a vassal, stipulating what the vassal must do to receive the lord's protection. These Hittite instruments were basically devices for securing binding agreements in international relations. The Hittite overlords were trying to cope with a problem that continues to plague nations to this day. While there are means of enforcing agreements, once made, within a nation, there is no effective, impartial institution capable of enforcing the keeping of promises between sovereign states if one of the parties should conclude that its interest is no longer served by keeping the pact. In such a case, the injured party has no choice but to accept the breach of faith or to resort to military force to enforce the pact. The purpose of the Hittite covenant was to give international agreements a binding character. This was done by the lord binding the vassal by an oath to meet the obligations stipulated in the agreement. An oath is a conditional self-curse, in which the person appeals to his own gods to punish him should he break the agreement. In the ancient Near East, oaths were initially effective in guaranteeing that a promise would be kept. As we know, they lost their effectiveness later on. We could also say that a covenant was a means of achieving unity of purpose between peoples that were bound to each other neither by ties of kinship nor by common ancestral gods. It was this aspect of the covenant that was to prove so important in its use in biblical religion.

According to George Mendenhall, perhaps the preeminant authority on the subject, the Hittite covenants had an elaborate form which was later used in the biblical covenant.[17] Among the elements that are of interest to us are the following: (a) a preamble identifying the king who was the author of the covenant; (b) a review by the king, speaking in the first person of the past benefits he had bestowed upon the vassal as well as an assertion that these benefits were the basis for the vassal's future obligation to the suzerain (both in the Hittite documents and the biblical covenant, historical events rather than the magical qualities of the lord were the basis of obligation; since history is the record of the ways in which men have used power that are considered worthy of memory, it was the lord's possession of and past use of power that constituted the basis of obligation); (c) a statement of the precise nature of the obligations incumbent upon the vassal. Moreover, in the Hittite treaties the vassal was explicitly excluded from entering into relationship with any other suzerain, just as in the biblical covenant Israel is excluded from having any God other than Yahweh.

An indispensable element of the Hittite past also found in the biblical covenant was the formula of blessings and curses.[18] While a breach of the Hittite covenant could lead to military action against the vassal, the only sanctions explicitly provided for were religious. The covenantal blessings and curses were thought to be the god's response to the vassal's behavior in either keeping or breaking his oath.

Another element of the Hittite pact that resembled the form of biblical covenant was the requirement that the text be deposited in the sanctuary of the vassal, as well as the provision for solemn ceremonies in which the pact was ratified, read in public, and periodically renewed.[19]

It is impossible fully to reconstruct the events surrounding the giving of the covenant at Sinai, but there is no reason to doubt that Moses had a revelatory experience at a sacred desert mountain and that that experience became the basis for the covenant between the new God and the escapees. It is also reasonable to assume that there must have been an enormous sense of wonder and triumph among the Hebrews after their escape. It was natural for them to believe that whoever was responsible for their revelation was a divinity greater than the god-king who sat on Egypt's throne. There may have been some temptation to regard Moses in that light, but Scripture insists that Moses made no such claim on his own behalf. Moses is always depicted as acting on behalf of and in obedience to a power greater than himself. Moses mediates between the new God and his people, but he always does so as a human being. Neither Moses nor any Hebrew experiences a direct, immediate, visible manifestation of the God who had been the author of their liberation.

The novelty of the encounter with the new God can also be expressed sociologically: Before Sinai there had been high gods, nature gods, ancestral gods, and gods of the polis, but there had never been a high God of escaped slaves and declassed fugitives. Moreover, by his election of the outcasts as his people, his "peculiar treasure," he had overturned all existing social hierarchies, in principle if not yet in fact. This was something utterly novel in human history and was to have revolutionary consequences. The Bible does not confirm social hierarchies. As we have noted, in the ancient world, and perhaps also in the modern, to be an outsider to all political structures can involve being deprived of all meaningful human status while possessing the full range of human capabilities and sensibilities. It is precisely such a band of outsiders who entered the covenant at Sinai.

The escapees had witnessed the dark side of Egyptian sacral kingship. They had good reason to reject its ethical and political values. A number of traditions are assigned by Scripture to the covenant at Sinai, but Mendenhall appears to be correct when he asserts that the new religion's values subordinated the power of the sovereign to the ethical concerns of human beings.[20] I would add that human status was no longer a function of membership in a political community in the new religion but derived from the God of the covenant. This was not explicitly stated at Sinai, but it was a corollary of that event, as later religious figures in Israel understood. In Egypt, where the ruler was a divinity, the interests of the state had a claim which transcended any possible claim of its subjects. There was, of course, a strong note of social protest in the new religion of the covenant. Escaped slaves, who had been the object of abusive power, were far less likely to give priority to the state's monopoly of force than were members of the ruling class. Nor is it surprising that throughout history oppressed classes have tended to identify themselves with Israel in Egypt and at Sinai. In place of the kingdom of Pharaoh, there was to be a new kingdom ruled by a very different kind of a God, the God who had brought them forth from Egypt.

Like the Hittite pacts, the Sinai covenant has a prologue, one in which Yahweh, the divine author, identifies himself and states his past benefits to those with whom he is to enter a covenant. "I am Yahweh your God who has brought you out of Egypt out of the land of salvery" (Ex. 20:2) identifies the author of the covenant and states the basis of obligation. Just as in the Hittite document, the memory of concrete historical events within the human world is the basis of the vassal's obligation. Similarly, just as the vassal is prohibited from fealty to more than one lord, so the Hebrews are excluded from loyalty to any other God. "You shall have no other gods to set against me ... for I am Yahweh, your God, a jealous God" (Ex. 20:3–5). Yahweh's insistence on exclusive worship had both political as well as religious import. It united those who accepted it into a community and effectively barred them from giving their loyalty to any of the sacralized kingships of the ancient Near East.

The second set of covenantal obligations dealt not with God but with the relations between man and man. Scholars identify several very old collections in Scripture that offer slightly different accounts of these obligations, but in all these collections the ethical relations between individuals have a priority over both political and cultic values.[21] Moreover, all accounts of the covenantal obligations are based on a new conception of the place of power in human affairs. The functions and the authority that had normally been ascribed to human rulers are depicted in Scripture as the prerogative of God alone.[22]

When, as in ancient Egypt, the ruler is declared to be a god, the state and its institutions are thought of as self-legitimating, a view rejected by Scripture. Where such is the case, whether in ancient sacralized kingdoms or modern secular states, there is no effective limit to the actions that can be committed and legitimated by those who command the political institutions and control the state's monopoly of power. This does not mean that those in command will invariably abuse their power. Nevertheless, when political power is self-legitimating, in principle there is no effective check on those in command. Even in the United States with its constitutional system of checks and balances, in a national emergency the normal checks on the executive branch of government can be suspended. The programs of mass enslavement, extermination, and expulsion that have been initiated by such governments as Nazi Germany, the Soviet Union, the Cambodian Pol Pot regime, Castro's Cuba, and North Vietnam are among the contemporary examples of the extremes to which the exercise of power can go when the authority of the state is regarded as self-legitimating. In the contemporary world, the balance of nuclear terror is the only credible restraint upon sovereign states that recognize no value as overriding their own requirements for security and self-maintenance.

Those who truly accepted the covenant at Sinai as binding upon them, rather than as mere pious rhetoric, were bound unconditionally by values that transcended and sometimes contradicted the state's requirements for self-maintenance. Murder, adultery, theft, false testimony, and coveting are forbidden by the covenant, although such categories of behavior can at times become legitimating means of maintaining or enhancing the power of the state. This is evident in the difference between the kind of behavior a state will tolerate in its citizens in peacetime and the kind of behavior it will not only tolerate but reward when carried out by members of its intelligence agencies. Violent behavior, often carried out in stealth, is legitimated as being in the national interest, a claim that cannot easily or realistically be disputed.

The case of the double agent highlights some of the more complex dilemmas of the assertion of the primacy of the interests of the state. In order to establish his credibility, a double agent may have to act as if he were a traitor and even be responsible for the death of many of his fellow citizens. Sometimes governments may knowingly sustain attacks on their own citizens rather than permit an agent to be uncovered. Thus, when the maintenance of the power of the state is self-legitimating, there can be situations in which there is no predictable relationship between the loyalty and trust of citizens and the actions of their government. In ancient times rituals of human sacrifice were a regular part of the life of almost every community. To this day, the state's insistence on human sacrifice, at least in emergency situations, has not and probably cannot entirely be done away with. There are situations even in peacetime when the state's requirement for self-maintenance may compel its leaders to endanger or imperil the lives of some of its loyal citizens. Undoubtedly, the age-old belief in the ultimacy of the state's interests provided the rationale for such questionable programs as the Army's secret introduction of dangerously infectious microorganisms into the ventilating systems of a number of American cities a generation ago, thereby making innocent citizens involuntary guinea pigs in biological warfare experiments. The list could be multiplied. It includes the involuntary administering of harmful doses of LSD to unknowing citizens by intelligence agents who were curious concerning the psychological effects of this drug. As is well known, a number of these experiments resulted in the death of the unknowing subjects. It could be said that the government agents were "playing God" by their abuse of power. There is no doubt that whoever has control over the state's monopoly of force, especially in wartime, does "play God" by virtue of his life-and-death power over others. It is not surprising that ancient man regarded those who possessed such power as gods.

I do not see any viable alternative to the idea that the state's requirements for self-maintenance ultimately override all other claims, if not in peacetime then certainly in times of national emergency. Nevertheless, Israel's ancient covenant with Yahweh was an attempt to create just such an alternative to the state's claim to ultimacy. By positing a God who possessed neither human image nor human incarnation as the power to whom the community owed its fundamental fidelity, the covenant had the effect of rejecting both the doctrine and the institutions that affirmed the ultimacy of the political order. Moreover, by insisting on the primacy of the ethical over the political in the new community's obligations to its God under the covenant, it set forth a principle that imposed unconditional standards on the behavior of men and nations alike. In addition, there was a harsh corollary to the idea that the community's obligations to its God were based upon the fact that he had redeemed them from Egypt and had constituted them a nation. It followed that if ever the new community failed to meet the ethical and religious obligations of the covenant, their God would withdraw his protection from them and they would be destroyed as a nation. In contrast to the sacralized kingdoms of both ancient and modern times that understand their religious traditions as giving assurance that the security and stability of their community is cosmically grounded, Israel's existence as a nation was tentative and conditional on her keeping the covenant.

In the Sinai covenant, we can discern many of the most significant features of Israel's later religious life. By subordinating the political order to the obligations of the covenant, the Sinai covenant laid the foundation of the prophetic protest against the ethical and religious abuses of the period of the monarchy as well as the prophetic idea that men and nations alike stand under the judgment of the God of the covenant. Over and over again, Israel's prophets reiterated their warnings that the very survival of the nation was dependent upon keeping the covenant.[23] Perhaps of greatest long-range significance was the fact that the covenant provided the basis for Israel's extraordinary ability to maintain its religious and communal integrity in the face of repeated military and political catastrophes. Since the political order had been denied ultimacy from the very beginning, it was possible for the community to survive the destruction of the Judean state as well as to interpret its misfortunes as evidence of the uniqueness and majesty of its God.

Nor did this essential community of faith and value based on the covenant come to an end with the close of the biblical period. The rabbis were very much within the tradition of the covenant when they refused to accept the Roman destruction of Jerusalem as involving the end of Israel's communal existence or its distinctive relationship with its God.[24] As much as we may admire the heroism of the men and women at Masada, their response would appear to have been less in keeping with that tradition. Given the biblical-rabbinic understanding of the subordination of the political order to the sovereignty of God, the rabbis were able to educate their community in a mode of life that permitted it to endure for almost two thousand years. Nor has that way of life yet lost its significance in our time. Although ritual was not stressed in the original Sinai covenant, the memory of the historic basis of obligation under the covenant was reinforced daily in the formula that the fulfillment of the commandments was a "remembrance of the going out of Egypt."

The covenant had yet other world-historical consequences, the most important and paradoxical being that its distinctive conception of the ultimate source of power and obligation eventually became the basis for the creation of the modern secular world. At first glance, the idea that the wilderness religious experience of a group of declassed, escaped slaves could produce the modern secular world seems farfetched, yet that conclusion has been increasingly persuasive in the analysis of the modern world since the time of Hegel.

Let us recall that the covenant's insistence that Yahweh alone is the God of Israel constituted a radical desacralization of the political institutions of the ancient Near East. For those who pledged themselves to the new God, both Pharaoh and the gods of Egypt were effectively dethroned. Similarly, the gods of Canaan, as well as their sacralized political and social institutions, were dethroned for those who came to accept the covenant in that land. The long-term effect of the covenant is everywhere the same: whereas sacral kingships see the continuity between the human and the divine orders, the covenant unconditionally distinguishes between them. It took a long time before the full implications of the original desacralization became manifest. Nevertheless, after the covenant had rejected the sacrality of the political institutions of the ancient Near East, it was only a matter of time before *all* human institutions were denied any intrinsic sacrality.[25] The cultural process whereby both the natural and the human worlds came to be regarded as devoid of any inherent sacrality has been called *Entzaüberung der Welt,* the disenchantment of the world. According to Max Weber, where such disenchantment occurs, "there are in principle no mysterious forces that come into play, but rather one can, in principle, master all things by calculation."[26] As we know, it is the aspiration of the modern secular, technological world to "master all things by calculation."

It is sometimes thought that this process of disenchantment is the result of modern intellectual skepticism. In reality, it is highly unlikely that modern secularism could have achieved its mass appeal on the basis of intellectual criticism alone. Only a religious faith that was radically opposed to the forces of magic and to belief in the existence of indwelling spirits could have initiated the profound cultural, psychological, and spiritual revolution that was necessary before entire civilizations could reject the gods and spirits men had revered as sacred from time immemorial. Without faith in the new God, it would have been impossible to dethrone the old gods. Only a God can overturn the gods. Only those who believed in their God's exclusive sovereignty had the emotional and intellectual resources with which to abandon belief in magic, spirits, and sacralized institutions. Thus, secularization is, paradoxically, the unintended consequence of a distinctive kind of religious faith. If one wishes to find the origins of the modern secular world, one must look for its beginnings at Sinai.

Yet, there is irony in such a paradoxical cultural achievement. Once the process of *Entzaüberung der Welt* is initiated, it is difficult to halt until the limit of radical atheism is reached. The same skepticism which the original believers applied to the sacred claims of the monarch of Egypt was eventually applied to the heavenly author of the covenant himself! In place of a world in which all values are ultimately a function of the state's requirements for self-maintenance, we finally arrive at a world in which values no longer have any ground whatsoever. Instead of a world in which only the outlaw, the man or woman who belongs to no political community, is treated with amoral calculation, kept alive and accorded decent treatment only if he or she is perceived to be useful, we arrive at a world in which all relationships are expressions of calculations of utility and no other standard need determine the relationships between man and man, save where the bonds of kinship remain unbroken. Put differently, we arrive at a world in which every man is a potential outlaw to his fellow. Although the covenant originally attempted to solve one kind of abuse of power, it had as its paradoxical and unintended consequence the creation of another set of problems of comparable gravity.

How then shall we evaluate the distinctive Jewish understanding of power and the record of its employment that we call history? Can we say that the entire enterprise was fundamentally mistaken in view of the fact that, against its original intentions, it eventually yielded an amoral, anomic secular world, or shall we perhaps say that the human world is amoral and anomic because it has never truly accepted the ethical obligations of the covenant? I would argue that the Jewish understanding was neither correct nor incorrect but functional in some circumstances and dysfunctional in others. It originally contained cultural and religious values that made liberation and the formation of a new community possible for a group of tenuously united, powerless fugitives who had been without access to the normal levers of power within an established community. Nevertheless, once the community of the covenant was established and in possession of its own territorial base, it found itself confronted with the same dilemmas of power and national interest that faced all the other kingdoms of the ancient Near East. The Israelite kingdoms had to defend themselves, sometimes by making war, sometimes by making alliances with their neighbors. Often, these alliances were ratified by the marriage of an Israelite king and a pagan princess. The covenant's demand for rendering exclusive homage to Yahweh simply could not be maintained by Israel's rulers without dangerously offending their allies and putting at hazard the security of the state. Of course, the prophets insisted that exclusive fidelity to Yahweh constituted the real security of the state, but which of us, had we been a ruler, would have deliberately endangered our nation's security in order to meet the prophetic demand for religious exclusivity? Similarly, the prophets accused the kings of favoring the rich over the poor, an accusation that is still heard in the land. Nevertheless, is it not possible that there are times when those who control large resources are a greater source of strength for the state than those who have no competence in the control of resources? It is not my intention to advocate that the rich be favored over the poor. My purpose is to suggest that there are times when the state must make decisions which do not always conform to our customary ideas of what is fair and equitable between individuals.

It is not surprising that, faced with political and social problems similar to those facing other rulers in the area, the rulers of the Israelite kingdoms began to respond as did those other rulers. Political values, especially the state's fundamental requirement that it maintain its monopoly of force against both internal and external opponents, took precedence over individual ethical values; the religion of landless, escaped slaves was found to be less functional than the agrarian religion of Canaan to men who now possessed and had to defend their own land.

We know how the prophets reacted to this development. We also know that the prophets' response formed the basis for much of the contemporary criticism of the state in countries with a strongly biblical culture such as the United States. What we regard as a natural and perhaps inevitable political and social evolution in ancient Israel was regarded by the prophets as unpardonable idolatry for which Israel deserved the worst kind of punishment. It can, however, be said in defense of Israel's rulers that a very different set of values is necessary to create a community, where none had previously existed, than to maintain that community once it is established. As soon as the problems of maintenance displaced those of creation in ancient Israel, some means had to be found to legitimate the interests of the state. One can dethrone the old gods when one is rejecting the old order. When one seeks a psychologically effective and cost-effective means of maintaining the new order, there will almost always be the strong impulsion to resacralize political institutions or, at the very least, to ascribe primacy to the state.

It can, of course, be argued that Israel's trust in political institutions proved futile, that both the kingdoms of Israel and Judah fell to the assaults of their enemies. Much of the continuing authority of the prophets came from the fact that their prophecies of doom did prove accurate. Nevertheless, it does not follow from the fact that the prophets were correct in predicting disaster that they were also correct in their analysis of its causes. This observation also applies to the contemporary would-be prophets of both the religious right and the religious left who offer their judgments on American politics. Is it reasonable to believe that the kingdoms of Israel and Judah would have been able to withstand the assaults of the Assyrians and the Babylonians if they had scrupulously maintained the personal and religious obligations of the covenant? What destroyed the two small kingdoms was their relative military weakness. Undoubtedly, national morale in ancient Israel would have been higher had the prophets' warnings against the exploitation of the poor been heeded, but even a perfectly just Israelite state could not have withstood the assaults that were directed against it.

After the catastrophe, the prophetic claim about Israel's failure to keep the covenant proved to be both psychologically and sociologically functional. Lacking realistic means to undo their predicament, the defeated at least retained the hope that, were they to repent and meet the obligations of the covenant, God would redeem them, as he had redeemed the Hebrew slaves in ancient Egypt. After 70 C.E. this hope served as the motive and the basis for the reconstruction of the catastrophically defeated Jewish society. It has continued to serve as a basis for Jewish faith to this day.

If one asks how the drama of human history is understood within Judaism, the fundamental answer has not really changed since Sinai: In Judaism history is ultimately regarded as the ways in which men have either met or failed to meet their obligations to their God who is absolutely sovereign over all things. These obligations are largely ethical rather than political. No human value, even the survival of those institutions that promise communal safety and security such as the state, is of sufficient importance to compromise the imperative to fulfill the divinely certified obligations, for the real safety and security of mankind rest with the God who alone is truly sovereign rather than with any human ruler or institution, all of whom ultimately stand under God's judgment and power.

There is both hope and consolation in this view of history. As we have seen, it is functional under certain circumstances. Nor were the Jews the only people to find hope in this view, which ultimately derives from the blessings and curses of the covenant. After the memory of the redemption of the slaves from Egypt and the subordination of the power of the state to that of the God of the covenant had become a part of humanity's permanent spiritual heritage, this perspective became a rallying point for the disinherited and the disadvantaged, as well as for those who identified themselves with their cause. It gave the disinherited a basis for hope and an ideological weapon in their struggle for liberation. In defeat it also gave them a profound source of consolation.

Unfortunately, while this view of power and history may on occasion enable the powerless to break their bonds and to form a new community, it is highly unlikely that it could ever prove capable of sustaining a community once it has been established, for an established community must inevitably deal with the challenges of power that are manifest and concrete rather than invisible. And, power that is manifest and concrete is human power. When confronted with problems of internal and external security, all governments must be functionally atheistic, no matter how sincere the religious commitments of their rulers or people may be and no matter what religious rituals are used to solemnize important communal efforts. Those in control of the monopoly of force have no choice but to respond appropriately and rationally when their monopoly is challenged, if they are to survive. The Jewish view of history is functional only for those who either do not have to face challenges of manifest power or for those who lack physical force and can only challenge the existing monopoly of force by psychological means.[27] Under such circumstances, the values of the covenant may prove to be a potent psychological weapon.

We do, however, know that the community created by the rabbis remained more or less faithful to the original attitude towards power of the Sinai covenant. It is my belief that this can be partly explained by the fact that the political situation of the Jews of the post–70 c.e. diaspora resembled that of the original wilderness band in important respects. Until the birth of the State of Israel, the Jews were never accepted as full members of any community that claimed a monopoly of force within its borders. Nor was it possible for the Jews to create such a community. Had they attempted to do so, their effort would have been speedily and violently smashed. Whether one characterizes the Jews of the diaspora as outsiders, exiles, or a pariah people, until the emancipation and in many countries until the present day, they were never given the same protection as were members of the dominant group. The relations between the Jewish outsiders and their overlords were usually motivated by considerations of utility. When their services were needed, they were tolerated. In some cases, they were even accorded privileges. When they were no longer needed, they were expelled and, in modern times, systematically exterminated. Had they lacked a religious basis for community, they would have become an atomized collection of anomic individuals. Covenantal religion, with its subordination of political to religio-ethical values, was indispensable for their survival.

Unfortunately, there is a great difference between recognizing (a) that covenantal religion was functional for Jews during much of their history, (b) that it was also functional for certain other disadvantaged classes, and (c) making the claim, as both Jewish and Christian theologians tend to do, that covenantal religion is the preeminent model for all of humanity at its finest. Not every person or group is an exile, a slave, or an outsider. For those who are more or less at home in their world, alternative religious options are likely to prove more appropriate than that of the God of the covenant, even when, because of family inheritance, one retains membership in a religion that formally affirms the sovereignty of the God of the covenant.[28]

There is, however, a situation in which a large number of people might once again turn to the God of the covenant: Even a cursory glance at biblical and Jewish history shows that faith in the God of the covenant tended to be firmest in times of crisis and catastrophe. Should the worldwide social and economic crisis continue to intensify, modern versions of both sacral kingship *and* faith in the God of the covenant might gain large numbers of new adherents. Those who feel that in a crisis safety and security can only be assured by hunting with one's own pack are likely to find some form of sacral kingship irresistible; those who have reason to distrust even the power structures of their own tribe are likely to find some form of the covenant attractive. Nevertheless, though the options of covenant and sacral kingship are perennial, they are not permanent. Each contains the seeds of its own dissolution.

Notes

1. Max Weber, *Economy and Society: An Outline of Interpretive Sociology* (New York: 1968), p. 53.
2. Max Weber, "Politics as a Vocation," in H. H. Gerth and C. Wright Mills, eds., *From Max Weber: Essays in Sociology* (New York: 1946), p. 78.
3. See George E. Mendenhall, "The Hebrew Conquest of Palestine," in *The Biblical Archaeologist Reader* (Garden City, N.Y.: 1970), pp. 25–53.
4. See George E. Mendenhall, *The Tenth Generation: The Origins of the Biblical Tradition* (Baltimore: 1973), pp. 122ff.
5. See Mendenhall, *The Tenth Generation*, pp. 23f.
6. Aristotle, *The Politics*, bk. 1, chap. 2, 1253a, 1–4.
7. This was evident in the term *Tiermenschen* ("subhumans") that the Nazis used to designate the Jews. On the subject of assigning a "paranthropoid" identity to those targeted for abusive treatment or extermination, see Gil Eliot, *Twentieth Century Book of the Dead* (New York: 1972), pp. 41, 94, 124.
8. Alan H. Gardiner, "The Autobiography of Rekhmire," in *Zeitschrift für aegyptische Sprache*, 60 (1925): 69, cited by Henri Frankfort, *Ancient Egyptian Religion* (New York: 1948), p. 43.
9. Frankfort, *Egyptian Religion*, pp. 43ff.
10. See Ernst Ludwig Ehrlich, *A Concise History of Israel* (New York: 1965), pp. 10ff.
11. See Gerhard von Rad, *Old Testament Theology* (London: 1973), 1:8–9, 20.
12. See Moshe Greenberg, *The Hab/Piru*, American Oriental Series, vol. 39 (New Haven: 1955), pp. 55–57.
13. This is stated by Montgomery Watt with reference to the origins of Islam. It also holds true of other traditions as well. See Watt, *Muhammed at Mecca* (Oxford: 1953), pp. 153ff.
14. See, for example, Exodus 3:13. After God reveals himself to Moses as the God of the Israelites' forefathers, Moses is depicted as asking him, "If I go to the Israelites and tell them, and they ask me his name, what shall I say?" indicating that the escapees did not know the name of the new God. See also Exodus 6:2, 3, in which God is depicted as saying to Moses, "I am the Lord. I appeared to Abraham, Isaac, and Jacob as God Almighty. But I did not let myself be known to them by my name YAHWEH."
15. See article "Covenant" in *Encyclopedia Judaica* (Jerusalem: 1972) 5:1012–22, and George E. Mendenhall, *Law and Covenant in Israel and the Ancient Near East* (Pittsburgh: 1955).
16. See George E. Mendenhall, "Covenant Forms in Israelite Tradition," in *Biblical Archaeologist Reader*, pp. 25–53, and Dennis J. McCarthy, S.J., *Old Testament Covenant* (Richmond, Va.: 1972).
17. Mendenhall, "Covenant Forms in Israelite Tradition," pp. 29ff.
18. Ibid., pp. 35f.
19. Ibid.
20. Mendenhall, *The Tenth Generation*, p. 30.
21. See von Rad, *Old Testament Theology*, 1:187ff., and Mendenhall, *The Tenth Generation*, p. 30.

22. Thus, when God is referred to as a "man of war," it is not the intention of Scripture to glorify war but to ascribe to God an authority previously ascribed to a human ruler. Similarly, when he is depicted as the sole proprietor of the land, this is meant to serve as a contrast to the idea that the monarch was the sole proprietor. See Mendenhall, "The Hebrew Conquest of Palestine," p. 110.

23. The relationship between Israel's fidelity to her obligations under the covenant and her fate are spelled out in many places in Scripture. See, for example, Leviticus 26:3–45; Amos 4:6–11; Jeremiah 44:1–4.

24. See Richard L. Rubenstein, *The Religious Imagination* (Indianapolis: 1968), pp. 127ff.

25. This point is implied in the discussion of the secularization process in Peter Berger, *The Sacred Canopy* (Garden City, N.Y.: 1966), pp. 106ff.

26. Max Weber, "Science as a Vocation," in *From Max Weber,* p. 139.

27. There is an obvious resemblance between the views expressed here and those of Friedrich Nietzsche. See Nietzsche, *On the Genealogy of Morals,* trans. Walter Kaufman and R. J. Hollingdale (New York: 1969), pp. 33ff.

28. It is obviously possible to retain membership in a religious tradition that strongly affirms faith in the covenant while at the same time "bracketing" the demands of that faith when one serves in a position of decision-making power. This was certainly true of both John Foster Dulles and his brother Allen when they served as secretary of state and director of the Central Intelligence Agency, respectively, under President Eisenhower. See Leonard Mosley, *Dulles: A Biography of Eleanor, Allen, and John Foster Dulles and Their Family Network* (New York: 1978).

Nine

History and Religion

The Ambiguous Uses of Jewish History

Ben Halpern

History, according to Henry Ford, is bunk. By this, no doubt, he meant to say that preconceived notions anchored in our past hamper our intelligence and prevent us from dealing with present issues effectively as straightforward technical problems. Santayana, on the other hand, told us that those who cannot remember the past are doomed to repeat it. The delicate suggestion here is that the *first,* fresh response to an experience, whether impulsive or deliberate, is likely to be foolish, narrow, and shortsighted. Only the wisdom of a well-formed identity, rooted in memory and tradition, safeguards the human enterprise. In any case, whether for good for ill, it is agreed that history, like memory, fixes human lives in patterns that transcend the random impulsions of immediate experience. It gives men direction amid the disjointed challenges and invitations of the here and now.

Formed identities are individual things, and every group identity is anchored in its own, individual history. Yet the history of every group involves the history of others; and this overlap is a prime source of the interminable controversies that bedevil the study of history. Some histories are generally held to have had an exceptionally wide-ranging influence: the wisdom accumulated in them penetrates the humane tradition of much of mankind. The whole of Western culture—as Heine and Matthew

Arnold were hardly the first to note—grew up under the aegis of the alternative traditions of Hellenism and Hebraism. The current decline in the study of the humanities was foreshadowed by the neglect of these core traditions in our academies; and it will not fill the gap so created to extend the curriculum by including other, non-Western traditions and "alternative" humane studies. Such wider options simply emphasize the lack of a common center which the older humanities provided. These other studies may enlarge our vision; they do not serve to focus it, nor do they yield a common universe of discourse.

Can one say, however, that the history of the Jews indeed yielded a common universe of discourse for Western culture? This is not a quibble that might be seriously raised with regard to the ancient Greeks. Greek philosophy and Greek politics, if not Greek science, continue to shape our ideas, to a significant extent, to this very day. While we speak about our "Judeo-Christian civilization," the coupling of the two terms "Judaic" and "Christian" does not suffice to eliminate the underlying tension between them. Judaism is one of a family of *rival* religions, and the scriptures of Jewish antiquity are texts employed by each scriptural religion in a sense contrary to the readings of the others. The classic literature of Hellenic culture, on the other hand, may be subject to varying scholarly and aesthetic readings, but it has not set the Greeks against the English, French, German, or any other of the national traditions of classical study.

The difference between the two cases lies in the fact that not only the Jewish *scriptures* but also—and indeed especially—Jewish *history* has been adopted by others as their own. Nothing like this happened to the Greeks. Rome and Islam both absorbed Hellenistic culture, as did the Jews, but none of these attached itself to Hellenistic history. After the fall of Byzantium, no race ever seriously considered Greek history as its own tradition until the modern Greek national revival. In contrast, Christians and Muslims took from Judaism not simply ideas and images, ritual and doctrines, detachable and transferable item by item into a new, independent tradition. They grafted themselves organically into the stock and root system of Jewish history. The church proclaimed itself the new Israel. The Islamic Arabs reclaimed for Ishmael the birthright of Abraham's heritage. They appropriated as theirs with exclusive right the Temple mount, where Abraham bound Isaac for sacrifice, and the graves of the Semitic patriarchs and matriarchs.

Having taken over Jewish history, the Christian and Muslim heirs of Israel could not concede much significance to the continuing history of the incongruously surviving aboriginal Jews. Muslims, until recently, had relatively little need to trouble themselves with the matter. The Jewish scriptures were easily disposed of, since the texts were assumed to be corrupted, unlike the Koran's pure transmission of the revealed Truth. As for the Jews themselves, they continued to be tolerated together with other scriptural *millets* throughout the sacred domain of Islam, but they were never a force significant enough to require an elaborate interpretation of their history after the Muslim conquests. Indeed, when the Zionist movement and the rise of Israel made Jews as grave a challenge as once the Crusaders of medieval times, the Arab and Muslim world had to look to the source books of European anti-Semitism for a doctrine of Jewish history, combining it with stray references from their own tradition.

The Christian world has always confronted Jewish history as a far more serious problem. The Jewish Bible is a sacred text for Christianity, not a humanly distorted transmission of revealed Truth—in the same way as for Jewish tradition. That Jews and Christians traditionally derived opposing conclusions from the same text made the rivalry more pointed than between Jews and Muslims; and it also focused the difference primarily on the rival versions of Jewish *history* drawn from the texts by either side. The Old Testament in Christian interpretations contained the proof texts that prophesied the coming, sacred mission, and ultimate second coming of Christ. Its primary function was to outline and prefigure the sacred history of mankind and of the cosmos; and it was the history of Israel, beginning with that of the Jews and culminating in the history of the church, the true Israel, within which all this was contained.

The persistence of the Jews, unregenerate and unconverted, among the Christians was also a more provocative presence than among Muslims. This was particularly true in the Roman Catholic lands, where the Jews were for centuries the *only* infidels tolerated by the church and the secular powers. Not only were elaborate legal safeguards—distinguishing marks, bans on intercourse, and eventually the ghetto—deemed necessary to protect Christians from the infection of Judaizing tendencies; an elaborate myth and ideology were developed to justify tolerating the presence of Jews and to interpret the repressive, increasingly hostile, and degrading conditions under which it was allowed to continue. On the one hand, the Jewish heroes of the Old Testament were charter members of the Christian college of saints; on the other hand, not only the New Testament but the continuing contacts of Christians with Jews provided a plethora of examples from which to fashion what has been called the "demonological" image of the unconverted Jew and his continuing history.

Thus, the impact of Jewish scripture and the Jews on Western culture is comparable to the influence of Hellenism in its magnitude, its extent; but it differs sharply in the form and channels of its diffusion. The scholarly study of Judaism—of the Bible, and more sporadically of the Talmud and Kabbalah—rose and fell with the tides of general humane scholarship, more or less in the same way as the study of the Greco-Roman classics.

But even in this restricted sphere, what concerned the scholars was far less the teachings and wisdom of the texts, the substantive issues which, in the study of Greek philosophy, preoccupied contending schools of patristic and scholastic thought. The main issue for Christian and Jewish philosophers alike in regard to biblical wisdom was to reconcile it as a body with the body of Greek philosophy, or to defend religion by discrediting philosophy. A close scholarly study of scriptural texts, and controversy over their interpretation, arose only in considering their historical, or "metahistorical," meaning—in debating the Christological reading of the Bible and the opposing Jewish version.

The Jewish impact on Western culture, unlike the Greek, was as strong in the lower orders and among the laity as among the scholars. It flowed through the channels of religious antagonism, reaching the remotest cells of the body of Christendom; and since the sacred history of the Jews served as the core of the Christian communion, it imposed upon the surviving Jews, and upon their continuing history as perceived by Christians, a fateful role in the drama of universal salvation. For this reason, awareness of the Jewish presence in one's own history did not depend, among the peoples of the Christian world, on the shifting attention span of scholars. It was a cumulative tradition broadly shared in the whole society; enriched by the changing experiences of new times and local conditions; but even in the recurrent absence of actual Jews—as in the aftermath of expulsions or massacres—it was nourished by the hagiography and demonography of the Jews that was part of the self-image of Christian peoples, rooted in their appropriation of Jewish history as their own.

The appreciation of Jewish culture may have been subject to variation, like that of classical literature, as scholarly interests and intellectual attitudes changed. But such shifts were confined by deeply rooted perspectives on the history and character of the Jews that pervaded society and formed the constraining environment of every developing mind. The attack of a Luther on the Catholic creed and institutions inverted some traditional perceptions of popular belief among Protestants. Where the pope became the Anti-Christ and the Inquisition an instrument of the Devil, roles previously assigned to Jews were preempted, and the Jews were now differently perceived. If they had remained stiff-necked and rejected Jesus under Catholic popes, this reaction could be traced back—apart from the other defects of Catholicism—to the persecutions committed against the Jews, persecutions still exemplified by the Inquisition. Protestants were entitled to expect a better response to their missionary efforts; including, for some pietist millenarians of the times, the hope that Jews, as a nation restored in the Holy Land, would join them in the apocalyptic battles against the anti-Christ and would then be converted, and saved, as a body. But later in Luther's life, when it became clear that Jews showed no greater liking for his teaching than Catholics, he reverted to a violent anti-Jewish style which differed in no way from the hostile imagery that was applied against the Jews traditionally and was endemic in Germany. The combination of new and old attitudes, and sometimes the same cycle of change as in Luther's case, were common among Protestant pietists in the heat of their revolt against Papism.

It was not very different with the Deists and rationalists, who began to question not simply Catholic dogma but all positive religion. Their attack on the sacred texts and their revisions of Jewish history departed from tradition more sharply and more radically than did Protestant dissent, but the constraint of popular imagery was no less evident in their perception of the Jews. The initial attack was on the Bible, about which skeptics fought a running battle with pietists in the seventeenth and eighteenth centuries, a battle that continues today. The reliability of biblical chronology as a base for history was contested first on the strength of conflicting evidence in classical literature and later because of the theories and findings of modern natural science. Not only the text came under criticism but also the heroes of the text—the patriarchs and prophets canonized by pious Christians, as well as the Chosen People as a whole, both the Hebrew tribes and their contemporary descendants. While the assault on Jewish antiquity might be rejected indignantly by pietist disputants, both sides drew their perception of the living Jews and their history from the same tradition—though the picture was enriched with references to classical authorities in the writings of Deists and Encyclopedists.

Among these precursors of our times there were also those who sought to better the condition of the Jews. Like Protestant reformers before them, they explained the character of contemporary Jews, perceived as corrupt, by their oppression under the regime inherited from the benighted Middle Ages. Together with the continuing interest in postbiblical literature that had inspired humanists, theologians, and millenarian enthusiasts to study and translate Talmudic and Kabbalistic works, there grew an interest in the history of the social conditions of the Jews. Ardent missionaries and rationalist reformers alike were soon found among the scholars who strove for religious toleration and, eventually, for the emancipation of the Jews.

The sources for such historical study were found initially in the historical works of Jewish scholars. These were traditional in their style and approach; and they were based on an eschatological view of the meaning of Jewish history similar to that of Christians. They differed sharply from the Christian version, however, in what they contained and what they omitted from the substantive record, and consequently in such elements of the form of history as periodization and perspective. The crux of history for Jews was not the Crucifixion but the destruction of the Temple and the beginning of the Exile. Neither Jesus nor such archetypical figures of villainy as Judas Iscariot are easily found in the Jewish sources; and traces of any contact with Christians in the first centuries are still the subject of ingenious scholarly conjectures. The Jewish chronicles, on the other hand, portray Titus and other villains, successors to Haman, in a light unknown to Christian and classical sources; and they record a whole roster of saints and sages unmentioned in the annals of non-Jews.

The chroniclers and hagiographers who composed Jewish historical records were, in a sense, performing rites essential to their religion, as their Gentile counterparts did for theirs. Lists of rabbinical luminaries and their tracts and treatises represented testimony to a continuous chain of legal sanction, overarching the unending disputations and differences of the sages and uniting all in common submission to the Law handed down on Sinai. The records of Jewish suffering offered incidental observations of the mundane causes and circumstances of persecution; but they were essentially a ceremony of mourning and penitential confession, an explication and acting out of the Jewish drama of Exile and Redemption. This martyrology, documenting pious submission to God's will, was a form of prayer, testifying that the Chosen People were faithfully carrying out their assigned role as God's Suffering Servant, with trust in the coming Redemption. The Christian perception of Jewish history was superficially similar but essentially different. The suffering of the Jews was, for some, a pointless consequence of social disorder; but in the more common view it was a just retribution for their crimes, administered by church and state within the bounds of Christian love.

For all their differences, these traditional perceptions of the Jews in history agreed in seeing little or no relation between the secular history of the realms and peoples among whom Jews lived and whatever Jews might record as a continuous, meaningful development in the records of their own experience. As time went on, Jews participated in the wars and affairs of the Gentiles only to protect themselves against their impact. What was meaningful for them, they did in the protected sanctuary of their insulated community; and in early modern times, behind the walls of the ghetto. The isolation from the currents of change around them, to the extent Jews were able to achieve such security, was especially marked in the Ashkenazic Jewries—above all, in Eastern Europe where emancipation was attained last. It was one of the ruling drives of those who sought emancipation to bring the Jews back into the mainstream of history, together with their Gentile countrymen.

This aim was one shared by both Gentile and Jewish reformers, but with a characteristic and decisive difference. All were agreed that the proposed emancipation of the Jews posed a problem of social rehabilitation—as we should call it nowadays—and of thorough reeducation. The long isolation of the Jews and their sharply skewed occupational distribution had to be overcome before they could be considered to deserve enfranchisement in full; and to achieve this the traditional culture and education of the Jews had to be replaced by those of their non-Jewish contemporaries and countrymen. So much was common to the reformers on both sides, but here their differences began.

The non-Jews, whether practicing Christians or not, saw as the natural end of the projected reforms the absorption of Jews into the larger community whose history they would now share. Having had no significant history of their own since Calvary, and having had a baneful significance in universal, that is, Christian history, they now, by dissolving their social bonds and disappearing as an identifiable group, would achieve two objects: they would acquire an adoptive right to the new national histories of their several homelands and they would be released from the burden of their special role in universal history.

There were, of course, some Jews who shared this perspective and hoped for a similar outcome. Others, however, while no less determined to be emancipated, were unwilling to renounce their Jewish identity—or understood that, as a rule to be universally applied by Jews, such renunciation was impossible. It became essential for them, in the Romantic secularist spirit of their time, not only to achieve citizenship in their country of birth and residence, and a share in its history, but to secure recognition of Jewish history as the legitimating principle of the Jewish identity they held fast to, as their fated destiny. A valid and significant history of their own was the mark of an authentic peoplehood in the nineteenth century; and without the recognition of a significant history of the Jews, survival of their identity would be the mere misfortune that it was tellingly named by Heine's fictional spokesman, Hirsch Hyacinth.

These were the circumstances under which modern, critical philological-historical studies, the so-called *Wissenschaft des Judenthums* or Science of Judaism, arose. The German scholars like Jost, Zunz, Geiger, Graetz, Steinschneider, and others who, together with their Italian and Austrian (that is, Galician) contemporaries, founded this discipline combined their erudition in traditional Jewish lore with the critical methods of the new German historical school. They collated texts, investigated etymologies, compiled massive bibliographies, constructed out of scattered references biographies of historic figures, and established the relations between Jewish and Muslim or Christian sources. Writing in Hebrew, they sought by historical studies to shed Western enlightenment on the self-image of their people; and writing in German, or other European languages, they aimed to speed the acceptance of the Jews, and of their place in history as well, by their fellow countrymen. For many of them in the Western countries, the accolade they sought most passionately was an appointment to teach their new discipline in a university. Only in our time has this measure of recognition been granted to Jewish studies in more than isolated cases.

Many reasons could be cited to explain the academic disregard of Jewish history and historians. The nineteenth century saw the displacement of universal by national histories, centered on the nation-state and its politics. Not only did Jewish postbiblical history lack a state and political life; those who wrote it—until the time of Dubnow—shared the qualms of their generation of Jews about acknowledging *any* political aspect of recent and current Jewish communal life and disavowed any hope for a Jewish state in the future. A history thus deprived of its central theme, as contemporary views held, could have no intrinsic justification; it might be of interest only as a sidelight on other histories, as in the transmission of Arabic and classic philosophy to the West or in the history of the rise of capitalism. The other topics favored by Jewish historians were disdained as lacking substance even when studies were carried out with impeccable methods. The modern Jewish historians found themselves dealing with the same themes as their traditionalist predecessors; the long chains of rabbinical transmission were succeeded by bibliographies and histories of Jewish literature, and the elegaic chronicles of Jewish martyrdom gave way to studies of "Jewish sufferings." At best, these could be regarded as historical irrelevancies by students of the mainstream of events. At worst, they were disdained as filiopietistic trivialities, marred by narrow vision and parochial bias.

But a more fundamental reason underlying such particular flaws explains the prolonged disinclination to absorb Jewish history in the academy and among the humanities. National histories, during their long season of unrivaled dominance, were based on the displacement of universal by local perspectives. The rule of Roman church and Holy Roman Empire yielded to national dynasties and parliaments, Latin succumbed to the luxuriant growth of vernacular languages and literatures, art and music cultivated national styles—and history began to be written from the same local perspectives. But this atomization of universal conceptions was less complete than it seemed—and the case of Jewish history aptly illustrates the point.

The national perspectives from which historians wrote their works rested upon tacitly assumed universal values common to modern—that is, Western—history as a whole. Political life, art, music, and literature may have been converted into expressions of the life of nation-states, but there remained universal Western values upon which the phenomenon of the modern nation-state securely rested. There was, on the one hand, modern Western science, its humanist tradition, and the technological civilization it had produced; and there was also the ethos of a Christian civilization defining the style in which modern Western peoples addressed themselves to universal demands of morality. As for the first, Jewish history could provide only footnotes to the history of humanism and was not otherwise significant for the history of science: eminent Jewish scientists in recent times have their place in other national histories, not often in that of the Jews. As for the Jewish share in the Christian ethos, it is effective in history in the form given it by Christians, not Jews; and if considered in the sequence of Jewish history, represents Jewish history after its purported death and transfiguration.

The modern Jewish historians, confronting this issue obliquely and unwillingly, have noted that, owing to the undoubted survival of the Jewish people, and its presence, over so many centuries and such a vast range of local settings, wherever Western history was made, Jewish history offered an exceptionally valuable alternative perspective and the rare opportunity of an experimental control group for the comparative history of modern nations. The facts referred to cannot be doubted; and the Jewish case has indeed been analyzed by comparative historians, notably in the debate over the origins of capitalism. But the transparent aim of legitimating on such grounds Jewish history in its entirety as a significant part of world history somehow fell short of its target. Despite the extraordinary effort of a man like Max Weber, it did not seem necessary even for him to penetrate the spirit of Jewish history as a continuous, integral whole in order to draw conclusions from some of its aspects for his particular purpose.

As to the suggestion that an alternative perspective on general history might be drawn from the individual history of the Jews, the attempt to apply this insight came to a fairly disheartening end. Heinrich Graetz's massive *History of the Jewish People* was a portrayal of its subject in the authentically Rankean mode of a saga of heroes and ideas—and, of course, also of villains and delusions. It presented what was, indeed, an alternative view—of German history, for example. What it provoked was a famous outburst of anti-Jewish rancor by Treitschke; and the Jewish voices heard in the ensuing discussion by no means united in defense of Graetz's "alternative." The preference of most modern Jewish historians—though not of some of the most daring, like Dubnow—has been to seek acknowledgment of Jewish history as a normal part of world history, not afflicted with the overheated intensity that has usually attended its interpretation—and which the awareness of its alternative perspective evokes.

There has been a remarkable rise in the acceptance of Jewish studies as indeed a normal part of the academic curriculum, and of Jewish history as a normal part of world history. In part, of course, the change is incidental to the great explosion of the academic curriculum that has been a typically American development, particularly in recent years. In part, however, it reflects events that, far from assimilating the Jewish case to a host of others—such as the rise of ethnicity and of women's studies as academic concerns—tend rather to focus a clear and piercing light on its singular, and yet universally significant, character. I refer, of course, to the Holocaust and the destruction of European Jewry and to the creation of Israel, the Jewish state.

It is impossible in the present context to do more than illustrate briefly some of the complex implications of these events for both Jews and non-Jews, and I shall confine myself to those that relate to our subject here most directly. What is most generally significant is that the Holocaust and the rise of Israel have brought the long-developing integration of Jewish and general history abruptly to a point where their inherently diverse perspectives constantly threaten to emerge in open confrontations.

By creating a state, Jews removed at one blow some of the prime objections of nineteenth-century historians to the claims for the validity of Jewish history as an academic pursuit. Moreover, Israel's location in geopolitical space is such that its affairs have a global impact of extraordinary intensity and become salient problems in the current history of virtually everyone else. But this very circumstance, which removes all doubts about the need for general history to concern itself with the Jewish state—and hence with the Jewish history out of which it sprang—does not simply render the Jewish case normal through its conclusive involvement in generally significant current issues. It has the paradoxical consequence of reviving a sense of the traditional exceptionalism of the Jewish experience. For one thing, the mere weight and intensity of attention given to Israel by the world is inconceivable in the case of any other nation-state of comparable dimensions. Whatever share chance may have in this matter, through the coincidence of Arab nationalism and oil wealth in the very area of Israel's rise, there are other, traditional forces at work. The restoration of Jewish sovereignty poses basic problems of self-identity and religious values equally for Jews, Christians, and Muslims. That Israel has become a new focus for anti-Semitic mobilization and that Jews now suffer a subacute crisis in self-understanding are some of the crucial consequences of this fact.

The Holocaust, unspeakably terrible in its material effect, has had similar, not fully realized, repercussions on the no longer firmly fixed identity systems of Jews and Gentiles. It forced the impact of anti-Semitism in world history upon the attention of rather reluctant historians; for the topic has not yet been given the full and probing consideration it deserves. As a source of symbolic imagery, the Holocaust—and indeed other aspects of postbiblical Jewish history—has been freely and widely drawn on; and it may be said that not since the Bible itself was appropriated by Christians and Muslims have Jewish experiences been taken over so decisively for non-Jewish purposes. The "ghetto" has become the accepted term for black and other "minority" settlements—while Jews are no longer accredited as minorities. "Genocide," the legal concept invented by Raphael Lemkin to cover the plight of Central and East European Jews, has been so broadly applied that it has lost all denotative meaning while conveying a heavy charge of emotional concern. The Jewish Exile, or Diaspora, while deeply questionable in the Jewish self-perception, has gained a certain vogue among Christian thinkers as a symbol of their own religious situation—not to speak of the wholesale appropriation of this and other Zionist concepts by Palestinian Arab nationalists, for baldly polemical purposes.

One can appreciate that the very same Jews most eager to normalize Jewish history, and the concepts that interpret it, should view such developments with some disquiet. There is first the wish to be freed of the burden of the Jewish-Christian eschatological "myth," as some critics have called it. There is on the other hand, the inescapable discomfort when Jewish experiences closest to the bone, like the Holocaust, are bowdlerized for indiscriminate application; and its gives special point to one's discomfort if one recalls that a fundamental reason for the unwillingness, or inability, of others to help at the time was the fact that the Jewish victims were not recognized in their own capacity but merged in a general mass not subject to their special forms of abuse. Similar, if of fairly trivial consequence, is the irritation Toynbee aroused when he first labeled the Jews "fossils" and then appropriated the Jewish Exile, converted into a universalized concept of "Diaspora," and proposed it as the form in which Western civilization was to escape the fate of all other civilizations and to survive impending universal genocide.

Given the inescapable complications of the Jewish situation in history, it has serious consequences when one brings this subject into the general academy. No partisan view formerly protected by isolation from opposed perceptions can now rest easy in its unquestioned assumptions. There may be a polite avoidance of open confrontations, but the issue lies near the surface, only barely covered. The constant scrutiny of evidence on more superficial matters, matters of social science or technical historiography rather than ultimate personal concern, cannot fail to put strain on the convenient clichés by which identities are sustained. The wearisome humanistic demand to "Know thyself" is rendered uncomfortably relevant. But this, after all, is said to be one of the primary purposes that a university must serve; and certainly it is a function aspired to by any faculty of the humanities.

Ten

Religion and Culture

Judaism as a Cultural System

David Buchdahl

"Wise men lay up knowledge; but the mouth of the foolish is
an imminent ruin."

Proverbs 10.14[1]

The Problem of Interpretation

Interpretation is simply a way of saying something about something; but saying something about
Judaism, or "modern" Judaism as a cultural system, presents a series of difficulties for anyone who
is foolish enough to open his mouth. The first difficulty, and by far the greatest, is the medium itself;
the words out of which any interpretation must be
fashioned have become an obstacle.

To the men of our age, nothing is as familiar
and trite as words. Of all things they are the
cheapest, most abused and least esteemed. They
are the objects of perpetual defilement. We all
live in them, feel in them, but failing to uphold
their independent dignity, to respect their power
and weight, they turn waif, elusive—a mouthful
of dust.[2]

Most interpretations simply make matters worse—
heaps of dust, debris from the tower of Babel piled
upon the echoing screams of a people. It has been
said that after the destruction of the Second Temple, prophecy was left to children and fools. After
the Holocaust (the day before yesterday) the same
might well be said for interpretation.

If we are bold or foolish enough to attempt the
task, we face a further difficulty—what Harold

197

Bloom somewhere called the anxiety of influence or the psychology of belatedness. Aware as we are of the role which interpretation has played in the formation of Judaism, who would imagine himself capable of saying something new? Interpretation is a central force in the development of Judaism. Joseph interpreting Pharoah's dream, Huldah interpreting an ancient scroll for King Josiah, the Levites interpreting the Torah read by Ezra to the congregation of Israel, or Kabbalists interpreting a verse from psalms—these acts and others are the formative events of Jewish tradition and represent the creative role which interpretation has played in its life. As Neusner has suggested, from the time of Ezra forward "the history of Judaism became the interpretation of Torah and its message for each successive age."[3]

Whether or not one chooses to accept this rabbinic equation between the history of Judaism and the interpretation of Torah, it certainly serves to underscore the significance of interpretation within Judaism, that long elaboration of meaning which has occurred through time. When we appreciate this process, and the brilliance of the prophets, rabbis, mystics, and scholars who have all participated in the task, how do we muster the courage to add our words to theirs? Whether our interpretation is intended to provide meaning for the Jew or the Gentile, can we, can I, really imagine ourselves equal to this task? Even if our words were somehow undefiled, what could they add to the meanings already elaborated? What would they be, coming at such a late time in the conversation which Judaism is—a conversation between Israel and God? What value could they have except to help keep memory alive?

This brings us to a third problem of interpretation, in addition to words which are defiled and a tradition in which we occupy such a late position. This is the difficulty with our intentions, which like our words, are no longer pure. Within the classical tradition of rabbinic Judaism, the intention of interpretation is always the same. It is a holy activity, a ritual act by which one penetrates more deeply into the meanings of Torah, thus to know and fulfill the will of God. In the modern context, however, the interpretation of Judaism may be guided by quite different intentions. Interpretation, from being an "instrument of faith," becomes the "exercise of suspicion."[4] Instead of a revelation of additional meaning, there is a destruction of traditional meaning. Or interpretation becomes another performance in the academic shrines of "Theory and Methodology" where the only intention is a display of erudition or wit—pilings of dust, vanity!

Interpretation thus becomes, as Cuddihy has named it, "the ordeal of civility," another chapter in the Jewish struggle with modernity.[5] It demonstrates the Jew's ability to participate in modern scholarship with its reasoned restraint, refined logic, polite language, and inoffensive tones.

Jews have helped to build this house of modern intellect, and the process
of dispassionate interpretation becomes the price of continued residence.
In the synagogue the Jew can cry and sing; in literature he can be crude
and obscene; in interpretation he can demonstrate decorum and a well-
disciplined mind.

If these difficulties were not by themselves enough, there is a further
problem of knowing or deciding what Judaism is. If it is itself the product
of centuries of interpretation, how are we to determine both its center and
periphery? Neusner comments that "as a concept, Judaism, understood
to mean Jewish religion (a datum to be studied by reference to creed, cult,
liturgy and even law) thus appears to be the most modern phenomenon of
all. The disintegration of Jewish *tradition* into Judaism on the one hand
and Jewishness or *culture* on the other, is the direct consequence of the
modern experience."[6] This contrast between Judaism on the one hand
and Jewishness or culture on the other is a familiar one: on the one hand,
faith, ritual, Torah, and the whole rabbinic tradition; on the other, the
various styles and customs of Jews around the world. But then what of
Judaism as a cultural system, a system of symbols and meanings contained in a set of myths and texts? And what is the relationship of a system
in this sense to tradition as an active force in Jewish life? These are the
questions which, with defiled words and dubious intentions, I want briefly
to consider.

System and Tradition

In his Friedland lecture to the Jewish Theological Seminary of
America in 1979, "The Talmud as Anthropology," Neusner extolled the
work of a few anthropologists for the light it shed on certain aspects of
Judaism and the study of religion. I expect most readers of this volume are
familiar with the examples which Neusner provided: Edmund Leach's
structural interpretation of "The Legitimacy of Solomon," Mary Douglas's original analysis of "The Abominations of Leviticus" in *Purity and
Danger,* and Clifford Geertz's widely influential discussion of "Religion
as a Cultural System."[7] What each of these contributions shared, and
what was articulated most explicitly by Geertz, is the notion that stories,
rules, or symbols cannot be usefully interpreted as isolated phenomena.
Their true importance is the part they play in a wider *system* of meanings
which it is the task of interpretation to reveal.

Leach, for instance, shows that the different stories in Chronicles
regarding succession to the throne of Israel mediate an important con-
tradiction between Israel as a purely separate, endogamous *people* on the
one hand, and a *kingdom* involved with exogamous political alliances on
the other. Douglas reveals the subtle relationships between dietary laws

and social boundaries, the way internal divisions can establish and protect external boundaries, and the way anomalies in one system can create regularities in another. And Geertz, though his examples are from Indonesia, not Israel, illustrates how a world view and a way of life are associated, or integrated, by a system of symbols.

It is not an isolated ritual here, or a particularly profound symbol there that provides a "religion" with its special force and appeal. It is rather its systemic quality, its ability to make a comprehensive order out of life's vicissitudes. "So far as life is to be orderly and trustworthy," Neusner observed, "it is a system which makes it so." For Mishnah and Talmud, therefore, the task of interpretation is "to look for the center of it all, to uncover the principal conceptions which unite the mass of detail."[8] The proper aim is to reveal the system which the ancient scribes and rabbis created after the system of Temple sacrifice had disintegrated.

Readers are likely to recall that Geertz defined religion as "a system of symbols which acts to establish powerful, pervasive and long-lasting moods and motivations in men by formulating conceptions of a general order of existence, and clothing these in such an aura of factuality that the moods and motivations seem uniquely realistic."[9] Oddly enough, however, when Geertz elaborates upon his definition, he has nothing at all to say about systems per se. He speaks instead of models, emphasizing the dual aspects of symbolic models—the fact that they are both "models *of*" and "models *for*" reality—pictures of the world and prescriptions for living in it. If they were only models *for* reality, the whole process of cultural change would be nearly impossible, since the lines of influence would flow only one way—from the model outward to the reality or the world—as with our genes whose molecular message reliably reproduces individuals of a species over and over again. If change takes place at all, it is a terribly slow and somewhat random process, the outcome of mutation and natural selection working together to bring new species into the world. Cultural change, on the other hand, is a more conscious process; and this is because cultural models are also models *of* reality. They can change in response to changing conditions within the world. The lines of influence work back in the other direction and new models are the result.

The dual aspect of symbolic models accounts for religion's special integrative power. As a model *of,* it is a picture of the world, a world view. As a model *for,* it is a way for living, an ethos. It works, when it does, because the symbols in both models are the same, so much so that it never appears as if there are two models, only one. Ethos and world view are thus inseparable.

Geertz's analysis of these issues served to emphasize the idea that religion was not simply a metaphysical doctrine, not "animism" or "animitism" or polytheism or monotheism, but a way of being in the world; not only how people imagine the world but how they respond to it.

Now it should be clear that, as a system, a religion will involve several different models, a whole array of symbolic forms that vary in their degree of complexity, significance, or art. Job as a story, for example, becomes a model *of* the evil that befalls men's lives. As a person, Job is a model *for* suffering. Or there is the story of Ruth, a model *of* social relations between Jews and gentiles, and Ruth herself, a model *for* devout conversion.

But where does this line of inquiry lead, this talk of "models" and "systems," as if religion were well served by discussing it with such mechanical metaphors? Even the phrase "a system of meaning" seems far removed from the passionate speech or intense love that lends importance to something as abstract as a model or a system. As an anthropologist, Geertz offered a definition of religion that was to end in the art of ethnography—not the analysis of a system but the description of real life, the moods and motivations that people exhibit in the course of their lives.

So we need to ask, as Neusner has asked in his analysis of Mishnah, "Who is the system for?" "Why is it created?" "Under what conditions and for whom?" If these contextual issues are not addressed, then systemic analysis, that is, structuralism, no matter how elegant or subtle, ends by "reducing the flesh and blood of reality to neat matchboxes."[10] Neusner shows us that we cannot understand the system of Mishnah, for example, unless we perceive that it was a response to catastrophe. It was the work of scribes and rabbis who sought an alternative to the moods of wild messianic longing or total despair. It became for the rabbis who used it, and the communities in which it became normative, a "map without territory,"[11] a system for making daily life holy outside the Holy Temple which lay in ruins. It substituted Torah for the Temple, recitation for sacrifice, reason for war. It made Torah itself into a dwelling place. Its six divisions are a model *of* how the world is arranged. Its purpose is to make life holy and it provides a model *for* a holy life. Its mood is a confident optimism in the face of catastrophes that could have otherwise been overwhelming to the point of ruin.[12]

I mention this situation with Mishnah because Neusner has been exceptionally clear about what he has been doing with the analysis of this system, and because it obviously plays such a great role in anything we might call Judaism. Certainly what is true for Mishnah—that we need to know the whys and wherefors of it—is true for any other system within Judaism, or even, as I would like to suggest, for Judaism as a whole.

Judaism, like Mishnah, can be viewed as a system of meaning created by particular people in a particular place and time—the Jews of modernity in Europe and America. Both are things that are made. For the rabbis of

Yavneh, Mishnah was a way of preserving whatever could be preserved, at first by memory and oral transmission, eventually in the form of a text. Judaism today is not nearly so systematic, but it too is something made, and made for very much the same reason—to preserve what is seen as essential to a tradition.

And what is tradition? Perhaps we could say that a tradition is the storehouse of elements out of which systems of meanings are made. When Jacob gave his final curse and blessings to his twelve sons, as recorded at the conclusion of Genesis, he created a system of tribes that contains, for the anthropologist anyway, evidence of a totemic tradition of which only a few faint residues remain. Judah is a lion, Isaachar a large-boned ass. "Naphtali is a hind let loose" (Gen. 49.21). Joseph is a fruitful vine. Of course one might say that this is only a manner of speech. But this is just the point. The manner of speech depends upon traditional forms of thought that make this system possible. In the same way, if there had not been a tradition of memory and oral recitation, then Mishnah would not have been possible.

Systems are created out of tradition, and then enter into tradition in turn. A tradition is the vast, unorganized, unsystematic consciousness of the past which is itself present. We speak of "it" but such reification is easily misleading, since "it" has no particular shape but changes continually as it absorbs new elements and sheds old ones. Mishnah was made to preserve a part of tradition, and in turn it becomes a part of tradition.

So we have this contrast between tradition on the one hand and system on the other—a total amount of information available for use, and an organization of a part of that information for practical purposes—a vague totality versus a systematic portion. Judaism is a system or a sequence of systems constantly made and remade out of Jewish tradition, out of the elements of the Jewish past. These elements can be ancient texts or modern events, faith in the messianic promise or in the names of kings and prophets, a word or even a sound or taste that evokes a particular meaning and finds its way into evanescent systems that provide a form and meaning to life.

I said above that the Jews of modernity make "Judaism." I think this is correct. It is made by rabbis and scholars who continue the classical tradition, who even insist that Judaism is Torah and Talmud, nothing more, nothing less. But it is also made by Zionists, reformists, secular Israelis, and other men and women who act out their own versions of Judaism or denounce a particular version of Judaism, whatever the case may be.

Of course it is not every Jew who participates in the making of Judaism into a "system of meanings." This is the task of interpretation, a task for critics and scholars afflicted with the need for order and meaning in a world that is, let us admit it, grossly obscene and quite mad. When the ancient rabbis created Mishnah, making a particular system out of tradition, they arranged it into six divisions. Those who make Judaism into a system frequently arrange it into three. We could represent the sequence of systems and periods in the following way, which is certainly not intended as a complete or definitive list, but merely a suggestive pattern:

Ancient Judaism
    Tribes
    Laws and Judges
    Kingdoms
    Prophecy

Rabbinic Judaism
    Mishnah
    Talmud
    Kehillah
    Kabbalah

Modern Judaism
    Hasidism
    Haskalah
    Holocaust
    Zionism

Objections will undoubtedly be raised against such a list, but as I said it is only meant to be suggestive, not terribly systematic. Certainly I do not imply that all these systems share an equivalent status. Obviously they do not. But how is it possible to speak of the Holocaust as a "system of meaning"? Is it not a gross indecency to couch such a monstrous crime in these terms? Yet for Jews of our own times, this is precisely what "Holocaust theology" and "Holocaust studies" achieve: the transformation of an incomprehensible horror into a system of meaning—a world view dominated by evil and an ethos permeated by fear and zealous determination—Never Again! Pilgrimages to the death camps become the ritual which brings the system to life. Here is where it happened. So the Holocaust assumes its place in the wider sequence of systems that we are calling Judaism.

It would be possible too, of course, to add items or systems to the list. Since there is no high court to arbitrate on such matters, and the divisions are not yet fixed, those who create Judaism are free to include whatever they believe is a valid expression of the tradition. Psalms for example, or Proverbs could both be added in this sequence. The psalms offer a world view which is overwhelmed by the presence and majesty of God in the world, and the moods of a warrior king that alternate between joy and grief. Proverbs provide a worldly wisdom and a mood of moderation that settles in after all of life's battles have been lost or won. Created at a particular time, Psalms and Proverbs, like all the other systems within Judaism, become a part of the tradition. Psalms remain as melodies repeated through the centuries, an oral transmission which links several generations through a shared performance. Proverbs persist as a model *of* wise speech and a model *for* righteous conduct in everyday affairs.

As a sequence of systems, all these different systems arrange themselves into a certain chronology—early or ancient, rabbinic or medieval, and modern. We have accepted current ideas of modernity and progress in order to see ourselves in a certain light. But as these systems become parts of a tradition, they lose their temporal orderliness, sharing instead a timeless contemporaneity, a past which is everywhere present. They become elements that undergo endless recombinations into new systems of meaning with a specific purpose until they too become a part of tradition. The process may be likened to a tree whose roots (tradition) grow ever deeper and whose branches (systems) extend ever higher into the air.

It is possible to carry out an interpretation for any one of these systems as separate phenomena, as Leach did for kingship or Douglas for a portion of the dietary rules. But such interpretations scarcely describe Judaism, nor are they meant to. We must at least try to remember that Judaism is never what we say it is, never a system, never even a sequence of systems, but a living faith, an "acted document."[13] The systems we identify are not its essence but merely its shells, external forms that provide access to internal states—the moods and motivations arising in different contexts serving different needs, meaning different things to different people—to women who have families and worry, to men who study and fear, to historians and mystics, to the foolish son, and to the wise.

God:Torah:Israel

Let us approach the question, the problem of Judaism as a cultural system, from another angle. In Judaism, as with other religious traditions, we find certain fundamental elements which become a foundation for all the various systems of meaning that appear. In Judaism, there are three—God: Torah: Israel.

I say there are three. Perhaps there are more. I do not have an argument as to why I choose these three and no others. I might say that the choice is self-evident, you either see it or you don't. And perhaps Mary Douglas is correct, that what appears as self-evident is dependent upon the basic perceptions we have of ourselves as social creatures made up of mind, speech, and body.[14] This perception (which may well be a cultural universal) then finds itself expressed on the cosmic level as God:Torah:Israel. It is the same in Buddhism—the Triple Gem of Buddha, Dharma, and Sangha is often understood as enlightened mind, enlightened speech, and enlightened body. We cannot even rule out the possibility of cultural diffusion of such ideas. It makes no difference, however, in the present context, why there are these three or why there are not more. Tradition presents them. That is enough.

God:Torah:Israel—not three separate elements but a pristine unity. The formation of the unity is the beginning of Judaism. What they in fact are, or what the unity means, is what Judaism as a cultural system is really all about.

God:Torah:Israel—though not primarily symbols, they do function as symbols, as words on a page or sounds in the ear that convey certain meanings. Symbols which are themselves symbolized. The symbol of God is his name—the tetragrammaton. The symbol of Torah is the scroll— black letters dancing in white space. The symbol of Israel is the circumcised foreskin—sublimated sacrifice. Name, scroll and skin: Naming as symbolic of the mind; scroll the symbol of speech; skin symbolic of the body.

God:Torah:Israel—a pure configuration, like Rosenzweig's *Star*.[15] Creation:: Revelation :: Redemption. Symbol and text. Another system out of the tradition. A primordial sign (see fig. 10.1).

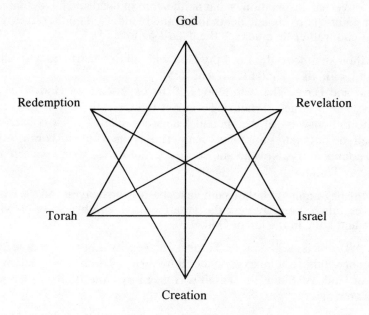

Fig. 10.1 The Star of Redemption

If symbols are things which essentially represent something else, then God:Torah:Israel represent only themselves. A pattern—a system of meanings—a model *of* life—a model *for* life—a way into life.

God:Torah:Israel: Interpretation can either bring us closer to these forms of life or lead us away into other systems of meaning—the meaning of modernity, perhaps, or meaningless talk. Systems are the products of interpretation carried out by particular people under certain circumstances—anthropologists or rabbis, phenomenologists or Kabbalists. Some become interior to the tradition. Others remain an exterior evaluation.

God:Torah:Israel—In a time when theologians, including some Jewish ones, have recently entertained the idea of the death of God, when fundamentalism and secularism compete for every mind, when science turns into mysticism and all words are defiled, is it not still dangerous to speak vainly of God? Or to speak of God without fear?

Proverbs teaches that "The fear of the Lord is the beginning of knowledge" (1:7).

And if God does not exist?

> God is not life. God is light. He is the Lord of life, but he is no more living than dead. To say the one or the other of him—with the old (philosopher) that "God has life," or with the new one that "God is dead," reveals the identical pagan bias. The only thing which does not resist verbal designation is that neither/nor of dead and alive, that tender point where life and death touch and blend. God neither lives nor is he dead; rather he quickens the dead—he loves.[16]

"And thou shalt love the Lord thy God with all thy heart and with all thy soul and with all thy might." (Deut. 6:5)

Fear and Love. The twin moods of the experience of God.

God:Torah:Israel—What is Torah? It is like asking "What is Zen?" We cite the answers of the ancient teachers. Hillel: "What is hateful to yourself, do not do to your fellow man. That is the whole of Torah. All the rest is commentary. Now go and study."[17] Before the world was created, there was Torah:

> In the beginning, two thousand years before the heaven and the earth, seven things were created: the Torah written with black fire on white fire and lying in the lap of God.[18]

God:Torah:Israel—Before Torah achieves its status as a text, as a system of symbols, it an experience. Pure terror. Torah is Revelation, the voice of God. At Sinai, the Torah was given by God to all the people of Israel—terror!

> And all the people perceived the thunderings and the lightnings, and the voice of the horn, and the mountain smoking; and when the people

saw it they trembled, and stood far off. And they said unto Moses: Speak thou with us, and we will hear; but let not God speak to us, lest we die (Ex. 20:15–16).

Centuries later, when Ezra read from the written Torah to the assembly of Israel gathered in Jerusalem, we read that

All the people wept, when they heard the words of the Law. Then he said unto them, Go your way, eat the fat, and drink the sweet, and send portions unto him for whom nothing is prepared, for this day is holy with our Lord; neither be ye grieved; for the joy of the Lord is your strength (Neh. 8:9–10).

Fear turned to joy—from fear at Sinai to joy in Jerusalem. Fear and joy—the twin moods of the experience of Torah.

Serve the Lord with gladness; come before his presence with singing (Ps. 100:1–2).

Tradition teaches that there are two Torahs. One written and one which is oral. "Eventually," according to Neusner, "the whole of the holy literature of rabbinic Judaism would, in time to come, be called Torah, and then would include both the written Scriptures and the rabbinic writings which were, in toto, claimed to be Oral Torah."[19]

But Heschel says, "The truth is that the oral Torah was never written down. The meaning of the Torah has never been contained by books."[20]

God:Torah:Israel—Israel, a patriarch, a people, a kingdom, a land, an enigma. Body and earth. When the people of Israel wandered in the desert after the Exodus from Egypt, Moses spoke to them saying:

Not for thy righteousness, or for the uprightness of the heart, dost thou go in to possess their land; but for the wickedness of these nations the Lord thy God doth drive them out before thee, and that he may establish the word which the Lord swore unto thy fathers, to Abraham, to Isaac and to Jacob. Know therefore that it is not for thy righteousness that the Lord thy God giveth thee this good land to possess it; for thou art a stiffnecked people (Deut. 9:5–6).

Israel—a stiff-necked people, so often and so consistently reluctant to fulfill the commandments of the Torah. From the Golden Calf to the present day, disobedience. Stiff-necked. The Holy Land can never be a secure possession:

To the eternal people, home is never home in the sense of land, as it is to the peoples of the world who plough the land and live and thrive on it, until they have all but forgotten that being a people means something besides being rooted in a land. The eternal people has not been permitted to while away time in any home. It never loses the untrammeled freedom of a wanderer who is more faithful a knight to his country when he roams abroad, craving adventure and yearning for the land he has left behind, than when he lives in that land. In the most profound sense possible, this people has a land of its own only in that it has a land it yearns for—a holy land. And so even when it has a home, this people, in recurrent contrast to all other peoples on earth, is not allowed full possession of that home. It is only "a stranger and a sojourner. God tells it: "The land is mine."[21]

Rosenzweig wrote these words during World War I. The history of the modern state of Israel has not contradicted them but only serves to demonstrate the inescapable burden of their truth. Even in the traditional homeland, secure possession remains an unobtained dream.

Today the state of Israel is the wider field in which the systems of modern Judaism take shape. If Mishna can be conceived as a map without territory, then Israel has now become a territory without a map. I do not mean this only in the obvious geopolitical sense of disputed boundaries, though this too is traditional. I mean it in a cultural sense, that there is no commonly accepted model for life in Israel. Secular Israelis, orthodox Jews, warriors, pacifists all struggle with competing visions of their home. Was it ever any different? Do we impose an order on the past that it never had?

God:Torah:Israel—Mind:Speech:Body. God is substance, not any ordinary substance, but still a substance of some kind, something to love. Speech, we know, is a code. Torah contains a code of law, but insofar as it emanates from God it has some substantive quality as well—letters of fire, primordial sound, speech as a body, as when we speak of the body of a text. Still, for the most part, it is a code. Mind and speech—substance and code. Israel is the coded substance, the body formed by the law, as with genes in our own bodies. The letters of Torah provide the body of Israel with all of its qualities—its shape, its sense of itself, its destiny.[22]

God:Torah:Israel—In the body of Israel there are individuals who have a direct link with the mind of God. In ancient days they were known as prophets. In medieval times they might have been mystics who scrambled the letters of the code in order to gain novel insights into the substance of God. They gave us a vision of his body. Who performs this function today for Israel? Perhaps it is anyone whose prayers are still heard by God, or anyone who keeps the love and fear of God alive.

God:Torah:Israel—Words pile up. We can say that ancient Judaism developed around the experience of God and based its systems on the charismatic authority of prophets, priests, and kings. Rabbinic Judaism centered itself on Torah and built its systems on the traditional authority that ancient Judaism had provided, the tradition of Moses and the rabbis. The tradition of rabbinic Judaism gave way slowly, assimilated to the rationalism of the modern Western world. But the Holocaust undermined reason and returned modern Judaism to Israel. Israel becomes the center of modern Judaism, and with the return to Israel we see the return of everything that reason by itself might have repressed—messianic yearning, traditional faith, and the charisma that attaches itself to the land. In Israel, even the air and stones have their own charisma—gifts from Heaven.

Antisystems

Whether we understand Judaism as tradition or system, no account of its forms and meanings would be accurate if it failed to consider the impacts it has had on the wider social field in which it occurs. Judaism has given rise to other systems of meanings that have engulfed the world. Sometimes these systems have resulted from individuals who left the social boundaries of the traditional community, as in the archetypal story of Ishmael, a castaway from Abraham who became the founder of all the Arab nations. But the greatest instance surely is Christianity, the teachings of the Jew born in Bethlehem and his disciple Saul. Christianity and Islam, these two systems grew out of Judaism, taking the God of Abraham and transforming everything else.

And along with these traditions has grown a different sort of system, another "ism" that has shaped the course of Western culture as profoundly as Christianity or Islam. This is anti-Semitism, the permanent shadow that accompanies Judaism's own transformations. For the anti-Semite, it is not God or Torah or even Israel that forms the basis of meaning. It is the Jew, a symbol of everything which is hateful and despised.

> Let us consider the real Jew [Karl Marx proclaimed], not the Sabbath Jew, but the everyday Jew. Let us not seek the secret of the Jew in his religion, but let us seek the secret of the religion in the real Jew. What is the profane basis of Judaism? Practical need, self-interest. What is the worldly cult of the Jew? Huckstering? What is his worldly God? Money![23]

Like so many other anti-Semites, Marx uses the Jew as a symbol for what he hates—money, private property, capitalism. It was Max Weber, of course, who years later demonstrated that the roots of modern, rational capitalism lay not in Judaism but in Christian puritanism, but the Jew remains a symbol of capitalist greed—Shylock seeking his pound of flesh. For the anti-Semite, the Jew is a symbol of impurity and defilement, the exact opposite of the condition of holiness which the Torah commands. As a liminal figure, forever outside the boundaries of the larger social communities in which Jews settled, the Jew always appeared as a dark and dangerous creature, a threat to the established social order. If this condition of liminality also contributed to the special creativity within Jewish culture, the price that has been paid is self-hate and persecution.[24]

Zionism sought a land where Jews could live without fear, a refuge from the ravages of anti-Semitism down through the centuries. After the Holocaust, Israel became a reality, but as a refuge from anti-Semitism it has been a complete failure. Modern Jews must face the realization that anti-Semitism will never cease, not as long as there is one Jew left on earth, or until the ancient messianic promise of redemption is fulfilled. Instead of being a refuge, Israel has become a focus for the concentrated hatred of Jews, for which anti-Semitism is still the polite name. As I write these words, Syria, the ancient enemy, sits with Russian missiles poised for war on the slopes of Lebanon where cedar trees once grew; and the whole Middle East is on a short fuse for nuclear war.

In America, the growing tide of conservative and fundamentalist Christians look toward Israel with wonder and fear. Here is where the ancient prophecies of the Last Days will be played out, with the remnant of the Israelites gathered into the Holy Land; then the great drama shall begin—Armageddon and the coming of the Lord. Arms for Israel support this kind of scenario as much as they might help Israel's "security."

The future of "modern Judaism" certainly depends upon the development of these situations, and upon the continued existence of the state of Israel, in war or in peace. So we wait, and we cannot prevent ourselves from asking the terrible question, when will the next war come, and how long will Israel survive?

Rest

Words pile up; meanings come and go; moods change. God, Torah, and Israel remain—a system of meanings for rabbis and children, scholars and mystics, widows and fools. Judaism is not one thing but a multiplicity, not even a sequence of systems but an infinite possibility of meaning arising from the constellation of God:Torah:Israel. It is a way for being in the world.

Words pile up, become defiled. In ritual, words are purified. They move into a different space. These words move into Sabbath. Interpretation seeks rest.

Remember the Sabbath day, to keep it holy. Six days shalt thou labor, and do all thy work; but the seventh day is a sabbath unto the Lord thy God; in it thou shalt not do any manner of work, thou nor thy son, nor thy daughter, nor thy man-servant, nor thy maid-servant, nor thy cattle, nor thy stranger that is within thy gates; for in six days the Lord

made heaven and earth, the sea, and all that in them is and rested on
the Seventh Day; wherefore the Lord blessed the Sabbath Day and
hallowed it (Ex. 20:8–11).

At Sinai, the former slaves were instructed to rest one day a week, to do
no work whatsoever, and to remember the process of creation.

Six days a week, Judaism lives in the world. On the seventh day it
contracts into itself, deep into a moment that is out of time, that hearkens
back to the original time when the world was new. Sabbath is the ritual
creation of the week and the recreation of eternity. Without Sabbath the
days are just an endless stream of days—"Tomorrow and tomorrow and
tomorrow"—the week is only work. Words pile up and turn to dust. On
Sabbath they find their true dimensions. Words turn into song. In the
space between the sixth day and the first, in the liminal realm of the
Sabbath, the way is opened to Israel, Torah, and God—not any longer as
symbols in some system of meaning but as sheer actuality, however it is
for each individual soul. There is no structure here, no system. The regularity of Sabbath worship and ritual practice become a way out of
structure, out of the taken-for-granted meanings.

The ritual of Sabbath is like an old reliable ferryboat that delivers a
person from one side of a river to another. On either side are the anxieties
and meanings of everyday life. But merely begin the Sabbath with a ritual
blessing and soon one finds oneself transported into the midst of the
Sabbath just as surely as the old ferry carries its passengers out to the
middle of the river. There, in the midst of the Sabbath, God:Torah:Israel
can remain hidden in deep places which consciousness cannot fathom, or
grow into life.

Words pile up; meanings change, moods flicker into life. The Sabbath
is set apart from this impermanence. It is a "dream of perfection,"[25] a
deep river that you can step into more than once, a river that flows
nowhere, but whose waters are always fresh and clean.

Words pile up. Dust and vanity. Judaism evolves out of centuries of
Sabbaths, following each other forever, until one day perhaps, as tradition
teaches, a Messiah will come to redeem the world. Time will cease. And
then every day will be as a Sabbath, and the whole world shall know peace.

On Sabbath, the body rests, levels of meaning are peeled off like layers
of a seed. The seed's meaning, its mystery, is its life. It will grow even on
Sabbath; without working, with no effort, it will continue to expand into
life.

The mind is like a seed. It too must rest after it has exhausted itself
with meaning. Then the heart beats quietly in time with Creation, and
Judaism is a moot point.

Notes

1. All quotations from Scripture are from the 1915 English translation published by the Jewish Publication society.

2. Abraham Joshua Heschel, *God in Search of Man* (Cleveland: World Publishing, 1959), p. 244.

3. Jacob Neusner, *The Way of Torah, an Introduction to Judaism* (North Scituate, Mass.: Duxbury Press, 1979), p. 10.

4. Paul Ricoeur, *Freud and Philosophy: An Essay on Interpretation*, trans. Denis Savage (New Haven: Yale University Press, 1970), pp. 28–36. I have tried to practice interpretation as an instrument of faith.

5. John Murray Cuddihy, *The Ordeal of Civility: Freud, Marx, Levi-Strauss and the Jewish Struggle with Modernity* (N.Y.: Basic Books, 1974).

6. Neusner, *The Way of Torah*, p. 123.

7. Edmund Leach, "The Legitimacy of Solomon," in Michael Lane, ed. *Introduction to Structuralism*, (N.Y.: Basic Books, 1970); Clifford Geertz, "Religion as a Cultural System," in his *The Interpretation of Cultures* (N.Y.: Basic Books, 1973), pp. 87–125; Mary Douglas, *Purity and Danger* (Baltimore: Penguin, 1970), pp. 54–73.

8. Jacob Neusner, "The Talmud as Anthropology," Annual Samuel Friedland Lecture, The Jewish Theological Seminary of America, 1979, p. 22.

9. Geertz, "Religion as a Cultural System," p. 90.

10. Jacob Neusner, "Beyond Historicism, After Structuralism: Story as History in Ancient Judaism," The 1980 Harry Spindel Memorial Lecture, Bowdoin College, Brunswick, Maine, p. 23.

11. Jacob Neusner, "Map without Territory: Mishnah System of Sacrifice and Sanctuary," *History of Religions* (1979).

12. Neusner, *The Way of Torah*, pp. 13–14, 19.

13. C. Geertz, "Thick Description," in *The Interpretation of Cultures*, p. 10.

14. Mary Douglas, "Self Evidence," in her *Implicit Meanings* (London: Routledge & Kegan Paul, 1975), pp. 276–317. I realize that I am distorting Douglas's idea of the social basis for self-evidence, but to develop the point here would take me too far afield.

15. Franz Rosenzweig, *The Star of Redemption*, trans. from 2d ed. 1930, William H. Hallo (Boston: Beacon Press, 1972), p. 300.

16. Ibid., p. 380.

17. Talmud b. Shabbat 31A, cited in Neusner, *The Way of Torah*, p. 21.

18. Midrash on Psalms to Ps. 90.3, Louis Ginzberg, *The Legends of the Jews*, trans. Henrietta Szold (Philadelphia: Jewish Publication Society, 1947). 1:3, cited in Neusner, *The Way of Torah*, p. 3.

19. Neusner, *The Way of Torah*, p. 14.

20. Heschel, *God in Search of Man*, p. 276.

21. Rosenzweig, *The Star of Redemption*, p. 300.

22. The idea of analyzing culture in terms of substance and code, which is only adumbrated here, derives from D. M. Schneider, *American Kinship, A Cultural Account* (Englewood Cliffs, N.J.: Prentice-Hall, 1968).

23. Karl Marx, "On the Jewish Question," in *Early Writings*, trans. and ed. T. B. Bottomore (New York: McGraw-Hill, 1964), p. 34.

24. The importance of liminality as a condition of social fields has been amply explored by Victor Turner. Cf. his *The Ritual Process* (Chicago: Aldine, 1969) and *Dramas, Fields, and Metaphors* (Ithaca: Cornell University Press, 1974).

25. Rosenzweig, *The Star of Redemption*, p. 313.

Judaism in the Comparison of Religions

Eleven

No Need to Travel
to the Indies

Judaism and the Study of Religion

Jonathan Z. Smith

In 1978, in the course of inviting participation in the reconstituted History of Judaism section of the American Academy of Religion, Jacob Neusner made a most important programmatic statement:

> I believe that section meetings in the History of Judaism should be planned so as to interest scholars in diverse areas of religious studies. If these meetings [on the history of Judaism] do not win the attention and participation of a fair cross-section of scholars in the field [of religious studies] as a whole, then they will not materially contribute to the study of religion in this country. There is no reason for the study of Judaism to be treated as a set of special cases and of matters so technical that only initiates can follow discussions—or would even want to.

This is a statement of the academic study of Judaism come of age. It is the perspective that informs this chapter.

I take it there is agreement that the topic "Judaism and the Study of Religion" is designed to address the question of the role of the study of Judaism within programs in religious studies in liberal arts colleges. I do not intend to discuss so-called Jewish Studies programs—programs which seem to me to lack any responsible academic war-

This chapter was first presented as a paper for the conference "Jewish Studies and the Humanities" at Brandeis University, March 19–20, 1981, sponsored by the Max Richter Foundation.

rant—or the older, indefensible notion of "Jewish presence" in programs in religious studies—Jewish professors primarily teaching Judaism to Jewish students. We are rather to ask what contribution the study of Judaism might make to the general curriculum. By implication, of course, to raise this question is to suggest how our graduate students ought to be trained, at least insofar as we take seriously the notion that graduate studies are, in part, preparation for teaching.

In order to ask this question, it is necessary to step back and reflect on the nature of the liberal arts curriculum. There are a multitude of spatial arrangements, the ways in which the blocks of courses are organized: general requirements, major requirements, prerequisites, electives, and the like. Each is appropriate to the peculiar ecology of particular institutions. What remains more or less constant is the temporal arrangements. Regardless of the academic calendar, there is almost always less than four full days of teaching time in a year-long course, less than one hundred hours of class meetings. And, there is no reason to presume that any student who takes one course on a given subject will necessarily take another one. Less than one hundred hours may represent, for a significant number of students, their sole course of study in a particular subject matter. It is at this point that curricular thought must begin—not with the major. For within such a context, no course can do everything, no course can be complete. The notion of a survey becomes ludicrous under such circumstances. Rather *each course is required to be incomplete, to be self-consciously and articulately selective.* We do not celebrate often enough the delicious yet terrifying freedom undergraduate, liberal arts education affords the faculty by its rigid temporal contraints. We do not have to "cover" everything. As long as we do not allow ourselves to be misled by that sad heresy that the Bachelor's degree is but a preparation for graduate studies (a notion that is becoming pragmatically unjustified and has never been educationally justifiable), there is nothing that must be taught, there is nothing that cannot be left out. A curriculum, whether represented by a particular course, a program, or a four-year course of study, becomes an occasion for deliberate, collegial, institutionalized choice.

I take as a corollary to these observations that each thing taught is taught not because it is "there" but because it connects in some interesting way with something else, because it is an example, an *exempli gratia,* of something that is fundamental, something that may serve as a precedent for further interpretation and understanding by providing an arsenal of instances, of paradigmatic events and expressions as resources from which to reason, from which to extend the possibility of intelligibility to that which first appears to be novel or strange. Whether this be perceived as some descriptive notion of the *characteristic,* some more normative notion of the *classical,* or some point in between, matters little. These are questions on which academicians of good will can profitably disagree.[1]

What ought not to be at controversy is the purpose for which we labor, that long-standing and deeply felt perception of the relationship between liberal learning and citizenship.

I take it as axiomatic that it is by an act of human will, through language and history, through words and memory, that we are able to fabricate a meaningful world and give place to ourselves. Education comes to life through the tensions generated by the double sense of fabrication: to build and to lie. For though we have no other means than language for treating with the world, words are not, after all, the same as that which they name and describe. Though we have no other recourse but to memory, to precedent, to what I have called fundamentals, if the world is not forever to be perceived as novel and, hence, remain forever unintelligible, the fit is never exact, nothing is ever quite the same. What is required at this point of tension is the trained capacity for judgment, for appreciating and criticizing the relative adequacy and insufficiency of any proposal of language and memory. What we seek to train are individuals who know not only that the world is more complex than it first appears but also that, therefore, *interpretative decisions* must be made, decisions of judgment which entail real consequences for which one must take responsibility, from which one may not flee by the dodge of disclaiming expertise. This ultimately political quest for fundamentals, for the acquisition of the powers of informed judgment, for the dual capacities of appreciation and criticism must be the explicit goal of every level of the liberal arts curriculum. The difficult task of making interpretative decisions must inform each and every course.

These matters become complex when we turn to a curriculum in religious studies. For, if we have correctly understood the archaeological and textual record, man has had his entire history in which to imagine deities and modes of interaction with them. But man, more precisely Western man, has had only the last few centuries in which to imagine the generic category of religion. It is this act of second-order, reflexive imagination which must be the central preoccupation of religious studies. That is to say, while there is a staggering amount of data, of phenomena, of human experiences and expressions that might be characterized, by one criterion or another, as religious—*there are no data for religion.* Religion is a creation of the scholar's study. It is created by the scholar's imaginative acts of comparison and generalization. *Religion has no independent existence apart from the academy.* For this reason, the student of religion must be exquisitely self-conscious. Indeed, this self-consciousness constitutes his primary expertise, his foremost object of study.

In this sense, religious studies are particularly appropriate for the liberal arts. For the self-conscious student of religion, no datum possesses intrinsic interest. It can be of value only insofar as it can serve as *exempli gratia* of some fundamental issue in the imagination of religion. The student of religion must be able to articulate clearly why "this" rather than "that" was chosen as an exemplum. His primary skill is concentrated in this effort of choice.

Implicit in this effort of choice are three conditions which need be met fully only at the professional level. First, that the datum has been well and truly understood. This presumes a mastery of both the primary materials and the tradition of their interpretation. Second, that the datum be displayed in the service of some important question, some fundamental theory, some paradigm, some element in the imagination of religion. Third, and of paramount importance, that there be some method for explicitly relating the datum to the theory, the question, the paradigm, and for evaluating each in terms of the other.

I have taken the title for this essay from a passage in *An Inquiry into the Original of Our Ideas of Beauty and Virtue* by that remarkable figure of the eighteenth-century Scottish Enlightenment, Francis Hutcheson:

> The late ingenious author [Lord Shaftesbury] has justly observed the absurdity of the monstrous taste which has possessed both the readers and writers of travels. They are sparing enough in accounts of the natural affections, the families, associations and friendships of the [American] Indians . . . indeed, of all their normal pursuits. They say, "These are but common stories. No need to travel to the Indies for what we see in Europe every day." The entertainment, therefore, in these ingenious studies consists chiefly in exciting horror and making men stare. The ordinary employment of the bulk of the Indians . . . has nothing of the prodigious, but a human sacrifice, a feast upon enemies' carcasses can raise a horror and admiration of the wondrous barbarity of the Indians.[2]

This passage, it seems to me, states with precision the most interesting dilemma of choice confronting the academic study of religion. Do we focus on those things which "excite horror and make men stare," or do we concentrate on "common stories," on "what we see in Europe every day"? It is a tension between religion imagined as an *exotic* category of human expression and activity, and religion imagined as an *ordinary* category of human expression and activity. This tension becomes particularly acute when we venture into the necessary endeavors of comparison, the imagining of the religions of other men, a central step in the imagination of religion.

It is at this point that we may usefully begin to join these most general considerations to our specific topic, Judaism and religious studies.[3] For these two options, the exotic and the ordinary, have been characteristic of the imagining of Judaism from the beginning—compare the fourth book of Apion's *Aegyptiaka*[4] with the royal symposium in Aristeas,[5] or the imagining of Jews as a "superstitious, "barbarian" race[6] with imagining them as a "philosophical race"[7] or as "cosmopolitans."[8] These continue to be options for the scholarly imagination. This is so, in part, because of the peculiar position of Judaism within the larger framework of the imagining of Western religion—close, yet distant; similar, yet strange; "occidental," yet "oriental"; ordinary, yet exotic. Emphasize the first set of terms and you get the anonymous Jew described by Clearchus of Soli as "a *hellene* not only in his language but also in his soul";[9] emphasize the other, and you may get the use of Isaiah 6:9–10 in early Christian discourse.[10]

Despite the sometimes painful and sorry apologetics, this tension between the exotic and the ordinary, the unfamiliar and the familiar is at the very heart of the imagining of Judaism and has enormous cognitive power. Indeed, I would go so far as to suggest that this is the prime reason for including Judaism in a program in religious studies in a liberal arts curriculum. This tension invites, it requires, comparison. Judaism is foreign enough for most of our students for comparison and interpretation to be necessary; it is close enough for most of our students for comparison and interpretation to be possible. (I play here, of course, with Dilthey's well-known formulation: "Interpretation would be impossible if expressions of life were completely strange. It would be unnecessary if nothing strange were in them. It lies, therefore, between these two extremes.")[11] Judaism ought to serve as a crucial exemplum for the enterprise of imagination, self-consciousness, and choice that characterizes religious studies.

Let me be clearly understood. I would insist that Judaism is not a proper or necessary object of study in religious studies programs in liberal arts colleges for historical or demographic reasons. We do not study Judiams because it is "there," because it has played an important role in our imagination of western civilization, or because some of our faculty and students happen to be Jews. As I have argued earlier, there is nothing in the liberal arts curriculum that must be taught, nothing which cannot be left out. We study Judaism for our own ends, for the purposes of the academy. We teach Judaism only insofar as it can serve as *exempli gratia* for our common endeavor at imagining religion.

Judaism, by virtue of its tensive situation between the near and the far provides religious studies with an ideal test case for central methodological issues such as definition and comparison. But I have discussed these matters elsewhere.[12] For the purposes of this essay, I should like to suggest some substantive topics for which Judaism might provide the most useful and compelling *exempli gratia* for our students, particularly at the most basic level of our curriculum in religious studies.

I will suggest four topics; they are by no means exhaustive. Rather they are intended, themselves, to serve as examples for our common enterprise. Each addresses what I perceive to be the fundamental problem confronting the teacher in a religious studies program, the overwhelming bias of our students toward conceiving of religion as something that is primarily individual, primarily a matter of faith and belief, and distinguished from the workaday world. Such notions, perhaps to be understood as crude generalizations out of certain impulses in the prevailing Protestant tradition, render the religious life of the majority of mankind wholly incomprehensible. Small wonder that, in a recent examination administered to three thousand college students by the Council on Learning, testing their knowledge of the world and other cultures, knowledge of "other" religions scored the lowest by a considerable degree.[13]

Given their general perspective, our students have great difficulty in conceiving religious systems for mapping significance in the world which do not require the postulation of moral values such as good and evil. Wherever they confront duality, it is immediately and instinctively translated into moral dualism. This is not surprising. The majority of textbooks, the majority of so-called classics in the field of religious studies do the same. Indeed, they go further. If such duality is not moral, it is somehow irrational.

Anthropologists have effectively addressed this issue in one form with the development of the distinction between "shame" and "guilt" cultures and the elaboration, cross-culturally, of the dynamics of "shame" and "honor" in terms of a set of classic texts and field reports.[14] The same must be done for the more pervasive religious categories of pure and impure.

A quotation from the first important academic treatment of this topic, William Robertson Smith's *Lectures on the Religion of the Semites,* makes clear the problem:

> The irrationality of laws of uncleanness, from the standpoint of spiritual religion or even of the higher heathenism, is so manifest. . . . I do not see how any historical student can refuse to class them with savage taboos.[15]

The equation "laws of uncleanness" = "savage taboos" = "irrationality" has haunted both the scholarly literature and popular perceptions ever since.

Much important work has been done to differentiate the various rules in nonliterate societies formerly lumped together under the title "taboo" and to display their logical coherence. But, beyond the problem of these materials being utterly exotic for our students, the logic is, more often than not, presented as a display of the anthropologist's interpretative ingenuity, and, as such, does not address the fundamental problem. For our students will ask: granted *we* can make sense out them, do *they?* Are taboos systems of articulate native thought or are they superstitious habits for those who hold them?

India has been the other major resource. But, aside from the fact that it, too, is exotic, the same situation prevails. There is remarkably little available to the college teacher from the rich Indian textual tradition of the systematics of purity and impurity. Rather, the decisive work has either been done on the grand theoretical level or by field anthropologists.[16] Again, we lack the articulate native.

Judaism presents the opposite case. While the priestly materials remain inarticulate (despite the ingenious attempts by scholars such as Douglas, Soler, Haran, Milgrom, and Levine to decode them),[17] there are other rich, almost obsessively articulate native systems available in excellent translations with outstanding scholarly commentaries: *Mishnah,* with Neusner's elaborate discussions of its purity systems;[18] Maimonides' *Mishneh Torah* in the Yale Judaica series.[19] There are, as well, quite different but equally articulate native systems that provide important proximate resources for comparison: Aristeas, Philo, Barnabas, Novatian.[20]

To discuss these materials with an undergraduate class is to display a fundamental element in religion. Through these materials, self-conscious as they are, one may raise important matters as to method in interpretation and comparison. But these materials may raise, as well, fundamental issues for a general education in the liberal arts—for example, *Mishnah*'s overwhelming concern for the definition and role of human intentionality.

My second example is no less pressing, although it is far more difficult to make precise. It is the notion of the domestic, the centrality of the domicile in religious activity. There is a well-known, rich, and convincing literature from a variety of disciplinary perspectives on the cosmic symbolism of sacred space, ceremonial space, the city and the temple.[21] But the house, when discussed at all, is treated merely as a miniature of these:

> The same cosmological symbolism, formulated in spatial, architectonic terms, informs house, city and universe. . . . Exactly like the city or the sanctuary, the house is sanctified, in whole or in part, by a cosmological symbolism or ritual.[22]

Yet one will search in vain in such works for the notion of the house as a distinctive locus of religious activity with an integrity of its own. One finds occasional studies of household shrines, but these are usually in works on folklore. The literature on domestic rituals is surprisingly sparse.[23] For this reason, it becomes all too easy for our students to oversimplify notions of the sacred and the profane—key elements in the academic imagination of religion.

Of course, there are exceptions, for example, the remarkable French tradition of scholarship on the Berber house.[24] But again, this is the exotic. Of far more use as a proximate yet foreign point of departure would be a work which describes the rich religion of the Jewish household, such as Zborowski and Herzog's *Life Is with People*.[25] One might then turn to specific domestic liturgical practices—although here the sources are disappointing. Despite the long tradition of scholarship, I know of no useful annotated translation of the daily or sabbath domestic services or the Passover *Haggadah* that is not marred by the kind of homiletics that are utterly inappropriate in the secular classroom.

Given the background and presuppositions of our students, it would be useful to have a discussion of the synagogue within the context of domesticity. To what degree is it best conceived as sacred space? as civil space? or are these categories inadequate? Again, the literature (except for histories of synagogue architecture) known to me is inadequate. Samuel Heilman's work, *Synagogue Life,* is the most useful, ethnographic point of departure.[26] But more classical materials will have to be introduced, particularly with respect to the tension between house (through the *haburah*) and synagogue as part of the enterprise of "domesticating" the Temple in early Judaism.

To discuss such matters with a college class is to do more than debate the question of origins, it is to raise fundamental questions about the adequacy of the dichotomy sacred/profane, it is to raise the issue of the relationship of the cosmological to the anthropological, it is, in the terminology of Francis Hutcheson, to insist on the "ordinary employment" of men as being of at least equal importance in the imagining of religion as the "prodigious."

The third topic, at first glance, seems more limited. I know of no thesis more secure in the imagining of early Christianity than that its fundamental generative problematic was the *Parousieverzögerung,* the so-called delay of the *parousia*. Not only the central texts of the New Testament,[27] but also the development of subsequent Christian traditions have been seen as a response to this problem. Thus Martin Werner can organize his magisterial work on the formation of Christian doctrine under the heading: "The Abandonment of the Basic Doctrine of Primitive Christianity consequent on the Non-Fulfilment of the *Parousia*."[28] More recently, New Testament scholars concerned with sociological questions have seized on Festinger's *When Prophecy Failed* as a major clue for reconstructing the social world of early Christianity.[29]

There is a serious problem of theory latent in this thesis. It not only suggests that religious communities are primarily constituted by theological issues (which I doubt), but that, in this case, the theology is to some degree negative, a response to the embarrassment of religious communities finding themselves having to live in the world! To quote Werner:

> The rise of Christian doctrine, i.e. the transformation of the Primitive Christian faith into the doctrine of Early Catholicism, was achieved as a process of the de-eschatologizing of Primitive Christianity.... Because of the unforeseen, but unavoidable, necessity of this de-eschatologizing, the development of Christianity in late antiquity acquired a decidedly critical character. Its course was not "normal," for it was burdened with special difficulties from the beginning.[30]

Aside from the awkward sociology, what are the implications of extending this "abnormal" model to other religious traditions as is now being done under the widespread rubric of millenarianism? For example, as I have argued elsewhere:

> The problem of cargo [cults] is *not* that the prophecy has failed or that the *parousia* has been delayed. It is rather that the prophecy has been fulfilled, but in an unexpected or "wrong" way.[31]

This is not all that uncommon in the history of religions. Simply ask Moctezuma!

The unexpected and unmessianic establishment of the state of Israel in relationship to the long tradition of yearnings for the restoration of Zion is *the* paradigmatic case. It has achieved surprisingly little scholarly attention.

To discuss Israel in this fashion with a college class is to do more than present a history of Zionism (which usually terminates in 1948, just when the problem for the imagining of religion becomes most interesting) or to engage in an exercise in Middle Eastern apologetics. It is to raise fundamental questions concerning the "adjustment" of traditions, the relationship of religious ideology to praxis and the world. It is to enrich our students' sense of history.[32] It is to raise, as well, the possibility of a different model for millenarianism and a different conception of the "practicalities" of religion and religious imagination.

For my final topic, I turn briefly to a theme so all-pervasive in the imagination of religion and the predisposition of our students that it cannot be subsumed under a single rubric. I refer to the privilege given to spontaneity as over against the fixed, to originality as over against the dependent, to the direct as over against the mediated. "The spirit quickens; the letter kills." This is expressed in the learned literature in a variety

of dichotomies: religion/magic, individual/collective, charisma/routiniza-
tion, communion/formalism, the text as direct speech over against the
commentary and the gloss, the original or primordial over against the
secondary or historical.

In elegant form this privilege is expressed in the writings of a scholar
such as Adolf Jensen for whom all truth, meaning, and value is located in
what he describes as a primal moment of ontic "seizure," a "revelation,"
a "direct cognition." The first verbal "formulation" of this experience,
its first "concretization" is an "intuitive, spontaneous experiencing"
which he terms "expression." All subsequent "formalizations" and
"concretizations" are reinterpretations of this primal experience which
Jensen terms "applications" (for him, a pejorative). All "application"
falls under the iron "law of degeneration" resulting in the original
"spontaneity" becoming a "fixed but no longer understood routine."

> According to the inescapable law, anything that culture has created
> must grow more distant from the [original] content of the creative idea;
> finally it will only be a pale reflection of its "original expression . . .
> [according to] the process of gradual semantic depletion along the way
> from "expression" to "application."[33]

To turn with our college students to the rich resources of a self-
consciously exegetical tradition such as Judaism is a direct challenge to
this sort of influential model. It is to discuss with them the value of the
prosaic, the expository, the articulate. It is to explore the creativity of
what I have termed in another context "exegetical ingenuity" as a basic
constituent of human culture.[34] It is to gain an appreciation of the complex dynamics of tradition and its necessary dialectics of self-limitation
and freedom. To do these things, which rise most naturally from the data
of Judaism, is to give expression to what I believe is the central contribution that religious studies might make to the liberal arts curriculum: the
realization that, in culture, there is no text, it is all commentary; that there
is no primordium, it is all history; that all is application. The realization
that, regardless of whether we are dealing with "texts" from literate or
nonliterate cultures, we are dealing with historical processes of reinterpretation, with tradition. That, for a given group at a given time to
choose this or that way of interpreting their tradition is to opt for a particular way of relating themselves to their historical past and their social
present. The study of this process of particular ways of relating, the
appreciation and criticism of these particular ways of relating, is how I
would define the enterprise of the humanities within the liberal arts and
why I find the study of religion so central to that enterprise. In this essay,
I have tried to suggest some ways in which the study of Judaism is pecu-
liarly appropriate to this endeavor.[35]

To echo an earlier call for a quite different vision of education and Judaism, "it is time," but only if the study of Judaism has truly come of age. Only if it is willing to be self-consciously selective with an eye toward serving as *exempli gratia* for fundamental issues in the imagination of religion.

Zeit ists!

Notes

1. I have in mind the distinctions sketched in J. Wach, "Der Begriff des 'Klassischen' in der Religionsgeschichte," in *Quantulacunque: Festschrift K. Lake* (London, 1937), pp. 87–97. The English version in J. Wach, *Types of Religious Experience* (Chicago, 1951), pp. 48–57, is not quite satisfactory.

2. F. Hutcheson, *An Inquiry into the Original of Our Ideas of Beauty and Virtue in Two Treatises*, 4th ed. (London, 1738), pp. 206f. The first edition was published anonymously in Dublin in 1725.

3. In what follows, I have drawn most of my examples from early Judaism. Equivalent *exempli* from other periods come readily to mind.

4. Jacoby, *FGH* 616 F4(i).

5. *Aristeas*, 187–300.

6. E.g. Agatharcides of Cnidos (*FGH* 86 F20), Poseidonius (*FGH* 87 F70), Cicero (*Pro Flacco* 67), Quintilian (*Institutio oratoria* III.7.1). This continues in early Christian discourse, e. g., *Diognetus* 1, Origen (*Contra Celsum* VIII.41).

7. E.g., Theophrastus (*FGH* 737 F6) et al. See the useful collection in M. Hengel, *Judaism and Hellenism* (Philadelphia, 1974), 1:255–61.

8. Philo is the first Greek writer to use the term "cosmopolitan" with any frequency. See *Opif.* 3, 142 et passim.

9. Clearchus of Soli *ap.* Josephus, *C.Apion* 180.

10. Acts 28:25–28; Matt. 13:14f.; John 12:40 et passim. See J. Gnilka, *Die Verstockung Israels: Isaias 6:9–10 in der Theologie der Synoptiker* (Munich, 1961).

11. W. Dilthey, *Gesammelte Schriften* (Stuttgart, 1926; rp. 1958), 7:255.

12. See "Fences and Neighbors: Some Contours of Early Judaism" and "In Comparison a Magic Dwells," in J. Z. Smith, *Imagining Religion* (Chicago, 1982).

13. Th. S. Barrows, S. F. Klein, and J. L. D. Clark, *What College Students Know and Believe about Their World* (New Rochelle, 1981), p. 16.

14. See G. Piers and M. Singer, *Shame and Guilt* (Springfield, 1953); J. G. Peristiany, ed., *Honor and Shame* (Chicago, 1966).

15. W. R. Smith, *Lectures on the Religion of the Semites,* 3d ed. (Edinburgh, 1927), p. 449.

16. For an outstanding example of the former, see L. Dumont and D. Pocock, "Pure and Impure," *Contributions to Indian Sociology* 3 (1959): 9–39; for the latter, M. N. Srinivas, *Religion and Society among the Coorgs of South India* (Oxford, 1952).

17. For a basic bibliography, see B. A. Levine, "Priestly Writers," *Interpreter's Dictionary of the Bible,* Supplementary Volume (Nashville, 1976), p. 687.

18. J. Neusner, *A History of the Mishnaic Law of Purities* (Leiden, 1974–77), vols. 1–22.

19. Esp. H. Danby, *The Code of Maimonides,* book 10, *The Book of Cleanness,* Yale Judaica Series, 8, (New Haven, 1954).

20. *Aristeas* 128–71; Philo, *Spec. Leg.* (there is a useful collection in J. Neusner, *The Idea of Purity in Ancient Judaism* [Leiden, 1973] pp. 45–50); *Barnabas* 7–10; Novatian, *De*

cibis judaicis (MPL III, 953–63, superseded by G. Landgraf and C. Weyman, *Archiv für lateinische Lexicographie* 11 [1900]: 221–49).

21. For a basic bibliography, see J. Z. Smith, *Map Is Not Territory* (Leiden, 1978), p. 104. See further the general works by Lord Raglan, *The Temple and the House* (New York, 1964), and H. W. Turner, *From Temple to Meeting House* (The Hague, 1979).

22. M. Eliade, "The World, the City and the House," in Eliade, *Occultism, Witchcraft and Contemporary Fashions* (Chicago, 1976), esp. pp. 24–27.

23. Most commonly, devoted to domestic shrines and worship in either China or Japan. E.g., H. Ooms, "The Religion of the Household," *Contemporary Religions in Japan* 8 (1967): 201–333; R. J. Smith, *Ancestor Worship in Contemporary Japan* (Stanford, 1974), esp. pp. 69–114; S. Feuchtwang, "Domestic and Communal Worship in Taiwan," in A. P. Wolf, ed., *Religion and Ritual in Chinese Society* (Stanford, 1974), pp. 105–30.

24. See R. Maunier, *La construction de la maison collective en Kabylie* (Paris, 1926); Maunier, *Mélanges de sociologie nord-africaine* (Paris, 1930); H. Genevois, *L'habitation Kabyle* (Paris, 1952); P. Bourdieu, *Esquisse d'une théorie de la pratique, précédé de trois études d'ethnologie kabyle* (Paris-Geneva, 1972), esp. pp. 45–69.

25. M. Zborowski and E. Herzog, *Life Is with People: The Culture of the Shtetl* (New York, 1952).

26. S. Heilman, *Synagogue Life: A Study in Symbolic Interaction* (Chicago, 1975).

27. E. Grässer, *Das Problem der Parusieversögerung in den synoptischen Evangelien und in der Apostelgeschichte,* 2d ed. (Berlin, 1960), is a rich recent treatment of this theme.

28. M. Werner, *The Formation of Christian Dogma* (London, 1957), p. 29.

29. L. Festinger et al., *When Prophecy Fails* (New York, 1956); see J. Gager, *Kingdom and Community* (Englewood Cliffs, N.J., 1975), esp. pp. 20–49, for the use of this model in a text designed for college students.

30. Werner, *Formation of Christian Dogma,* p. 297.

31. J. Z. Smith, "A Pearl of Great Price and a Cargo of Yams," *History of Religions* 16 (1976): 16.

32. I have in mind the sort of approach to history taken by Bernard Lewis in his 1974 Gottesman Lectures at Yeshiva University, *History Remembered, Recovered, Invented* (Princeton, 1975).

33. I have taken the various phrases in quotation marks from A. E. Jensen, *Myth and Cult among Primitive Peoples* (Chicago, 1963), pp. 5, 6, 66, 171, 176, and 194.

34. J. Z. Smith, "Sacred Persistence: Towards a Redescription of Canon," in W. S. Green, *Approaches to Ancient Judaism* (Missoula, 1978), 1:11–28.

35. I would be remiss if I did not call attention to the remarkable, sustained meditation on these themes represented by J. Neusner, *The Academic Study of Judaism: Essays and Reflections* (New York, 1975–80), vols. 1–3. Any contribution to this topic must be in serious and constant dialogue with these volumes.

Twelve

Alike and Not Alike

A Grid for Comparison and Differentiation

Jacob Neusner

When we compare one thing to another it is in order to gain a measure of perspective on each. What we seek is an account of likeness and difference, a mode of comparison. Jonathan Smith concludes his account of the problem with that point at which I wish to begin mine: "Wittgenstein's last question ["How am I to apply what the one thing shows me to the case of two things?"] remains haunting. It reminds us that comparison is . . . never identity. Comparison requires the postulation of difference as the grounds of its being interesting (rather than tautological) and a methodical manipulation of difference, a playing across the "gap," in the service of some useful end" (*Imagining Religion*, p. 35). There are two sides to the matter: comparison and differentiation. One without the other leaves us at that impasse at which Smith ends his reflections. But to escape therefrom we have to look beyond the barrier. We need to obtain a picture of the road beyond, that is, to define that useful end for which the work is done, the journey undertaken.

When we propose to differentiate, we postulate a fundamental commonality. When we propose to compare, we do so because we perceive some basic point of difference that bears significance. Comparison in a methodical way is a methodical manipulation of difference. Comparing and contrasting is to play across the gap. So let us begin with that "gap."

For historians of religion, the gap is not only between different religions but between different versions of the same religion. For historians of Judaism, the gap is not solely diachronic, that is, comparing the state of "Judaism" in Ezra's time with the "Judaism" of the Essene community of Qumran, or with the "Judaism" of Maimonides. Indeed, the diachronic problem—how to construct or postulate a single "Judaism" spread out over so many centuries and countries, encompassing so vast a range of significant and definitive differences—is only part of the difficulty of description and definition in Judaism. The synchronic problem is no less acute. The varieties of ways of life and world views exhibited by people who stoutly claimed for themselves the title "Israel" impress us in our own day. But it is hardly anachronistic to discern these same varieties in earlier times, whether we choose the second century B.C. and focus upon the diversity of Greek and Aramaic speaking Jews; or the second century A.D. and select Jews responsive to hopes for the end of days for comparison with those engaged in building an eternal system of sanctification; or address the third century and fourth centuries A.D. even in a single country, Babylonia, and notice there a quite severe conflict in theories of salvation with consequent difference in modes of attaining it; or speak of the ninth century with its Qaraites and Rabbinites; or the seventeenth with its Sabbateans and (from the Sabbatean viewpoint) infidels. This long catalogue is meant to underline a simple fact. The diversity of Judaisms generally characterizes not only the diachronic continuum but also the synchronic frame, which sets bounds around the data deemed definitive of, and appropriate to, "Judaism."

It must follow that a sound definition of the labor of comparison and differentiation, a clear notion of what we do when we compare, and a defensible program of the exercises of description and interpretation—these three tasks have successfully to be carried out, if a religious tradition exhibiting any historical and cultural diversity whatever is suitably to be grasped and subjected to analysis. Descriptive analysis of "a religion" is a labor of comparison and differentiation. To begin with, subject to the work of comparing and contrasting are the diverse systems of life and thought, the various societies or cultures, finding a place within said "religion." Because these systems or societies or cultures are alike, they can be shown to differ. Because there will be points of difference, one can discern commonalities and important traits of sameness. What the one thing shows me can be applied to two things *only* when both things show the same one thing (among other things).

The diachronic phenomena available for comparison in the history of Judaism pose one kind of problem, the synchronic phenomena another.

In the case of Israelite systems of sanctification extending over that mythic "four thousand years" of current discourse the problem is to establish grounds for comparison. Such a basis permits juxtaposing one world view and way of life, constructed in the name of "Israel," with some other world view and way of life, also constructed in the name of "Israel." The atomistic and nominalistic attack on a notion of a "Judaism" meant to deal with so vast a temporal range hardly requires amplification. When we ask what unites the historical David with David Ben Gurion, we come up with three answers, only the third of which is relevant in common discourse. The first is the theological answer, deriving, therefore, from the authoritative Talmudic stories about David as a master of Torah. So the diachronic unity gained through theology is imposed by theology; it need not detain us. Neither element of the comparison is taken seriously in its own context. The second is the psychological answer, deriving from the mind of David Ben Gurion, who (we may postulate, for the sake of argument) can have looked back upon a putative ancestor for inspiration and example. While the psychological answer provides ample insight into the mind of an important twentieth-century examplar of "Israel," it provides nothing interesting for insight into the mind of an important tenth-century B.C. framer of "Israel." So the two parts of the comparison are not equal. The third is constituted by the claim that there indeed are points in common between King David and Prime Minister Ben Gurion. That claim proves less preposterous upon inspection than it does when it is laid down. For, after all, a common geographical location and a common set of military and political problems as points of commonality cannot be dismissed out of hand. That is what the one thing shows me which applies to the case of two things. But the diachronic comparison and contrast may rapidly collapse into a rubbish heap of platitudes, generalities, and commonplaces. The reason is that the fundamental justification for the exercise of comparison and contrast is not really well grounded to begin with. A running jump across the abyss of time and change between the one David and the other, as I said, cannot be confused with a leap of faith. Yet it is only a highly contemporary faith which justifies and validates the exercise of comparison.

That is why I think a more reliable route toward a theory of comparison and contrast is to be located in the diachronic setting; located, that is, by comparisons within a given age, defined by a common set of characteristics of a gross and obvious sort. These should be, to begin with, historical and geographic, cultural, political and economic and social. That is to say, within a given religious tradition extending over a long period of time and many countries, we must seek moments at which we may fairly and reliably speak of a particular place and time of proximate uniformity. Then, and only then, will the exercise of differentiation become possible, so that we may apply what the one thing shows me to the case of two things.

Finding what is unlike in the like is legitimate, in a way in which finding what is like in the unlike is not, because in the former case the datum is similarity, which is not imposed, imputed, or invented, but obvious and superficial. In the latter case the datum is difference, but this may be imposed, imputed, and invented; it is subjective and deep. Then, if we wish to compare, our mental experiment is to differentiate among available similarities rather than to wander aimlessly in search of connections among things unlike one another. The latter process seems to me too much a labor of imagination or theology to serve well in the work of analysis and the gaining of insight.

So let us now specify those common grounds which make possible the mapping of diverse contours of a single social-religious group. If we are to compare artifacts of mind, then in common among the framers of those artifacts should be a common language and mode of discourse, even a shared holy book and doctrine about which to dispute. If we are to compare modes of constructing a holy way of life, we should locate a homogeneous population, making its living within a single ecological and economic framework. Only in that way shall we be able to ascertain that points of difference do not express a merely economic or ecological diversity. If, finally, we propose to compare diverse visions of the meaning of history and the destiny of a group to which all parties claim to belong, we should begin the labor of comparison within the framework of a single political structure, or, at the least, a shared experience of politics. Otherwise those questions raised in peoples' minds about the meaning of history and the destiny of the group may turn out to be expressions of a diverse and incomparable political setting: different people ruled by different kings in different ways, so to speak. Finally, in common must also be sufficient data, so that we have not only ample knowledge of the several groups subject to comparison but also knowledge of the same sort about these several groups. We cannot accomplish much, if for one group we know much about eschatology, and, for a second, about liturgical and cultic matters, and, for a third, about facts suitable for the comparison of the family and the writing of marriage contracts and writs of divorce. That rather obvious perquisite of comparative work has to be specified, because so much comparison has so far treated one thing about one group in juxtaposition with a totally incongruous thing about some other.

Having listed what I think are the necessary outlines of a map for comparative studies, I may fairly be accused of traveling in search of an intellectual utopia. And yet, I think the conditions I have postulated can be met in more than a single moment in the history of Judaism(s) (to refer to the source of examples useful to the present exercise). Certainly the Jews of the Holy Land from the time of Ezra to the Moslem conquest can be shown to share a common language of mind and mode of discourse—Scripture. The economic and ecological framework remains fundamentally uniform, because of an unchanging natural habitat and enduring modes of production and exchange. All of the Jews of the country normally lived under a single government, even though, over time, the character and sponsorship of that government exhibited significant variation. Finally, a fair amount of data, both literary and material, have come under intensive study for a very long time. While we do not know all of the same things about a long series of diverse groups, all claiming to be "Israel," we do have access to some of the same things. The Gospels and the Mishnah come into contact at more than a few points, even though, on the surface, they are talking about different things to different people. So a labor of synchronic comparison, within a given period, will be worth attempting.

But the important question remains to be asked, and it is phrased by Smith: "We know better how to evaluate comparisons, but we have gained little over our predecessors in either the method for making comparisons or the reasons for its practice. There is nothing easier than the making of patterns. . . . But the "how" and the "why" and, above all, the "so what" remain most refractory. . . . It is a problem to be solved by theories and reasons, of which we have had too little" (*Imagining Religion*, p. 35). To phrase matters in another way: Having defined an arena for comparative study, why is it urgent to undertake this work of playing in the arena of comparison? What do we learn, which we did not know before, when we juxtapose two congruent, (available) facts? What questions do we answer which we could not answer before the act of juxtaposition, comparison, and contrast? Or, to put it more accurately: *What else do we know, what more do we know than we knew before we tried to apply what the one thing shows me to the case of two things?* This is the significant issue.

My answer to this question comes out of a problem of interpretation thrown in my path by my own research, so, with apology, I offer a minute of autobiography. In the course of studies leading to my *History of the Mishnaic Law of Purities* (Leiden, 1974–77, vols. 1–22), as in those culminating in the other components of the whole history of Mishnaic law, I was struck by the problem of parallels. That is, I was well aware that in diverse cultures the corpse was a source of uncleanness, or that the transfer of a woman from man to man (e.g., from father to husband) was carefully regulated, or that the advent of certain days in the lunar-solar cycle provoked in many social groups beside the Israelite one the application of taboos. I had to figure out what, if anything, I should do about those facts. I had to decide whether to assemble a range of parallel facts,

and, if I did assemble them, whether to choose those contexts that were
suitable for a search for parallels and to eliminate those that were unsuit-
able.

If composing a catalogue of cultures and circumstances in which a
corpse produced "uncleanness" would have materially assisted in my
labor of describing and interpreting the Mishnaic law under discussion, I
should have been ready (if not eager) to make up such a catalogue. It was
at that point in my thinking that, I must admit, I began to raise questions
about the value of comparison undefined by context and purpose. The
"So what?" of Smith's statement reinforced my instinct that the work
was to no good end. This guess that the labor would be futile provoked a
search for how to make the work worthwhile. I could not ignore the
obvious fact that corpses do "contaminate" nearly everywhere. I also
could not make sense of how to utilize that fact, e.g., for the interpretation
of the same fact in the setting of Mishnaic Law. That is to say, What else do
I know, what more do I know, than I knew before I discovered that one
thing, the fact of corpse "contamination," is the case of two things (indeed, of many things)?

Two steps forward marked my progress. The first came with the work
on *Purities,* the second with that on *Women.* In the former, I noted that a
fact has to be interpreted within its own context, and, once in that context, becomes particular to it. In this regard I found particularly suggestive the statement of Mary Boyce on the simple fact that eschatological
doctrines of Zoroaster occur in four great religions, Judaism, Christianity,
Islam, as well as in Zoroaster's own religion. She states:

> Zoroaster's eschatological teachings ... became profoundly familiar
> through borrowings, to Jews, Christians, and Muslims, and have
> exerted enormous influence on the lives and thoughts of men in many
> lands. Yet it was in the framework of his own faith that they attained
> their fullest logical coherence.

In that context, this judgment of Boyce's means that comparison yields
little insight beyond the simple fact that the same thing is found in more
than one place. My own comment at that point was this: "While a woman
after childbirth is deemed unclean for the same forty days in both the
Zoroastrian and the Israelite Levitical systems of uncleanness, the
meaning of that shared detail is different for each context, and knowledge
of the fact on its own produces no insight." The presence of one rule in
two different cultures could not be interpreted or explained. For whatever
significance that shared fact had was peculiar to the cultures in which it
made its appearance. Differing verbal explanations were all that I had in
hand, unless I wished to follow the example of Goodenough in positing
some meaning of a universal and a psychological character present in the

underground of a given fact. That example did not seem to me promising or fructifying. It follows that had matters stood as they then appeared, the entire exercise of comparison should have proved futile. Even if we found logical grounds for uncovering similar patterns in a diversity of situations, we could not then say, "So what? Because...."

The second step, in the context of my *History of the Mishnaic Law of Women,* was to recognize that, if a fact appearing in many systems became consequential only in the context of those several systems, then comparison may be attempted among systems joined by said common fact. Specifically, what was to be compared was the principle of selection which led a given society to choose for its sustained attention one fact, rather than some other. Why a given system talks about the documentation of the transfer of women while another speaks about the prohibitions of consanguinity, the behavior of mothers in relationship to children, or the sexual activities of women at diverse points in their relationship to men—these are questions which may lead to comparison of system with system. Answers to these kinds of questions about principles of selection and their practical exegesis and application permit us to compare and contrast the *choices* made by diverse groups. We thereby may hope to understand the taxonomy of systems, both within a given cultural framework and even across frontiers of space and time. The work of systemic description is to compare one system with some other, to uncover principles of selection and the logic operative within each, and the relationships of those principles and that logic to the encompassing ecological framework (using the word "ecology" in a social and historical sense) among the several systems under study. Our work then is to locate the logic of a given system and to relate that logic to the context of the system. Meaning is to be perceived in two dimensions: first, within the system located and constructed in context; second, between diverse systems yielded by a shared context. Context then is not a priori, but merely prior to the work of interpretation. So the work, as it seemed in connection with *Women,* was to find out what makes a system systematic.

At this point I must digress to emphasize that when we speak of system, we mean only a social system. That is a way of seeing the world and living life characteristic of a specific, bounded group of people, way of life, and world view that work together to define the group and make sense of its collective life, keeping the outsider outside and joining the insiders together into the group. The boundaries of a system are the boundaries of the group, the things which make the group distinctive among systemic constructions. These things are the encompassing mode of living, the comprehensive mode of explanation. The limits of the system are not literary but social, even though, in historical research, we tend to begin with literary evidence. But we end with a material description of a system of a social group, a description so composed as to permit the juxtaposition and comparison of one system created by one social group with another system expressive of the totality of being of some other.

Having offered an answer to the question of "How?" I turn now to the twin questions "Why?" and "So what?" Once more I find it best to offer an answer out of my own autobiography. Why do I wish to construct a system out of law and to make sense of the whole by seeking other wholes, other systems? The answer is given in the question, in use of the language, "to make sense." In my judgment, knowing what a given group has to say about its life by itself does not help us to make sense of what that group wishes to say. It is only in discovering the choices, the contexts in which statements are made, in defining the persistent questions to which statements constitute answers, that the statements begin to make sense. Discovering similar patterns in a diversity of situations makes possible the juxtaposition for purposes of contrast and of comparison of the people who live in those circumstances and make their lives within them.

Only when we take account of the things people might have done are we able to make sense of the things they actually did do. Confronting the range of choices, we make sense of the chosen. Now, since a given group generally does some one thing, constructing the requisite group of choices is rarely possible within the range of artifacts of a single group. I suppose in theory all the things all groups might choose constitute the true range of alternatives, a social and cultural equivalent to the unlimited range of sounds we are able at birth to replicate. But in practice, a broader synchronic context, defined in terms of commonalities of politics, economics, and culture, defines the proximate range of alternatives, equivalent to the sounds we actually hear, which rapidly deprive us of our innate power to make all sounds ever heard. I apply what the one thing shows me to the case of two things by demonstrating that, faced with both things, one group chose one thing, one group the other. In the comparison and contrast of groups standing within a single, clearly defined continuum, I am able to make sense of one group by playing it off against the other. The useful end of the game of comparison, then, is to discover, through the might-have-beens of culture, the meaning of what was.

The chief perplexity, the purpose of contrast and comparison, and the end of insight, is to show the relationship between peoples' ways of viewing the world and living out life on the one side, and the context in which sight becomes insight and a way of life, the stuff of living. These then are the decisive questions: What questions are answered, and how are they answered, in the system of historical and social ecology framed and founded by a given group? How do others answer these same questions, within the same systematic structure of history and economy? And, finally, what do we learn about both groups in the comparison and contrast of each with the other? These are the three exercises which respond to the questions of "Why?" and "So what?" For the answer to "so what" must be, So this is one way in which people made choices, and that is another way, and in the variables between the one and the other lie rich insight even into how we are and might be.

What I propose, therefore, is a way beyond the historicizing atomism which treats all things as unconnected to all others, and which therefore closes off the path to insight worth sharing, method worth repeating. Historians treat events as singular. That is why events deserve careful description. But if there are patterns, they reduce the singularity, the givenness, of the singular. To historians the search for insight is a task for philosophers, theologians, or social scientists—people who wish to bring things into relationship and to find out the universally useful truth in diverse things. Now the power of historical study also is its pathos, just as the strength of philosophy and theology is their weakness. To take the case at hand, the theological construction of "Judaism" falls before the wrecking ball of historians, with their exceptions, their various examples, their particulars. And yet in the detritus of history still are bricks and stones. The iron ball does not smash all. Out of the ruins will emerge new buildings, made of the bricks of the old—of the irreducibles of society, the not to be pulverized facts of ongoing material life and the shared, enduring imagination.

So there is no possibility of claiming there never was, nor is there now, such a thing as "Judaism" but only "Judaisms." For once we take that route, there will be no "Judaisms" either, but only this one and that one, and how we feel from day to day, and this morning's immutable truth and newly fabricated four-thousand-year-old tradition. But to find the alternative way historians of religion need not magically turn themselves into philosophers or theologians. Their work of patient description of some one thing, one at a time, which is their power, cumulatively yields descriptions of diverse things, all together, all at once. Seeing the whole whole, finding out what makes it whole, establishing definitive context, discovering the questions to which systems constitute answers—this is the sort of description which makes possible the labor of interpretation. And that work of interpretation begins when the work of description has made available two or more sets of interesting facts; it begins, I mean, when the work of description has shown that the one thing applies to the case of two things. Out of description comes that work of interpretation which, in my judgment, is an exercise of comparison and therefore of contrast: a labor of nuanced comparison and differentiation.

Contributors

David R. Blumenthal	Jay and Leslie Cohen Professor of Judaic Studies Emory University
David Buchdahl	Georgia, Vermont
Arthur Green	Associate Professor of Religious Studies University of Pennsylvania
William Scott Green	Associate Professor of Religious Studies University of Rochester
Ben Halpern	Professor Emeritus of Jewish History Brandeis University
Charles S. Liebman	Professor of Political Studies Bar Ilan University, Ramat Gen, Israel
Ivan G. Marcus	Associate Professor of Jewish History The Jewish Theological Seminary of America
Jacob Neusner	University Professor and Ungerleider Distinguished Scholar of Judaic Studies Brown University
Richard L. Rubenstein	Robert O. Lawton Distinguished Professor of Religion and Co-Director of the Humanities Institute Florida State University
Richard S. Sarason	Associate Professor of Rabbinic Literature and Thought Hebrew Union College–Jewish Institute of Religion, Cincinnati
Jonathan Z. Smith	William Benton Professor of Religion and the Human Sciences, Professor of New Testament and Early Christian Literature, and the Committee on the Study of the Ancient Mediterranean World University of Chicago

237

Index of Biblical and Talmudic Texts

Index of Names and Titles

35,820